PAUL
THE APOSTLE
TO AMERICA

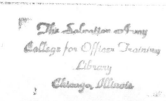

PAUL
THE APOSTLE
TO AMERICA

Cultural Trends and
Pauline Scholarship

ROBERT JEWETT

Westminster/John Knox Press
Louisville, Kentucky

Permission to use material adapted in chapter 3 has been granted for "The Law and the Coexistence of Jews and Gentiles in Romans," *Interpretation: A Journal of Bible and Theology* 39 (1985): 341–56.

Permission to use material adapted in chapter 4 has been granted for "The Conflict over Sexual Roles in Pauline Churches," in *Weslyan Theology Today: A Bicentennial Theological Consultation*, edited by Theodore Runyon (Nashville: Kingswood Books/United Methodist Publishing House, 1985), 151–60. Some material in this chapter is also adapted from "The Sexual Liberation of the Apostle Paul," *JAAR Supplement* 47 (1979): 55–87, also used with permission from the *Journal of the American Academy of Religion*.

Chapter 6 is reprinted by permission from *Quarterly Review: A Journal of Theological Resources for Ministry*, volume 14, number 1 (Spring 1994): "Tenement Churches and Pauline Love Feasts," by Robert Jewett. Copyright 1993 by the United Methodist Publishing House and the United Methodist Board of Higher Education and Ministry. A more technical version of this chapter is appearing in *Biblical Research* 38 (1993) under the title "Tenement Churches and Communal Meals in the Early Church: The Implications of a Form-Critical Analysis of 2 Thessalonians 3:10."

Permission to use material adapted in chapter 9 has been granted by the Christian Century Foundation for "Zeal Without Understanding: Reflections on Rambo and Oliver North," *The Christian Century* 104, (September 9–16, 1987), 753–56.

Book design by Drew Stevens
Cover design by Kevin Darst, KDEE Design Inc.

First edition

Published by Westminster/John Knox Press
Louisville, Kentucky

This book is printed on acid-free paper that meets the American National Standards Institute Z39.48 standard. ∞

PRINTED IN THE UNITED STATES OF AMERICA
9 8 7 6 5 4 3 2 1

Library of Congress Cataloging-in-Publication Data

Jewett, Robert, date.
    Paul the Apostle to America : cultural trends and Pauline scholarship /
Robert Jewett.—1st ed.
        p.   cm.
    Includes bibliographical references and indexes.
    ISBN 0-664-25483-7 (alk. paper)
    1. Bible. N.T. Epistles of Paul—Criticism, interpretation, etc.—United
States.   2. Christianity and culture.   I. Title.
BS2652.J477   1994
227'.06'0973—dc220   93-46597

Contents

Preface

Like its companion piece, *Saint Paul at the Movies: The Apostle's Dialogue with American Culture*, this book arises from a longstanding interest in relating the results of critical Pauline scholarship to the cultural setting of the United States of America. It is the product of a gestation process that began more than thirty years ago when my wife and I studied in Europe and then returned to a pastorate and later to teaching posts in this country. Looking back, I can see that my intellectual development has been shaped by critical interaction with European scholarship to which I remain profoundly indebted.

Numerous colleagues and students contributed to the development of an American approach to Paul that has crystallized in this book. Some read earlier drafts of this project and helped me to gain clarity, including Patrick H. Alexander, Roger Bourland, William Doran, Dean Lanning, George W. Schreiner, and R. Franklin Terry. Others contributed their expertise by reading drafts as they evolved, including Jacob W. Elias, Charles Mabee, Emery Percell, David Rhoads, Graydon F. Snyder, and John L. White. Seminary colleagues and former students who provided evaluations of parts of the project include James B. Ashbrook, Phyllis Beattie, Keith A. Burton, Constance DeYoung Collora, Reta Halteman Finger, Neal F. Fisher, Craig C. Hill, Rosemary Skinner Keller, Wolfgang M. W. Roth, Jack L. Seymour, Douglas E. Wingeier, Khiok-Khng Yeo, and Henry J. Young. Critical assistance in refining my views of Paul has been provided by colleagues in the Association of Chicago Theological Schools and the Chicago Society of Biblical Research, by participants in the Pauline Theology group of the Society of Biblical Literature, and by other friends and colleagues in the Society of New Testament Studies, and others too numerous to be mentioned here. I would, however, like to acknowledge several European scholars who contributed to the formation of my outlook, including those under whom I am grateful to have studied: Markus Barth, Otto Betz, Ernst Käsemann, Otto Michel, and Horst Moehring; others whose lectures were influential in Chicago and Tübingen included Karl Elliger, Daniel T. Jenkins, Hans Küng, Paul Schubert, Paul Tillich, and Artur Weiser.

Biblical scholarship today is an international enterprise, requiring mutual dependence on the contributions and criticisms of colleagues in many countries, reflecting many different approaches and commitments. My effort to develop an American approach to Paul is not intended as a declaration of independence. It expresses instead the convictions that contextual interpretations are a necessity for every cultural setting for the gospel to be effective, and that scholars from various cultural arenas can best contribute to the ecumenical dialogue if the distinctive insights derived from their situations are allowed to mature. My goal is to lend a tentative voice with an American timbre to the ecumenical chorus anticipated so long ago by Paul the Apostle to the Gentiles, "so that unanimously with one voice you might glorify the God and Father of our Lord Jesus Christ" (Rom. 15:6).

Introduction

I do not wish you to be unknowing, brethren,
    that I have often planned to come to you,
and until now have been hindered,
    in order that I might reap some fruit also among you as among
        the rest of the nations.
Both to Greeks and to barbarians,
    both to the wise and to the uneducated I am under obligation,
hence my readiness also to preach the gospel to you who are in
        Rome.[1]

(Romans 1:13–15)

In contrast to the predominantly European legacy of Pauline studies, this book relates his life and thought to distinctive features of American culture. It explores the cultural frontier between Paul and the United States of America. That Paul felt "obligated" to become an apostle to cultures like ours is strongly suggested by the caption from Romans. While North America is among the "nations" and continents that Paul had not reached in his lifetime, it fits to some degree the appellation "barbarians," referring to people incapable of discourse in the classical languages. If Europe has continued the legacy of the "Greeks," remaining in continuity with a classical legacy, we have continued a somewhat separate cultural development whose barbarism we are increasingly willing to affirm.

Among the writers in the New Testament, Paul should be the most adaptable to cultural differences. The obligation he felt to adapt his message "to Greeks and to barbarians, both to the wise and to the uneducated" (Rom. 1:14) explicitly "embraces all races, both those whom Hellenism owns and those it despises, and all levels of society, both those highly regarded within Hellenism and those disregarded," in the words of biblical commentator James D. G. Dunn.[2] Paul spoke of himself as being a Greek to the Greeks and a Jew to the Jews, all for the sake of the gospel (1 Cor. 9:20–23). He developed a conscious strategy of sympathizing with the weak as well as the strong (Rom. 14:1–15:7). Each of his letters takes up peculiar issues in particular congregations, reflecting different cultural and racial backgrounds. We know that he was a successful apostle to Galatia, Thessalonica, Corinth, Philippi, Ephesus, and elsewhere, and that his missionary colleagues had worked successfully in such places as Colossae and Laodicea. The cultural adaptability of Paul's proclamation made it possible in later generations for him to become the apostle to the Armenians, the North Africans, the north and central Europeans, and many others. Paul's theology was basic to the development of the Augustinian theology that dominated Roman Catholic Europe during the Middle Ages. It decisively influenced Martin Luther, John Calvin, and Menno Simons, and in later centuries theologians such as John Wesley, Friedrich Schleiermacher, Ernst Troeltsch, Adolf Harnack, Karl Barth, Emil Brunner, Paul Tillich, Jürgen Moltmann, and Wolfhart Pannenberg. Given the involvement of Pauline theology in crucial developments from the Reformation through neo-orthodoxy to the present day, one could easily speak of Paul as the "Apostle to the Europeans." Why not also to the Americans? Is it not possible that the cultural flexibility of this theology might throw light on the situation in the United States at a time when our culture is feeling itself more and more independent of its European roots?

Actually, given the traditionally European orientation of Pauline scholarship, this book should be viewed as a preliminary exploration, a small-scale Lewis and Clark expedition to probe potential routes through the American wilderness in the hope of finding viable paths for others to follow. Lewis and Clark and their companions were not the first people calling themselves "Americans" to travel west, and they could not have completed their journey without the resources, expertise, and hospitality of Native Americans who had known and lived in portions of the West for generations. Their expedition was also preceded by explorers like DeSoto and Coronado, whose expeditions were seeking cities of gold, and by Nicolet, Radisson, Marquette, Jolliet, La Salle, Cadillac, Mackenzie, and others in search of furs or converts. But Lewis and Clark represented the first systematic exploration using modern, scientific methods of observation that transversed the continent from St. Louis to the mouth of the Columbia and back. More definitive explorers and surveyors were to follow, stimulated in part by the record of their expedition through a barbarous region.

In a similar sense, *Paul the Apostle to America* offers some preliminary explorations of the relevance of Paul's letters to the American scene. It exploits the resources of scientific biblical research that might allow Paul's message to be clarified and related in new ways to modern culture. The exploration covers majestic mountains as well as plains and even deserts, from elegant expressions of high culture to the less ethereal realms of popular entertainment. Important trends in American culture, including popular entertainment and books, are brought into interaction with freshly discovered aspects of Pauline thought. By a nontechnical presentation of recent research and a sometimes whimsical treatment of contemporary cultural artifacts, Paul is allowed to engage and challenge contemporary American society in unexpected ways.

The argument in these chapters is shaped by trends in American culture rather than by traditional polemics against alternate interpretations of Pauline theology. None of these essays claims to be the definitive word on a particular Pauline passage. I have no illusion that Pauline theology supports all the causes that my denomination or I personally may espouse, nor do I believe that my judgments about Paul are final. In fact, I have found myself surprised again and again to be led to conclusions that are far from what I had originally thought were the implications of his thought for our time. Light has a way of dawning when and where we sometimes least expect it, even if we glimpse it only "through a glass darkly" (1 Cor. 13:12). My hope is that you will find some of these ideas both surprising and enlightening, even if they comprise only preliminary explorations of a vast and significant terrain that Paul might well have traversed had the Apostle to the Gentiles lived in our time.

PART 1

PAULINE SCHOLARSHIP
INTERACTING
WITH CULTURAL TRENDS

1. Overcoming the Eurocentric View of Paul

From now on, therefore, we regard no one according to the flesh;
  even though according to the flesh we once knew Christ,
    we know him that way no longer.
So if anyone is in Christ, there is a new creation:
  everything old has passed away;
    see, everything has become new!
All this is from God,
  who reconciled us to himself through Christ,
    and has given us the ministry of reconciliation.[1]
                                        (2 Corinthians 5:16–18)

In current American scholarship there is probably no area that stands closer to its European origins than Pauline theology. The main lines of interpretation remain largely within the historical-critical framework that arose a century and a half ago in Europe, having emerged out of the theological warfare initiated by the Protestant Reformation, the Counter-Reformation, and the Enlightenment. Consequently Paul's proclamation of a "new creation" tends to be understood by scholars in categories that are rather far removed both in time and space from the current American scene. This situation is quite different from other areas of biblical scholarship in which distinctively American approaches have emerged. With regard to Pauline studies, one could hardly say that they follow the innovative trajectory suggested by the message that "everything old has passed away; see, everything has become new!"

In this ecumenical era, why should European domination of Pauline studies be a matter to overcome? It is clear that many other arenas of American culture have inherited much of the best from Europe, not only from Anglo-Saxon and Spanish origins but also from the rich variety of other European traditions in later immigrations. We are just as clearly an extension of European culture as imperial Rome was an extension of Greek civilization. I myself am a product of the European legacy in various ways. The Jewett family came from England in the 1630s and my other forebears emigrated shortly thereafter. My Methodist church tradition originated in eighteenth-century England and my theological orientation was shaped by sixteenth-century Germany. My education began in institutions based on European models and ended in a classic center of theological study, Tübingen in Germany. Perhaps in part because of this educational legacy, I have been preoccupied with the question of the uniqueness of my American identity, separate from, yet influenced by, European impulses. Out of reflections that began during the four years my wife and I studied abroad, there has emerged a conviction that at least part of the problem in properly understanding Paul derives from features in European culture itself. This mitigates to some degree the pioneering work that critical Pauline scholarship of the European type has produced. While often claiming scientific objectivity, such scholarship has tended to know Paul "according to the flesh" (see 2 Cor. 5:16), that is, on the basis of culturally shaped preferences.[2]

The Eurocentric Paul—Painted in Blood

A book by Stuart Miller, who is neither a biblical scholar nor a theologian, offers a provocative entree into some distinctive features of European culture that have a bearing on Pauline study. *Painted in Blood: Understanding Europeans*[3] is a penetrating analysis of the European character, written by a classicist and journalist who lived for years in Europe, discovering in this encounter the uniqueness of his own American perspective. These essays first appeared in *Der Spiegel*, the German counterpart to *Time* magazine. Much of what Miller writes tallies with my own experience of living in Europe and interacting with European scholarship over the years.

A prominent feature of the European intellectual tradition is what Miller calls "defensiveness," the tendency to have a well-worked-out viewpoint, a philosophy, about virtually any subject one could discuss. The European loves a well-developed system, a consistent perspective. The "drive toward system-building"[4] inclined European scholars to think of Paul as a systematician.[5] His letter to the Romans has consequently been used as the lens through which the lesser occasional letters are interpreted. But Paul was not a system-builder. He was a conversational thinker who devised his theology as he went along in response to new situations.[6] The subtitle of Calvin J. Roetzel's introduction to the Pauline letters expresses this current consensus among North American scholars: *Conversations in Context*.[7] J. Christiaan Beker has popularized the idea that a tension between contingency and coherence characterizes the "dialogical" thought of this pastoral leader: "Paul is not a philosopher. . . . A contextual-dialogical method must resist . . . the topical-dogmatic method that is employed in most Pauline theologies."[8]

Closely related to the European love of systematic thought is the tenacity, even to the point of ill temper, with which European intellectuals sometimes defend their systems. Miller uses the terms "eristic" and "irenic" to describe the difference between European and American scholarship. "Eristic" comes from the Greek term *eristikos*, meaning "fond of wrangling," "warlike." "In the eristic style, the European advances ideas like batallions of tanks, holds the ground he wins, blasts you as you come toward him, brings in other batallions to reinforce a position."[9] The irenic style, on the other hand, seeks to find common ground, remaining tentative and open. Reflecting on why the eristic style, so despised by the ancient Greek philosophers, could have become dominant in European intellectual life, Miller suggests the influence of the "passionate tradition of Christian theologizing" that shaped Europe from the medieval period onward. "It broke the pagan tolerance and made argument into an ardent enterprise, one upon which whose outcome your very salvation might depend."[10]

The eristic preference is clearly evident in the traditional picture of Paul. The occasionally combative qualities in writings such as Galatians and 2 Cor. 10—13 were brought to the forefront and read into the rest of the Pauline corpus, distorting the record at many points. Paul's extensive efforts to find common ground with his conversation partners, his tolerance of divergent points of view, his support of persons and groups suffering discrimination, and the extensive evidence of his pastoral tenderness—all this tended to be diminished.[11] Paul the intellectual warrior remained dominant. A classic statement of this may be found in Auguste Sabatier's widely read biography of Paul.[12] Since Paul's conversion was "a radical negation of the Jewish principle,"[13] it followed that "it was over circumcision that the great battle came to be fought."[14] Since the original twelve apostles were intellectually incapable of taking sides, "Paul, on the other hand, naturally became the apostle of Christian freedom. To defend the independence of the Gospel was to defend his own work, his apostleship, his faith, his conversion. This great cause became his personal cause."[15] After the conflict with the circumcision party at the apostolic conference in Jerusalem, Paul became a theological warrior who defended the gospel against the attacks of the Judaizers. All of his major letters are understood as expressions of this theological combat, according to Sabatier:

> Attacked almost simultaneously at every point of his work, Paul does not shrink from the contest; he redoubles his energies, and makes himself almost ubiquitous, everywhere confronting his adversaries and never for one moment doubting of victory. For four or five years this great controversy absorbed his whole thought and energy; it was the leading fact

which dominated and distinguished this second period [of his ministry].
Our great epistles are the issue of these truly tragic circumstances, and can
only be thoroughly understood in their light. These epistles are not theological treatises, so much as pamphlets; they are the crushing and terrible
blows with which the mighty combatant openly answered the covert
intrigues of his enemies.[16]

Not only was the picture of Paul distorted by this eristic legacy, but it also
shaped the style of scholarly discourse about Paul. Scholars have wrangled
over every verse and word in the Pauline letters, sometimes with such bitter-
ness that the Pauline vision of new creation through reconciliation was
clouded. The Paul who struggled against the competitive and divisive spirit
in his church has been presented in such divisive, harsh tones, with such
severe rhetoric directed against alternate views, that the truth has sometimes seemed smothered by eristic controversy. For instance, a large part of
the excitement that captured the huge audience of theological students in
Tübingen listening to Ernst Käsemann's lectures on Romans in the early
1960s came from his impassioned battles against alternative interpretations.
In any of these brilliant lectures, one might hear passionate polemics against
the pietists, the Roman Catholics, the Bultmannian liberals, the Protestant
conservatives, and virtually every interpreter from other cultural traditions.
This host of alleged theological heretics was repeatedly accused of distorting
and diluting the pure Pauline gospel. A small sample of this eristic polemic,
toned down for publication but following in the track of the Sabatier citation above, is the following:

> Paul's doctrine of justification is in fact a militant one. We are not to
> weaken this element in the least by letting (cf. Cambier, L'Évangile,
> 420ff., 417ff., 421ff.) the "polemical coloring" serve only to underline the
> sola gratia, as it was understood as early as the Pastorals. Nor should we
> relativize the material significance of the polemic historically (as Cerfaux,
> Christian, 383f.) by relating it to the phase of the most intense discussion
> of Jewish Christianity. It is the inalienable spearhead of justification
> because it attacks the religious person and only in so doing preserves the
> sense of the justification of the ungodly. Otherwise the Christian message
> of grace will become a form of religion and Paul's doctrine of justification
> will be reduced, as happens throughout modern exposition, to a proclama-
> tion of salvation which speaks profoundly of the love of God and therefore
> does not seriously set the pious person before his Judge.[17]

This eristic spirit captures even those who do not share Käsemann's style of
polemic. In a tradition marked by sharply defined controversy on each
minute point, even polite scholars feel obligated to refute a wide range of

supposedly erroneous views. Many books on Pauline theology deal far more extensively with scholarly controversies about Paul than with Paul himself. One thinks, for example, of the host of complex studies on Paul and the law, written from every conceivable point of view, that exhaust every nuance of the relatively few references to this topic in the Pauline letters.[18] An important aim in most of these studies is to combat alternative points of view, which allegedly jeopardize the Christian faith or undermine public morals.

When scholarly self-images and prestige are so tied to intellectual systems that are defended at all costs, often the only way to prevail is to resort to authority. One seeks to destroy the opposition by the superior weight of one's own prestige. In European scholarship there is little confidence in the power of persuasion. "Over and over again," Stuart Miller observes, "I have found that beneath the polished appearances of culture, if you hold them long enough in your view, you will hear among Europeans the grunt and clash of weapon on shield, the bang of egotistical mace on heavy buckler, the harsh splintering of a lance and the puffing into temporary retreats: all the back and forth of the armored conflict of social selves endlessly contending for place and mastery."[19] Pauline theology has been "painted with blood," to use Miller's title, not only in the fierce struggles between Protestants and Catholics and others over sectarian construals of his thought but also in the way Paul himself is perceived. The emphasis has been on his authority rather than on his persuasive strategies.[20] Paul has been pictured primarily as the one who used his "absolute"[21] authority to proclaim the gospel in the face of heresy. Only recently has attention been drawn to his rhetorical skill, his elaborate strategies to persuade his audiences in various churches.[22] A number of recent studies have indicated the care with which Paul takes up the viewpoint and even the vocabulary of his conversation partners, how he devises proofs out of the shared assumptions of his churches, how skillfully and pastorally he guides his congregations into mature and independent judgments.[23]

Hierarchy versus Solidarity

The kind of community that Paul wished to encourage is far removed from the hierarchical pecking order and the harshness bred by European intellectual life. Miller writes: "A vague habit of social intolerance, fueled by remembered hierarchy and the fury of revolution both, allows each individual, no matter what his social position, to feel not only that he is right but also that what he thinks in fact represents the right, as embodied in the group." As an Italian professor told Miller half jokingly, "We don't argue to convince; we know we are right and that only a fool would not have seen our point long ago."[24] The "harshness of religious warfare"[25] in European history tends to be read back into the Pauline communities, exaggerating their conflicts.[26] As Miller observes, "It takes some historical imagination to understand the fierceness with which Europeans sometimes foolishly cling to their boxes and their often self-destructive habits. Old blood and divinity blind their eyes."[27] As a consequence, European scholars find it natural to downplay the egalitarian joy of early Pauline communities, to discount the evidence of their remarkable solidarity.[28] European habits of hierarchy tend to be imposed on the organizational structure of those early communities.[29] The few wealthy and respected members were thought to dominate early house churches.[30] As Miller explains,

> Most fundamentally, the ancient social hierarchy of Europe, surviving intact until very recently and now existing in a debased form, provided men with a continuous visible model for the hierarchy of worth in all things. . . . Even in the kingdoms of the supernatural, there was a hierarchy of saints, angels, and archangels, all leading up to God himself. This sense of an inherent, proper, vertical scheme to everything, with an established aristocracy at the top of the human social order, so un-American, still runs like a current of influence and meaning in the European character.[31]

This legacy has made it difficult for traditional scholarship to understand the cooperative solidarity that marked the early Pauline communities, to take seriously the insights of sociologists about the unusually democratic social structure. While European scholarship has been preoccupied for centuries with the background, order, and legitimate participation in the Lord's Supper,[32] only recently has the obvious become visible. Elisabeth Schüssler Fiorenza states the consensus that is now dawning:

> The Christian house churches had the same unifying center: the communal banquet or meal which regularly gathered together all members of the group for table companionship. Eating and drinking together was the major integrative moment in the socially diversified Christian house community. The *diakonia* at tables was crucial for early Christian community. . . .
>
> Christians . . . all are equal, because they all share in the Spirit, God's power; they are all called elect and holy because they are adopted by God, all without exception: Jews, pagans, women, men, slaves, free poor, rich, those with high status and those who are "nothing" in the eyes of the world.[33]

Clearly what was most distinctive about the communities Paul founded was their solidarity, not the hierarchies carried over from Greco-Roman culture. But this remains very difficult to acknowledge for those bound by traditional parameters.

Paul as the European "Great Man"

The aristocratic legacy has tended to interpret the evidence concerning leadership of the Pauline churches as dominated by the "great man" at the top. Only in the past quarter century has it become clear that Paul's ministry was collegial, that he worked as a member of a large team of male and female missionary colleagues.[34] It now appears that only five of his co-workers, all of them male, functioned as Paul's subordinates at times in various letters. The rest, including all the women mentioned in his letters, were more or less equal colleagues.[35] Moreover, despite the fact that in several letters Paul was forced to defend his apostolic authority, he did not advocate what Miller calls "the Imperial Self" characteristic of later European aristocracy.[36] Paul did not think of himself as the commanding center of attention and action, but rather as a servant in a divine drama in which someone else was Lord. As Jeffrey Crafton has shown, Paul saw himself as the agency through which divine action flowed, rather than the agent of such action: "An agent-orientation assumes that apostles are the actors, that they are essentially in control as distinct entities. An agency-orientation assumes that God acts through the apostle, that God determines the parameters, the scope, the purpose, the means of that ministry; it diverts attention away from the apostle as an individual to the apostle as a channel, a vessel, a window upon the divine character and will."[37]

Paul would not have recognized himself as a "great one" in the European sense, matching "the old aristocratic notion of glory," someone not only good with a sword but a "glorious man—a paragon of many virtues, who legitimately and intrinsically towered over others in his very essence."[38] On the basis of traditional depictions of Paul as such a paragon, it was awkward to accommodate Paul's admission that "his bodily presence was weak and his speech contemptible" (2 Cor. 10:10). It was impossible to acknowledge that he sometimes worked under the patronage of others, who in the social context of the Greco-Roman world, were far higher up the social scale than he was, the prime example being Phoebe (Rom. 16:1–2).[39] Although reportedly a Roman citizen, Paul functions as a lower-class handworker, subject to the contempt with which such persons were held in his day, as recent American scholarship has demonstrated.[40]

Admittedly, the view of Paul as the great man is not entirely the result of European influences. The Pauline letters are framed in the Christian canon by the book of Acts on one end and the Pastoral Epistles on the other, both of which promote the heroic dominance of Paul. The entire second half of Luke's history of the early church traces the travels of Paul from Jerusalem to Rome, suppressing references to more than a few of his associates, all of whom are depicted as subordinate to his authority. None of the female missionary colleagues referred to by Paul with such respect in Romans 16 appear in Luke's story of the spread of Christianity, with the exception of Prisca, whom Luke calls by her diminutive nickname Priscilla. Paul alone transcends every barrier and prevails in every encounter, blithely resisting death by stoning (Acts 14:19) or snakebite (Acts 28:3–6). He is the center of attention in every crisis from the Philippian jail to the Areopagus in Athens, from the riot of the silversmiths in Ephesus to the storm at sea when all the sailors lost their nerve. He triumphantly preaches before kings and governors, ending his story by preaching openly in Rome despite his imprisonment. It is wonderful entertainment, as Richard I. Pervo has shown,[41] but it varies considerably from the troubled life reflected in the authentic Pauline letters. The Pastorals continue this vision, with Paul passing on his charisma, message, and authority to his disciples Timothy and Titus. It is a combination perfectly suited for the great man premise of European culture, even though the evidence in Paul's letters points in another direction.

Discomfort with the Presence of a New Age

The misunderstandings influenced by the European legacy reach to the very core of Pauline thought. His most distinctive doctrines are salvation by grace alone and freedom from the law, yet in broad streams of traditional European exegesis there is a persistent effort to show that such salvation and freedom were only "in principle," that they could not have been socially embodied. Numerous studies have aimed to show that Pauline freedom for slaves and women was largely theoretical.[42] The background of this distortion is explained by Miller: "Europeans still don't have a sense of practical freedom."[43] They are impeded by what he calls "boxification," a compartmentalized world in which various professions and political groups occupy well-worn locations on the social scale, and in which each group is locked in constant battle with other groups.

In America, the experience of freedom from European boxes has opened up spontaneous forms of cooperation and neighborliness reminiscent of early Pauline churches. Miller describes a Parisian intellectual who was told when moving to America that she would

> find people totally selfish and individualistic, lacking any solidarity. But compared to Paris . . . Cleveland was social. Over there, mothers shared children and people were active in community organizations. An example: two days after having my baby in the university hospital, I went home, terrified at being alone. But all my neighbors were there. People I'd never seen. And they kept coming back to hang up curtains, give advice, pass on some old baby clothes, two strollers, and a used playpen. When I needed milk and the shops were closed, I just went next door.[44]

That freedom and cooperation can be socially embodied is a natural premise for Americans, while remaining difficult for Europeans to conceive, either for themselves or in their portrayals of Pauline Christianity. This distinctive feature of the American experiment was visible in the first settlers on the Mayflower who "pledged not only as particularly devout Christians to love all men but also as members of a more or less hastily assembled group to love each other. Wilderness circumstances led to the repetition of this pattern of warm affiliation. Total strangers gathered together to make up the wagon trains,"[45] treating each other with the kind of love and self-sacrifice that Paul seems to have expected from his churches. The idea of America as the nation "with the soul of a church," to use G. K. Chesterton's famous phrase,[46] was influenced by Paul's writings. This legacy makes it understandable that some Americans are more likely than European scholars to accept at face value the evidence that freedom, love, and cooperation were actually to some degree embodied in the Pauline communities, flowing from powerful conversion experiences in which the "boxification" of Greco-Roman culture was overturned.

Finally, the European mindset has hindered the grasp of Paul's apocalyptic worldview. In the European tradition, "pessimism is a collective basic assumption. As the French are given to say . . . 'The worst is always certain.' "[47] This makes it difficult to understand a Paul whose most distinctive outlook was marked by apocalyptic hope. In Beker's words, "the apocalyptic hope for Paul is an existential reality that is part and parcel of Christian life, inasmuch as it sighs and hopes for the resolution of death, suffering, and evil in the world."[48] Paul was a revolutionary who saw a new creation coming. Christ had defeated the principalities and powers, and soon the bridgeheads of hope in the tiny house churches and tenement churches would expand to cover the world, bringing the age of pessimism and cynicism to an end.

Americans are the inheritors of this optimistic intellectual tradition, derived from early Christianity.[49] We have a cultural affinity for the apocalyptic orientation of early Christianity, having shared it in the peculiar American notion of being "the new order of the ages," the national motto printed in Latin on our currency. This produces many problems for us and is sometimes hopelessly unrealistic, yet it links us to the Pauline churches with a direct intellectual affinity not shared by most Europeans. We are closer to Paul the founder of revolutionary, countercultural communities than are most Europeans. Americans have typically been willing to break from the past, to shape a new world. Like optimistic apocalypticists convinced that history is on their side, we like the prospect of a new future. We periodically select leaders who offer change, even when the precise shape and wisdom of such innovations remain somewhat vague. As Miller explains, Americans "are adaptable and change exhilarates us. Europeans, on the other hand, suffer 'future shock' as we do but with no habit of pleasure in change."[50] Their experience of revolution has repeatedly been disorienting and destructive, so marked by blood that it remains difficult for them to share Paul's apocalyptic optimism.

The Abiding Contribution of European Exegesis

It hardly needs to be said that it is often easier to see the blind spots of other cultures than to confront those of our own. The critique of European exegesis does not entail the suggestion that we simply substitute one culturally induced opaqueness for another. Having struggled to understand and to resist the "principalities and powers" of my own culture for the past several decades,[51] inspired in part by the Pauline vision, I entertain no belief in American superiority in intellectual or moral insight, regardless of our affinity with Pauline radicalism. It remains clear to me that the modern study of Paul rests squarely on critical foundations now accepted by international scholarship, developed in large measure by Europeans and their intellectual allies. I continue to admire what many of us have derived from this tradition: the ideal of critical objectivity, the passionate quest for the truth, the relentless criticism of popular hypotheses on the basis of a close examination of the evidence, the courage to dismantle the beliefs and prejudices that lie at the root of one's own tradition, the love of methodological innovation. In Pauline studies particularly, I rely on the traditional European grasp of the dialectic between faith and works, law and gospel, light and darkness, between the indicative and the imperative, the already and the not-yet. I continue to appreciate the sensitivity of European scholars to Pauline realism, to the ongoing struggle reflected in his letters against the excesses of enthusiasm and freedom. But I am committed now to adapt these insights and methods for the American scene. Since his thought has been extensively related to the modern European inheritors of the "Greeks" and the "educated" of Rom. 1:14, the goal in this exploration is to bring Paul the Apostle to the "barbarians" and the "uneducated," to those less directly shaped by the Latin and Greek roots of our common civilization. His "ministry of reconciliation" (2 Cor. 5:18) is relevant to us all.

2. Interpreting Paul in the American Context

For though I am free with respect to all,
   I have made myself a slave to all,
      so that I might win more of them.
To the Jews I became as a Jew,
   in order to win Jews. . . .
To the weak I became weak,
   so that I might win the weak.
I have become all things to all people,
   that I might by all means save some.[1]
          (1 Corinthians 9:19–20, 22)

In view of the distortions caused by the Eurocentric domination of Pauline theology, it makes sense to explore the possibility of an American approach. Given the impact his thought had on early colonists, is there evidence of a distinctively American approach among the Pauline scholars and preachers of recent times? Have they followed the logic of his missionary strategy, which was to adapt himself to the Greeks as well as to the Jews, the weak as well as the strong? To what extent is his theology, which had so decisive an impact on the original shaping of the American character, being indigenized for the recent American scene?

The Adaptation of Paul in American Preaching

I decided to explore this issue by listening to sermons and reading popular books on Paul, hoping to detect the way Paul might be functioning as the "Apostle to America." Popular writing and preaching tends to distill scholarly interpretations of biblical material, often a generation later, so that they may provide important indications of how a figure like Paul is being understood in the culture. While I was on a recent sabbatical leave, my wife and I gave up our normal church obligations to become guest listeners, visiting other churches principally of Methodist, Presbyterian, and Congregational orientation to hear sermons and to gain a renewed sense of which theological and biblical resources are currently the most used. Several things struck us in the sermons we heard, confirming impressions made on other occasions over the past thirty years. Our first impression was the paucity of preaching on Paul. Inquiries about the cause of such avoidance typically result in comments reported by a colleague in Pauline theology, that ministers "usually respond by complaining about 'the difficult Paul,' especially about the trouble they have in conveying to their people the argumentative texture of his letters and the seeming irrelevance of many of Paul's concerns."[2] The result is that Paul's gospel is typically limited to three occasions in contemporary Protestant churches: "on Reformation Sunday (Rom. 1:16–17), for weddings (1 Corinthians 13) and for funerals (Rom. 8:31–39)!"[3] This pattern of avoidance is linked, I believe, with the alien orientation of the dominant interpretive pattern for Pauline texts. Of the relatively few sermons I have heard on Pauline theology, most seemed to have a strongly European cast, as if Paul had still not been fully adapted to the situation in the New World. With the exception of Lutherans who still use Pauline texts with great frequency to develop their traditional themes, preachers in North America appear to be more comfortable with material from the Gospels or the Old Testament. The situation seems quite different in the United States as compared with Germany, where we attended services for four years in one of the Lutheran state churches. Sermons on the Pauline letters were frequent and elaborate, with roots obviously going back to the powerful theological heritage of Protestant orthodoxy.

Several tendencies surfaced in the American sermons I have heard on Pauline texts in recent years. One is a kind of doctrinal preoccupation. Sermons on Pauline texts seem to be more doctrinal than exegetical. The unique historical situation behind a particular Pauline letter is rarely considered. At most there will be a description of the account in the Book of Acts related to the city addressed in the letter. A tone of theological abstraction seems quite characteristic of such preaching, and generally speaking it is individualistic in its scope. When a Pauline text related to grace or faith is used, for instance, it usually is interpreted as related to individuals rather than to groups. The points that are developed, moreover, seem very close to the sermons we heard so often in Germany. They are shorter and less developed, for the most part, but the doctrinal emphases on justification, grace, freedom, and the like seem quite similar—at least to this listener.

This leads me to the key generalization about the interpretation of Pauline material in the United States of America: It remains strikingly European in orientation. Whereas there are distinctively American approaches to the exodus and exile materials of the Old Testament, the kingdom of God sayings in the Gospels, the pilgrim motifs in the Epistle to the Hebrews, to the necessity of practical ethics in the Epistle of James, and in some traditions at least, to the apocalyptic material from the Book of Revelation, it seems to me that Pauline interpretation has been less clearly touched by the American experience. When one hears sermons on the distinctively Pauline themes of the grace of God, justification by faith, works-righteousness, the law, and the body of Christ, they seem to follow the same tracks I heard developed in those powerful Lutheran sermons in Tübingen during student years from 1960 to 1964. I have never heard an application of the distinctively American interpretation developed in this century, Josiah Royce's adaptation of Paul's doctrine of love in terms of loyalty to the beloved community.[4] One clear exception in my limited experience of sermon listening is the Pauline doctrine of freedom, which I have occasionally heard linked with American traditions of liberty and responsibility. Although I have been deeply influenced by Reinhold Niebuhr's writings on such Pauline themes as sin and the ambiguity of collective behavior, I have not heard many sermons on such themes. So there is little evidence that Paul is functioning to his full potential as the Apostle to America. Despite the flexible resources of his thought detected in the scholarship of the past several decades, Paul still seems to have been only partially indigenized in American preaching.

Paul's Despisers

When one looks beyond officially sponsored sermonizing, the most prominent impression one receives is that Paul tends to be despised as an authoritarian chauvinist who is fundamentally out of step with our democratic, egalitarian society. Although this rap is contradicted by many of the discoveries of modern Pauline research and is based in part on evidence in materials that were probably not actually written by him, it persists as a culturally shared suspicion that probably accounts in part for the sparsity of preaching on Pauline texts. J. Christiaan Beker refers to "a large-scale alienation from Paul's gospel coupled with a widespread dislike for the person of Paul" that is prevalent in contemporary culture.[5] Many "intelligent church members" he has met "cherish a dislike for Paul because of his presumable arrogance, his doctrinal stance, or his 'perversion' of the gospel of Jesus."[6] This spite extends far beyond the American shores, because a European scholar has recently observed that in the feminist literature she has surveyed, Paul is "the most attacked person in the New Testament. . . . Unconcealed hatred is directed against Paul."[7] Conversations with students and audiences for public lectures suggest that Paul's despisers form a vehement majority of those who have an opinion on the subject.

The doctrinal preoccupation that is offensive to our culture derives in part from misunderstanding the situational context of Paul's authentic letters and the larger conversation between Paul and his congregations. The impression of dogmatic authoritarianism, however, comes primarily from 1 and 2 Timothy and Titus, letters whose non-Pauline vocabulary and theology lead most contemporary scholars to conclude they were written a generation after Paul's death by an increasingly conservative Pauline school.[8] The post-Pauline tradition tended to abandon the revolutionary radicalism of both Jesus and Paul, replacing it with doctrinal certitudes. These three writings are the primary source of the violent religious prejudices that seem to be promoted by Paul, leading many Americans to agree with Thomas Hardy's critique of the alleged Pauline foundation of Mr. Clare's destructively doctrinaire outlook in *Tess of the D'Urbervilles*. Clare's orientation was "less a Christiad than a Pauliad. . . . less an argument than an intoxication."[9] It is 1 and 2 Timothy and Titus that replace rational argument with dogmatic assertion, not the authentic letters of Paul, whose argumentative interactions with early Christian congregations are now becoming understandable to scholars employing modern techniques of historical reconstruction and rhetorical analysis.

The rejection of critical biblical scholarship by fundamentalists, resulting in their confusing the dogmatic Paul of 1 and 2 Timothy and Titus with the Paul of the authentic letters, leads to the widespread impression that Pauline theology supports anti-intellectualism. This allegation is supported by a simplistic reading of Paul's critique of "wisdom" in 1 Cor. 1–4. Such allegations lead many contemporary Americans to share Herman Melville's assessment that Paul was "a subverter not only of reason but also of faith." His dogmatic irrationality "makes him a doubtful prophet or an unreliable guide to ethical praxis."[10] In Melville's words, Paul belongs among the "destroyers of confidence" who corrode the human prospect.[11] But in fact, in the reliable assessment of a recent philosopher, Paul never criticized the "use of reason in the service of faith. . . . Paul's critique cuts not at reason itself but at its inflated pretender—intellectual conceit."[12] This insight will be developed in chapter 8 of this study, dealing with Paul's self-critical intellectual openness that seems well suited to the scientific consciousness needed for the present age.

The charge that Paul is an advocate of intolerant attitudes toward women also rests primarily on evidence in the Pastoral Epistles, 1 and 2 Timothy and Titus, which forbid any leadership role for women and demand their silence in public.[13] One of the few arguable interpolations in the authentic Pauline letters also supports this chauvinistic view, 1 Cor. 14:33b–36, as I shall show in chapter 4 below. Winsome Munro has gone even farther in attempting to identify a "pastoral stratum" of interpolations throughout the Pauline corpus beyond 1 Corinthians 14.[14] Even if one chooses to ascribe this passage to the historical Paul, its prohibition of female involvement in public worship must have been temporary and localized because there is so much evidence in other Pauline passages of his collaboration with female missionary colleagues and congregational leaders. Yet this passage, in conjunction with the pastorals, leads people to identify Paul as the "most influential, and therefore perhaps most dangerous" of the world's "sex reactionaries."[15] Numerous supporters of liberated values still concur with George Bernard Shaw's dictum that "Paul is the eternal enemy of woman."[16] Mary Daly takes this spite a step further by referring to Paul as the "archhater of life in general and women in particular."[17] A responsible revision of this bias is available in numerous feminist scholars, most prominently in the work of Elisabeth Schüssler Fiorenza.[18]

The charge that Paul was the father of Christian anti-Semitism derives in part from misinterpreting Paul's critique of the Judaizers in Galatians and of the Jewish law in Galatians and Romans. This leads a prominent critic like Rosemary Radford Ruether to discuss Paul under the rubric of "the Philosophizing of Anti-Judaism."[19] Paul's attack on the law and the type of Jewish zealotism he had formerly expressed in persecuting the early church is frequently taken as a sign that Paul became an apostate who hated Judaism. The most extreme statement of this perspective is found in the work of Hyam Maccoby,[20] whose work creates frequent echoes in American scholarship. He attempts to show that Paul was a renegade pagan who faked a Jewish background in order to pose as the authoritative apostle who could steer Christianity toward anti-Semitism.[21] Several of our most prominent American scholars have devoted themselves to clearing away such misconceptions, as the treatment below will suggest.

The suspicion of Paul in the African American community centers on his alleged support for the institution of slavery. A memorable example of this is Howard Thurman's report that despite her love of the hymn to love in 1 Cor. 13, his grandmother disliked Paul because of sermons she had heard from white preachers advising slaves to obey their masters.[22] Although the texts for such sermons came from deutero-Pauline writings like Colossians and Ephesians, Amos Jones, Jr., reports that "as recently as the 1960s, Paul has been held culpable by black theologians of making the burden of bondage heavier for black people."[23] While working with African American students in college and seminary settings, I have encountered this concern many times. In the recently published study of black biblical interpretation, Stony the Road We Trod, Clarice J. Martin confirms that the influence of this misunderstanding remains pervasive: "Few New Testament narratives have exerted as profoundly a malefic and far-reaching impact on the lives of African Americans as have the Haustafeln—the table of household codes or domestic duties found in Colossians 3:18–4:1; Ephesians 5:21–6:9; and 1 Peter 2:18–3:7."[24]

The various forms of suspicion about Paul felt by many current Americans provide the foils for a number of crucial chapters in this book, resulting in the contention that a clarified view of Paul would place him, paradoxically, alongside rather than against many of his critics. For, as some of our most perceptive prophets have discerned, Paul is on the side of freedom and equality. He is the defender of cultural pluralism. Within the context of the New Testament, he is a preeminent advocate of a humane fusion between the seemingly incompatible strains of religious ecstasy, faith, rationality, and ethical responsibility.

Pauline Themes in Books for the Popular Market

For the most part, books written for the religious book market do not respond to American spite against Paul. Conservative authors are unwilling to distinguish between authentic and inauthentic Pauline writings, and thus are unable to separate the true historical Paul from the despised, authoritarian framework provided by Acts and the Pastoral Epistles. Others seem more interested in European criticisms of Paul than in correcting his distorted image in American culture. In my sample of books that attempt to popularize Paul's theology, distinctively American criticisms, themes, and interests surface only occasionally, though the record is more positive in recent years. I would like to start with works that reveal the Pauline picture of the past generation of American expositors.

Rollin H. Walker's popular book on Paul[25] opens with an episode in a German railroad station when he saw a pamphlet on the newsstand featuring a mailed hand choking a serpent with the title, "Back to Jesus! Away with Paul!" He responds to the European debate over the dogmatic image of Paul by affirming the power of Paul's spiritual enthusiasm. Paul had discovered that "God is exhausting divine ingenuity for the salvation of each one of his children, and all that is needed on their part is to respond to his initiative and to believe in his goodness."[26] In a manner consistent with European modernists from 1900 to 1914, Walker stresses Paul's commitment to religious ideals, hope in the progress of Christian civilization, and a belief in individual immortality. The ethical task of controlling the flesh by concentrating on Christ is stated in witty, modern terms: "According to Paul, we must do our moral typewriting by the touch method. That is to say, we must keep our eye on the copy and let our fingers caper freely over the keys of life."[27] In contrast to the Nietzschean ideal, Paul insists that "power comes from the closest union with the brotherhood, and that the superman must be, like Jesus, the superlover."[28] The style is picturesque in a folksy, American mode, but the thought is European. And the cultural spite that Walker corrects is exclusively European.

Holmes Rolston's *The Social Message of the Apostle*[29] is an example of a study that raises a characteristically American question, to which a characteristically European answer is given. He attempts to do for Paul what had frequently been done for the Jesus material during the era of the social gospel. To a degree, Rolston tries to understand Paul's original cultural setting and to relate his message to the twentieth century. The framework he uses to understand Paul's ethic is the church struggle led by Karl Barth and others in Germany, whose principal theme was resistance against culture. Paul is seen to advance "radical" as well as "conservative" principles in his ethic, each interacting on the other, calling for bold decisions on the part of individual Christians and the church. Rolston uses Emil Brunner's concept of the "orders of creation" to describe Paul's attitudes toward sexual relations, economic conditions, political decisions, and the social order. He uses many citations from contemporary theology and ethics, mostly European in origin, referring frequently to the ecumenical movement. Karl Barth is constantly cited and when theological precedents are sought, they are invariably found in Luther and Calvin.[30] One gains the strong impression in Rolston's work that the United States still remains, in biblical hermeneutics at least, a cultural colony of Europe.

In the popular exposition spun off from his writing of the Romans commentary in the *Interpreter's Bible*, John Knox presented a timeless biblical theology in traditional, European terms. He defines "peace" and "justification" in terms of "forgiveness" in a manner that would have pleased Luther and Calvin,[31] but he attempts to counter the individualistic misunderstanding of this doctrine by stressing the corporate quality of life in Adam or Christ[32]. This corporate sensitivity comes much closer to the essence of Pauline thought than the individualistic approach of traditional interpretation. But Knox does not attempt to adapt Paul to American culture. No concrete issues either within the church or the society are mentioned in his exposition; no hint of the global or national situation is revealed. I found only one personal illustration, drawn apparently from Knox's own experience. The only citations are the poems of Millay and Hopkins in connection with the theme of death in Romans 8. In the effort to present a timeless biblical theology, this is actually a characteristic product of neo-orthodox exegesis of the 1950s, an approach that would probably repudiate on principle any effort to make Paul the Apostle to America.

An example of evangelical exposition is represented in Kingsley G. Rendell's *Expository Outlines from 1 and 2 Corinthians*.[33] After brief introductions to the Corinthian letters, using the standard, nontechnical resources, Rendell provides outlines in propositional form on every preachable text. His work reveals a healthy consciousness, however, that the unique circumstances of the Corinthian congregation are not always directly applicable to modern congregations.[34] But for the most part Rendell suggests a glib application of the ancient text to the modern church.[35] No effort is made to relate Paul to a particular historical or cultural situation in the modern world. The individualistic implications of traditional Protestant theology are constantly presented as the obvious relevance of Pauline texts. That this individualistic interpretation derives from the European tradition is nowhere acknowledged. The interpretive line has simply become habitual. It also surfaces in the more recent book by Lewis B. Smedes on 1 Cor. 13.[36]

A substantial break with the naively traditional view of Paul surfaces in William Baird's *Paul's Message and Mission*.[37] He follows the track of the historical-critical method to recover Paul's missionary message in the first-century context marked by "pervasive pessimism," a pathetic view of history as meaningless, and a frustrated yearning for salvation.[38] The critical perspective derives from European exegesis, stressing that Paul's conversion was identical with "the call to world mission" and that "all the attempts to explain the conversion experience on human grounds—as a mere psychological experience or a case of sunstroke—are totally inadequate for Paul."[39] He shares the emphasis of European neo-orthodoxy that "though the difference between the word of God and the words of men must always be maintained, it does not represent a radical cleavage; the transcendent God can actually speak through the mundane language of Paul."[40] The traditional dialectics of strength and weakness, grace and works, freedom and law are faithfully maintained: "We are saved by faith. Man cannot justify himself before God by some feverish righteous activity nor by the rigorous following of some prescribed steps of salvation. Faith is not a work to be accomplished, but a unique action of man's freedom whereby he accepts God's action in the secret heart of his inner being."[41] The premise here is that Pauline theology as interpreted by leading European critics has universal validity and therefore requires no cultural adaptation.[42]

Even the popular commentaries written on the Pauline letters in recent years tend to retain the characteristic European cast. The exegetical discussions in the *Interpreter's Bible* betray none of the cultural interests of the expositional sections, retaining the traditional European orientation. The newer commentaries in the Proclamation series do not attempt to bridge the gap to American culture any more than those in the Word or Glazier series. These series reflect the ecclesiastical interests of publishers and writers, most of which appear to follow traditional European tracks of development. Roy Harrisville's commentary on Romans provides a simplification of Käsemann for the most part,[43] while Paul J. Achtemeier provides a Calvinist counterpart, still very European in its orientation.[44] Ralph Martin's commentaries on Philemon and Colossians have a strongly British orientation,[45] while James Reese's commentary on the Thessalonian letters is virtually indistinguishable from its European counterparts.[46] The contributions in the Anchor series lack a common viewpoint or method, but one finds nothing distinctively American in the interpretation of Pauline letters by Markus Barth,[47] Victor Furnish,[48] or James Walther and William Orr.[49] The New International and the Word Biblical Commentary series also remain within traditional European boundaries, as visible in the work of Gordon Fee,[50] James Dunn,[51] and others. Several commentaries published outside of series break from these traditional boundaries, but their impact has been marginal thus far. For example, John Heil's commentary on Romans employs reader response criticism but does not attempt to relate the text to the American cultural setting.[52] Graydon Snyder's commentary on 1 Corinthians combines archeological and historical research with an American Anabaptist orientation, applying the text at a number of points to cultural trends. This last work may prove capable of overcoming marginal status.[53] But it still can be said that commenting on the Pauline letters has been a predominately European game. It is no accident that many of the most popular commentaries in this country have been written by non-Americans. One thinks of the widely used commentaries by C. K. Barrett on Romans and Corinthians; by Anders Nygren, C. H. Dodd, Ernst Käsemann, Matthew Black, and James Dunn on Romans; by Ernest Best, F. F. Bruce, and Charles Wanamaker on Thessalonians; by James Moffatt, Jean Hèring, and Hans Conzelmann on 1 Corinthians; or Jean Hèring, R. H. Strachan, and Ralph P. Martin on 2 Corinthians.

There are exceptions, of course, such as Robin Scroggs's *Paul for a New Day*.[54] He relates Pauline themes to post-Freudian psychology, making particular use of Norman O. Brown, the American Freudian whose work was widely influential in the 1960s and 1970s. But even here the frame of reference is the allegedly universal structure of psychological development rather than the cultural orientation shaped by the North American experience. A more conspicuous exception is available in some of the sermons of Martin Luther King Jr., which utilized Pauline texts to speak directly to dilemmas in American public ethics.[55] But he never devoted a book to the specific task of popularizing Pauline theology.

A sensitivity to the communal dimensions of Paul's thought surfaces with a measure of independence from European perspectives in several Roman Catholic interpreters in recent years. Joseph A. Grassi developed the concept of "fraternal union" between church members who follow "the ideal of the Christian commune" that is not limited to celibates in religious orders but is "shared by married people and children as well."[56] He stresses Paul's tolerance of diversity and the egalitarian quality of Pauline communities.[57] Paul's gospel is understood here as "a gospel of freedom. He saw the risen Christ as a truly liberating person who could deliver people from the terrible social and racial barriers. Paul presented the image of a God of love who would free men and women from the bonds of legalism and necessary religious observances."[58] A similar independence surfaces in William G. Thompson's book, which reinterprets Pauline thought for Catholic adult education.[59] He interacts with James Fowler and Evelyn and James Whitehead, American specialists in adult development, rather than with European scholarship on Paul.[60] The book describes Thompson's scholarly journey away from the sterile, doctrinal approach to the Pauline letters, discovering the liberating potential of placing Paul "in his historical context."[61] Thompson poses questions about the parallels between that ancient context and the contemporary situation in the United States, even taking account of popular films and television series.[62]

A contextually relevant picture also emerges from Amos Jones's effort to approach Paul "from a black point of view with an interest in what he might say to the black situation in America."[63] He repudiates the picture of a Paul "who has been misrepresented, corrupted, perverted, and misused by the white church of the pre-Civil War era in America and, to a large degree, by the white church of today. . . . So what we have today is a Paul who is trapped. On the one hand he is [used] . . . to perpetuate institutional racism. On the other hand black theologians castigate and disparage Paul for his seeming proslavery position. . . . Blacks and women have yet to liberate the liberator."[64] Jones carefully examines the passages dealing with slavery in the authentic Pauline letters, showing that "the slave who was called in the Lord is liberated from civil and social servitude and becomes the Lord's freedman."[65] He concludes from 1 Cor. 7:23 "that slaves were to resist any attempt to be made slaves once again" and that consequently current-day Christians should oppose the division of the church "into two distinct segments, one white and the other black."[66] He interprets Galatians as an epistle of freedom and boldly argues that "it is not fantasy to speak of American people as the offspring of the Galatians of the New Testament."[67] The flaw in American civil religion, he argues, is "fickleness" in carrying through with the Puritan vision of freedom and equality, enslaving blacks, and failing to provide equal rights for women. On the basis of Pauline theology, Jones urges black Christians to maintain their faith in freedom, to hold on to moral decency, to avoid relying on materialism, and to overcome the antipathy toward productive work that continues over from slavery.[68] He relates Pauline passages on discipline, the body of Christ, and economic independence to current circumstances within the black community, contending that if the church follows Paul's message of freedom, it will contribute to the transformation of the culture as a whole and also "serve as an agent of liberation for black people and the black community by providing them a haven of refuge from a cold and hostile world about them."[69]

In contrast to the cultural focus of Jones, a recent book by J. Paul Sampley approaches Paul's ethic by taking his eschatology into account.[70] The idea of living between the old age and the new, a major theme in European exegesis for the past generation, is developed with balancing emphases on the community as the "primary context" for ethical discernment,[71] on the Spirit's revitalizing power to make ethical behavior possible,[72] and on the role of a traditional sense of what is "fitting" or "appropriate."[73] While Sampley points out the areas of "dissonance" between Pauline and contemporary thought,[74] he does not focus on the North American context. Most of his book could easily have been written by a contemporary European scholar.

My study of *Christian Tolerance* attempts to relate Rom. 14—15 to conflicts in American churches and culture between conservatives and liberals, providing a biblical basis for humane pluralism. Noting that Romans has "never played a role in the discussion of tolerance in North America," this study argues that Paul "remains an unacknowledged ally in the quest for the foundations of a tolerant society."[75] By bringing Paul's argument in Romans into interaction with American discussions of civility and pluralism, a distinctive approach is suggested in which "genuine tolerance of one's competitors is a logical step for those who are conscious that they themselves have been treated tolerantly by God."[76] This book was followed by curricular materials and a laypersons' commentary on Romans that extend Paul's message into other arenas of American life.[77]

The last study to be mentioned in this survey of books for the popular market was written by a church leader rather than a Pauline scholar. Marva J. Dawn was free to depart from the traditional perspective by presenting Paul as an advocate of the "hilarity of community," based on the reference to *hilarotês* ("cheerfulness") in Rom. 12:8.[78] This word describes "the ideal Christian community . . . that thoroughly enjoyed being itself" in embodying a transformed life in Christ.[79] With an unusually clear understanding of the communal dimension of Pauline theology, she construes Paul's admonition to "present your bodies as a living sacrifice" (Rom. 12:1) as referring to cooperation between Christian groups in service to the world, thus countering the isolating alienation of contemporary life.[80] Relating experiences in various forms of communal ministry in recent years, Dawn argues that Paul's concept of "one body in Christ" (Rom. 12:5) encourages believers "to work and share together more closely as a community."[81] This involves forms of *koinônia* ("fellowship") that draws "partners together in meeting the needs of the set-apart people of God . . . actually becoming immersed in the other's situation" and sharing material resources.[82] This book boldly presents Paul as an advocate of a "beloved community" that can be socially embodied, even in the North American setting that is so distant from Paul's environment. It suggests a line of argument I intend to develop later in this study, analyzing the tenement churches and the Pauline Love Feasts.

Paul as an Apostle to America in Scholarly Writing

When one surveys recent books written by Americans for the scholarly audience, a lack of interest in culturally indigenous intepretation remains typical. But the orientation of many Pauline scholars is departing from

European paradigms and prejudices, and is making significant advances against traditional biases about Paul, both of which are to be traced in subsequent chapters. The three most influential contributors in the past twenty years have been E. P. Sanders, J. Christiaan Beker, and Wayne A. Meeks, who interact intensively and critically with European scholarship. Yet each has provided powerful arguments against the cultural despisers of Paul in this culture as well. In *Paul and Palestinian Judaism* and subsequent studies, Sanders overturns the Lutheran orientation of classical European exegesis, with its anti-Jewish implications.[83] He shows that the Judaism known by Paul did not encourage earning salvation through conformity to the law, and thus that Paul's critique of the Jewish law centered on its incapacity to bring people into relation to Christ, which was only possible through faith. It follows that justification by faith is not the center of Pauline theology, as the dominant European matrix has assumed. Paul's entire interest in "faith" and "law" was to clarify the entrance requirement into the Christian community. Only faith was required for Gentiles, who did not first have to conform to the Jewish law as some Christian Judaizers were insisting. The polemic in Pauline theology is thus against conservative Jewish Christians, not against Jewish religionists themselves, as the traditional matrix has taught. Paul's only complaint about fellow Jews, according to Sanders, is that they did not accept Christ as the Messiah. Far from favoring an anti-Jewish outlook, Paul was involved in creating cross-cultural communities, "the body of Christ, in which all—Jew and Greek, male and female, slave and free—become one person."[84]

Beker goes beyond Sanders by replacing justification by faith with apocalyptic triumph as the center of Pauline theology. While developing this classical European alternative to Lutheranism in the form of a Calvinistic emphasis on the triumph and sovereignty of God, Beker further repudiates the traditional anti-Jewish stance of Pauline theology, showing that Paul retained the doctrine of the priority of Israel by stressing God's faithfulness "to his promises to Israel."[85] This means that the Israel that repudiates Christ retains a crucial place in God's apocalyptic plan for the salvation of the entire world. Beker denies that the phrase "all Israel will be saved" (Rom. 11:26) legitimates the conversion of Jews, insisting that it points toward an eschatological event of global salvation.[86] The coherent center of Pauline theology is thus hope "for the resolution of death, suffering, and evil in the world."[87] The concern for the hermeneutical adaptation of this idea is clearly visible in Beker's next book *Paul's Apocalyptic Gospel*, which concludes that "the cosmic implications of Paul's gospel drive us out of our cultural ghettos—to the larger concerns of our interdependent and pluralistic world."[88] The theme of apocalyptic hope was further developed in Beker's more recent study *Suffering and Hope*, which enters into a dialogue with Jewish and European scholarship to show that "in Paul . . . notwithstanding

God's saving intervention in Christ and the gift of the Spirit to the church, the weight of suffering has the effect of making God's present rule over history and creation opaque. It seems that only at the end of history is the hiddenness of God's rule lifted and clearly recognized."[89] Although oriented to an ecumenical, that is, European style of biblical theology, Beker allows himself one tangential step in the direction of a culturally contextual hermeneutic by proposing this approach to Christian hope as "an antidote to all Christian egoism and privitization of bliss so common in American celebrations of the instant immortality of the individual soul after death."[90]

Among the three leading Pauline scholars in recent decades, Wayne Meeks has made the most fundamental departure from the approach shaped by European orthodoxy. Responding to the puzzlement of American students over the traditional presentation of Pauline theology, Meeks sets out to create a social history of the urbanized groups of Pauline Christians, as reconstructed from evidence in the authentic Pauline letters.[91] He establishes the revolutionary, apocalyptic, and countercultural ethos of these charismatic converted communities, showing their commitment to egalitarianism in the midst of the hierarchical structures of the culture both inside and outside the church. In *The Moral World of the First Christians*, Meeks goes on to show how early Christians incorporated the great traditions of Greece, Rome, and Israel into a new type of apocalyptic sectarianism resting on the belief that a new age had dawned with Christ and that a new humanity was arising in various cells throughout the Roman Empire.[92] The social and moral ambiguity of this movement and its ethical outlook, which provides some of the raw material for a spiteful construal of Paul, is affirmed as productive for contemporary thinkers:

> In the first generations of Christians, moreover, we see many people who have a kind of double vision. Two different kinds of symbolized universe overlap in their minds and in their social experience. On the one hand there is the world so commonplace that no one in everyday life would think of speaking of it as "symbols." . . . On the other hand there is the strange new world of the creating, caring, and judging God, of the crucified Messiah raised from the dead. There are the little groups of fellow believers, of brothers and sisters, children of God, with their simple but powerful rituals, their vigorous admonitions of one another, their moments of high emotion, sometimes trances, ecstasy, experiences of the Spirit—in these meetings this other world seems more vivid than the ordinary one. . . . From them everyone who craves a vision of a juster, kinder world . . . may have something to learn.[93]

This work goes a long way to correct suspicions about Pauline theology and the communities it helped to create. It provides the basis for what Meeks has called "a hermeneutics of social embodiment" that takes the community of faith as the point of departure.[94]

This provocative work was accompanied by a number of other studies informed by the social sciences, written by such scholars as John Gager,[95] John Howard Schütz,[96] Norman Petersen,[97] Abraham Malherbe,[98] Dale Martin,[99] Bruce Malina,[100] Jerome Neyrey,[101] Robert Atkins,[102] and myself[103] who have broken away from the traditional parameters of Pauline scholarship. For the most part, it should be acknowledged, this scholarship is oriented to the international disciplines of anthropology and sociology rather than to distinctively American trends. Nevertheless, a vast amount of fresh raw material has been made available in this work to construct innovative approaches to culturally contextual hermeneutics.

Equally innovative is the work of American rhetoricians and classicists such as Hans Dieter Betz,[104] Wilhelm Wuellner,[105] David Aune,[106] Stanley Stowers,[107] George Kennedy,[108] Frank Witt Hughes,[109] and Jeffrey Crafton,[110] who are recovering a long-suppressed tradition of examining the rhetoric of Paul's letters and their intended interaction with audiences. During most of the period of historical-critical research, this method remained peripheral because it appeared to compromise the abstract, theological substance of Pauline theology. My own recent contribution to Pauline studies is indebted in part to this method,[111] which can be used in coordination with social scientific reconstructions of the communities addressed in Paul's letters. Some of these scholars remain ecumenically European in their scholarly orientation while making contributions, in some cases unintentionally, that are potentially relevant for American cultural hermeneutics. For instance, one of Betz's potentially most cogent books for the American scene has never even been translated into English.[112]

Although marked by a lower level of methodological innovation than some mentioned above, Krister Stendahl stands among the most influential Pauline scholars in the past quarter century. His work was shaped by the classical Pauline tradition of European scholarship but proved responsive to American cultural trends such as pluralism, respect for women in ministry, and interest in glossolalia.[113] He has sensitized an entire generation of American scholars to the fact that "the main lines of Pauline interpretation . . . have for many centuries been out of touch with one of the most basic of the questions and concerns that shaped Paul's thinking in the first place: the relation between Jews and Gentiles."[114] A number of American and Canadian scholars have taken up the impulse articulated by Stendahl, and along with Beker and Sanders have created perspectives with a high level of relevance for the North American intellectual context. The work of such scholars as John Gager,[115] Lloyd Gaston,[116] Norman A. Beck,[117] and others will be discussed in chapter 3.

A distinctive feature of American scholarship on Paul is the participation of Jewish colleagues whose contributions have been widely read and respected.

Samuel Sandmel's study *The Genius of Paul* has gone through three editions since its initial publication in 1958.[118] Using critical methods to evaluate the evidence, Sandmel depicts Paul as a Hellenistic Jew with apocalyptic leanings whose "conversion provided for him the solution to the human predicament," which he understood as the "inability to live up to the Law."[119] Strongly opposed to the influence of European neo-orthodoxy that "threatens to make a shambles of what was once an intellectually honest endeavor to find the truth," Sandmel insists that Paul creatively fused Hellenistic, Jewish, and early Christian influences to create a new religion based on grace.[120] While disapproving Paul's Christology, Sandmel lauds the genius that contributed to "those attitudes toward the individual, toward freedom of the conscience, and toward the inviolability of the conscience which made the transition from the middle ages to modern times. There is a sense in which Galatians and Romans are the spiritual charter of modern men who believe in personal liberty and personal freedom."[121] This wording makes plain that the American context is primarily in view in assessing Paul's contribution.

Another book that reflects the context of a Jewish theologian and psychologist in an American university is Richard Rubenstein's *My Brother Paul*.[122] Approaching Paul from the perspective of a Jew who had followed a "secularized form of the law" of academic accomplishment,[123] Rubenstein discovered that the tension between the high demands of the law and human rebellion could be resolved by a modern, psychological form of Paul's experience of grace. He interpreted Paul's view of the Lord's Supper in Freudian terms: "Both Freud and Paul understood human solidarity as rooted in primordial criminality; by partaking of Christ, the true 'tree of life' at the Lord's Meal and thereby becoming 'like God,' men confess, repeat and represent the original crime. . . . By consuming the body of the indestructible, life-giving redeemer, the believer reenacts his craving to cannibalize his parental life-giver without harming either himself or others. . . . In true sacrificial worship the believer achieves at least momentarily . . . *an end of repression*."[124] Paul's view of Christ as the last Adam symbolizes an overcoming of the repressive split between subject and object, offering "the final restoration of God, man, and the world to each other and the primordial bliss the orientals have named Nirvana."[125] By interpreting Paul as the precursor in a kind of psychological counterculture, Rubenstein is able to affirm the "attempt at self-liberation" that has much to teach contemporary humans.[126] This is an audacious and sympathetic effort to interpret Paul with modern psychoanalytic categories, moving beyond the traditional parameters of Eurocentric Pauline scholarship of the 1970s.

The outstanding Jewish scholar in the current discussion is Alan F. Segal, who places Paul's conversion on the solid foundation of "the Jewish apocalyptic-mystagogue of the first century," whose vision linked Jesus as "a vindicated hero and the image of the *Kavod* [i.e., the "divine glory"], the manlike figure in heaven."[127] Like other early Christians, Paul "identified the son of man, the human or angelic representative of God, with the risen Christ."[128] In beholding the "glory of the Lord" in 2 Cor. 3:18, Paul is claiming a mystical encounter with the "human form of God" which causes his own "transformation into his image."[129] Segal does not hesitate to use the mystical and communal metaphors that are traditionally avoided in Eurocentric exegesis, describing Paul's "new creation" as a conversion process that "takes place in community. Like many visionaries, Paul suggests not just a personal transformation but a transformation of community and of the cosmos as well."[130] Paul thus set about creating communities of converted persons whose faith overcomes the traditional boundaries between Jews and Gentiles, and whose unity comes not from obeying a single law but by sharing the same conversion experience and the same apocalyptic intensity. "Fervently expecting the end, living communally, and doing only what was necessary to support one's family in the interim, the cells of early Christian apocalypticists . . . formed a highly motivated group of proselytizers"[131] that Segal compares with American hippie groups in recent decades.[132] This bold synthesis, firmly based on social scientific insights as well as a judicious sifting of comparative religious sources, represents mature North American scholarship at its best.

Another influential trend in the American context is to use literary-critical methods in analyzing the Pauline letters. Daniel Patte's book *Preaching Paul*[133] is based on his definitive study of structuralist exegesis, *Paul's Faith and the Power of the Gospel: A Structural Introduction to the Pauline Letters*.[134] Both books offer an innovative interpretation of Pauline texts, using the techniques developed by French structuralism. Although the orientation tends toward the timeless, it allows Patte to relate the Pauline critique of idols to the nuclear arms race[135] and to reflect on the relevance of Pauline ethics for the unemployed.[136] The focus, however, is not so much on American cultural dilemmas as on the "post-Christian culture" in the Western world as a whole.[137] Another form of French literary criticism is employed in Robert Hamerton-Kelly's provocative study *Sacred Violence: Paul's Hermeneutic of the Cross*.[138] Building on the scapegoat and mimesis theories developed by Renè Girard, he interprets the death of Christ as "an epiphany of sacred violence."[139] To accept the gospel therefore commits one to resist the principalities and powers that encourage "exclusiveness and scapegoating" and to join "the new community of freedom and mutual acceptance."[140] The Pauline doctrine of original sin is reinterpreted as a manifestation of "mimetic rivalry within the system of sacred violence"[141] since it focuses so intensively on the elements of coveteousness and desire that corrupt the law. This study shares my interest in dealing with the religious motivations of violence, but it mentions "the resurgence of ethnic and nationalist conflict . . . in

Europe and Africa, and its dreary continuance in the Middle East"[142] rather than specific trends in the American scene.

In a category by itself, in part because it deals with a theme that reaches beyond the Pauline letters, and in part because of its innovative focus on American imperial culture in the context of international trends, is Walter Wink's three-volume study of the "principalities and powers." In *Naming the Powers* Wink shows that the Pauline and Deutero-Pauline letters use a fluid group of categories to refer to the "outer and inner aspects of one and the same indivisible concretion of power"[143] by which the reality and spirit of institutions are marked, often leading, as in recent American experience, to the destruction of life. In *Unmasking the Powers* the Pauline critique of the social and ideological embodiments of such institutions is developed with an eye to the evil constellations of power that have emerged in contemporary societies.[144] Finally in *Engaging the Powers* Wink explores the myth of the domination system that has arisen in American culture and attacks it with the Pauline analysis of the fallen world, the world of the flesh, and the old age.[145] He analyzes the "spiral of violence," using some of the same analytic categories that Hamerton-Kelly develops,[146] and shows the relevance of Paul's idea of community and of nonviolent resistance against evil for current circumstances in this country. Using the resources of international biblical scholarship, here is a culturally contextual theology in a mature and provocative form.

Richard B. Hays employs the techniques of intertextuality popularized by American literary critics in his study *Echoes of Scripture in the Letters of Paul*.[147] He shows that Paul's faith "is one whose articulation is inevitably intertextual in character, and Israel's Scripture is the 'determinate subtext that plays a constitutive role' in shaping his literary production."[148] His study concludes with suggestions about contemporary hermeneutics following the Pauline model, which should read scripture "primarily as a narrative of election and promise," taking its function in churchly sermonizing seriously, accepting its definition of the faith community as "participants in the eschatological drama of redemption," and learning "to appreciate the metaphorical relation between the text and our own reading of it."[149] The large number of studies stimulated by this book and presented in recent meetings of national and regional meetings of the Society of Biblical Literature are an indication of how fruitful such appropriations of American interpretive trends can be.

The ambivalence of current scholars about placing Pauline theology firmly within the context of American intellectual trends is visible in the first volume created by the Pauline Theology group of the Society of Biblical Literature, published in 1991.[150] Although it seeks to overcome the traditionally European point of departure of starting with Romans and Galatians, understood as doctrinal treatises, there is no attempt to complete the interpretive arch so as to relate the results to the American cultural setting. The participation of several key European scholars in the enterprise makes it an admirably ecumenical enterprise. The contribution is formidable, throwing an innovative light on five of Paul's shorter letters and showing that American biblical scholarship is functioning in parity with its European counterparts. The American intellectual orientation is partially visible in the pragmatic pluralism of approaches, the lack of a single, dominating matrix, a suspicion of received systems of thought, and attention to the probable sequence of Paul's letters. But most of the categories used in these chapters, including my own,[151] are well worn by generations of European scholars.

An emblem of the ambivalence toward the American cultural setting and hermeneutical tradition surfaced in Dieter Georgi's recent book *Theocracy in Paul's Praxis and Theology* in reference to Josiah Royce's interpretation of Romans 7 that anticipated key exegetical developments by several decades.[152] This is the first reference in Pauline scholarship to Royce's contribution that I have ever seen, and it comes from a colleague who returned to a European university after years of teaching in this country. He points out that "by using social categories and concentrating on social psychology rather than individual psychology," Royce was able to understand the conflict between individualism and the law that functions as the consensus of society better than leading European interpreters.[153] It is stunning to reflect that as early as 1913, Royce explained Paul's view "that the moral self-consciousness of every one of us gets its cultivation from our social order through a process which begins by craftily awakening us" by the lure of individual transcendence, "which taints his conscience with the original sin of self-will, of clever hostility to the very social order upon which he constantly grows more and more consciously dependent."[154] Paul's solution to this problem, according to Royce, is loyalty to "a certain divinely instituted community . . . the body of Christ. The risen Lord dwells in it, and is its life. . . . In the universal community you live in the spirit. . . . Paul's doctrine is that salvation comes through loyalty. Loyalty involves an essentially new type of self-consciousness—the consciousness of one who loves a community as a person."[155] Royce affirms Paul's faith that "loyalty . . . is the only cure for the natural warfare of the collective and of the individual will."[156] It is understandable that this distinctively American construal of Paul was so quickly set aside, buried under the avalanches of cultural pessimism and neo-orthodoxy that swept Pauline studies after the First World War. But it remains an extraordinary confirmation of cultural amnesia that such a distinctive contribution by an important philosopher and the founder of an American tradition of hermeneutics could have gone unmentioned by Pauline scholars for almost eighty years. It was off our mental map because it relied too heavily on an American attitude toward the "beloved community," affirming those very qualities in Paul that the dominant Eurocentric tradition tended to despise.

In conclusion, while in a theoretical sense Paul should be the most flexible resource within the entire New Testament to relate to the extraordinary community of varied cultural groups in this country, becoming "all things to all people," one would have to conclude that the traditional parameters, so powerfully established in European exegesis, have remained largely intact. One finds a few scattered references to American values and problems and even fewer efforts on a larger scale to relate his theology to the the distinctive issues of the American ethos, civil religion, or cultural trends. I believe it is time to begin following the example of Lewis and Clark, exploring some tracks across the New World, and clearing the way for Paul to begin functioning as the veritable Apostle to America.

3. Law and the Coexistence of Jews and Gentiles

I speak the truth in Christ,
   I do not lie,
      my conscience bearing me witness in the Holy Spirit,
that my pain is great
   and [there is] unceasing grief in my heart.
For I would have wished myself to be accursed and set apart from Christ
   for the sake of my brethren, my kinspeople according to flesh
who are Israelites,
   whose [are] the sonship
    and the glory
      and the covenants
        and the lawgiving
and the worship
   and the promises,
     whose [are] the patriarchs
       and from whom [came] the Christ according to the flesh,
      who is God over all, blessed for the aeons, amen.[1]
(Romans 9:1–5)

One of the most important challenges to current scholarship on Paul's letter to the Romans is to come to terms with an interpretive tradition marked by largely unacknowledged anti-Semitism while remaining true to Paul's purpose in writing the letter. If a "paradigm shift" is occurring in the study of Romans in this country,[2] stimulating scholars to revise the traditional anti-Judaic approach, the task is to provide a more adequate alternative. Pauline scholarship in the American setting is particularly called to this task because in the post-Holocaust era, ours is one of the few remaining societies where Jewish and Christian scholars interact constantly. We graduate from the same universities and work together in the Society of Biblical Literature, on university faculties, and in local scholarly organizations and projects. Bonds of personal friendship link Jewish and Christian scholars all over North America. An emblem of this cooperative situation is an acknowledgment page in Alan F. Segal's recent book *Paul the Convert*, on which this brilliant Jewish scholar expresses appreciation to twenty-five Christian and Jewish colleagues who participated in various scholarly consultations and then read sections of his book.[3] I believe that the discussion now has advanced toward a clarification of Paul's position in support of respectful coexistence between Jews and Gentiles in the context of a mission of world transformation and unification.

My plan is to begin with a response to the debate over the past two decades concerning the role of Pauline theology in the rise of anti-Semitism. In two subsequent sections, I will deal with the major issues that comprise the core of the problem: Paul's view of the future of Israel and the debate whether Rom. 10:4 refers to Christ as the "end" or the "goal" of the law. These details will lead to some concluding reflections on the contemporary implications of Paul's doctrine of tolerant pluralism, which has a high level of relevance for the American scene.

Romans and Christian Anti-Semitism

Most of the biblical scholars working in the United States since the Holocaust have been troubled by the traditional reading of Paul's critique of the law. Two prominent European scholars who taught in America may be taken as representative. In 1963 Krister Stendahl published the English version of "The Apostle Paul and the Introspective Conscience of the West,"[4] which contributed to his lifelong campaign to show that "Paul is not carrying out . . . a polemic against the Jews, but is rather giving an apology for his mission."[5] In 1977 Nils Dahl reprinted essays written since 1947[6] that show that Paul's doctrinal development was related to the Gentile mission rather than to a program of anti-Judaism and that he always viewed God's oneness as "demonstrated by the impartiality of his judgment and of his grace upon Jews and Greeks without any distinction."[7]

Picking up strands of this discussion in the mid 1970s, Rosemary Radford Ruether provided a provocative centerpiece for the subsequent discussion of the formation of Christian anti-Semitism.[8] She discussed Paul under the rubric of "the Philosophizing of Anti-Judaism," which involves a fusion of Philonic, Gnostic, and apocalyptic dualism. "Paul's theological thinking is governed by a remarkable fusion of Gnostic and apocalyptic dualisms. . . . Paul has fused this Gnostic world picture with the apocalyptic dualism between this 'present age' of world history, dominated by the powers of wickedness, and the new 'age to come,' which Paul sees as eternal and spiritual in character."[9] The model for this dualism is Gal. 4:21–31, which

contrasts the offspring of Hagar and Sarah, flesh and spirit, the present
Jerusalem and the heavenly Jerusalem, slavery and freedom.[10] That this
material sustains Ruether's contention that "Paul's position was unques-
tionably that of anti-Judaism"[11] is plausible as far as Galatians and Philippians are concerned, the letters where Paul is engaged in polemic against the
Judaizers. But Ruether uses this dualistic model to interpret the entirety of
Pauline theology, overlooking the very real differences in the perspective of
Romans. While Galatians suggests that "the reign of Torah is equivalent to
the reign of these demonic powers and principalities of the finite realm,"[12]
Rom. 7:7 denies that "the law is sin," and Rom. 3:31 contends that Paul and
his theology "uphold the law."

A particularly controversial aspect of Ruether's interpretation relates to
the conversion of Jews in Rom. 11. Her forthright reading of Paul's "mystery" concerning the conversion of the Jews leads her to reject ecumenists
who suggest he defended the ongoing validity of the Mosaic covenant. "In
this sense, he enunciates a doctrine of the rejection of the Jews (rejection of
Judaism as the proper religious community of God's people) in the most radical form, seeing it as rejected not only now, through the rejection of Christ,
but from the beginning. The purpose of Paul's 'mystery' is not to concede
any ongoing validity to Judaism but rather to assure the *ultimate vindication of
the Church.*"[13] I believe she is correct in acknowledging that Paul did expect
"that all Israel will be saved" (Rom. 11:26) through acceptance of Jesus as
the Christ, but this did not necessarily entail the abandonment of Jewish
culture or obedience to the Torah as Rom. 3:30 and 14:1–15:8 reveal. It is
hard to maintain that Paul eliminates the ongoing validity of Judaism in
light of Rom. 3:1–2 and 9:1–5, where he acknowledges the "advantage" of
possessing the "sonship, the glory, the covenants, the giving of the law, the
worship, and the promises . . . the patriarchs, and of their race, according to
the flesh, is the Christ." But the difficulty in providing a satisfactory explanation of these data is evident in the subsequent debate over Ruether's
provocative sketch of the radical kind of anti-Judaism that can be derived
from selections of Paul's writing.

The response to Rosemary Ruether's construal of Paul has been less vigor-
ous than to other aspects of her thesis. According to John Gager, most
scholars have accepted her view.[14] As the major predecessor of the reinter-
pretation Gager wishes to offer, Lloyd Gaston from Vancouver School of
Theology is cited.[15] Both scholars flatly reject the contention that Pauline
theology contains elements of anti-Judaism and that Pauline Christology
leads to anti-Semitism. Though quite different in their approach, one could
consider the recent work of J. Christiaan Beker[16] and E. P. Sanders[17] as
offering alternatives to Ruether's perspective. The first issue that arises from
this debate concerns the status of Israel and its relation to faith in Jesus as
the Christ.

Paul's View of Israel and Its Salvation

Although the question of Paul's attitude toward Israel has been debated rather intensely for the past thirty years,[18] a provocative starting point for the recent discussion is the work of Krister Stendahl. He argues persuasively that Romans research has long been "out of touch with one of the most basic of the questions and concerns that shaped Paul's thinking in the first place: the relation between Jews and Gentiles."[19] In contrast to the traditional view of justification by faith as the theme of the letter, he argues that "the real center of gravity in Romans is found in chapters 9—11," which describe the divine plan for Paul's mission involving the inclusion of Jews and Gentiles.[20] This interpretation offers a striking alternative to the widespread view that Paul's opponent in Romans is the pious Jew.[21] It is therefore understandable that Stendahl rejects the traditional interpretation of Jewish conversion that Ruether had advanced, insisting that the "salvation of the Jews" in Rom. 11:26 does not imply their acceptance of Jesus as the Christ.[22] Stendahl's contention that Paul intentionally fails to mention the name of Jesus Christ in this context is considerably less convincing than Ruether's forthright exegesis, particularly in light of the prominent references to Christ in the crucial, early stages of Paul's treatment of the status of Israel (Rom. 9:1–10:17) and his insistence that the gospel of Christ must be preached "to the Jew first and also to the Greek" (Rom. 1:16).

Nils A. Dahl advanced this discussion by placing Paul's statements about the future of Israel in the context of the rhetoric of Romans and the situation of the early Christian mission.[23] Some of the distinctive features of Rom. 9—11 are explained by reference to the unique "epistolary situation" that required the Apostle "to refute false rumors that Paul had rejected the law and his own people."[24] It follows that Rom. 9—11 deals not with theodicy but with the issue of divine faithfulness to Israel, advancing the thesis in Rom. 9:6, that God's word has not failed. By a detailed analysis of the argument, Dahl shows that faithfulness to the divine promises to Israel is consistent with the inclusion of the Gentiles and with faith in Christ, hence with the doctrine of the justification of the ungodly by faith. When Paul maintains that "all Israel will be saved," he "does not affirm that every individual Israelite will attain salvation, but that God will grant salvation to both parts of his people, to those who have rejected Christ as well as to those who have believed in him."[25] Dahl acknowledges, however, that a historical reversal of Paul's hopes occurred after writing Romans. The Jerusalem offering failed to provoke the envy of Israel, encouraging conversion, and the Gentile Christians continued the tendency to make themselves "great at the expense of Israel."[26] Ultimately Christians came to believe that God had rejected Israel and, with the emergence of Christianity as a state religion, that discrimination against unconverted Jews was required. Dahl goes some distance to raise questions about the legitimacy of Christian missionizing of Jews: "Paul does not envision any mission among the Jews by Christians of Gentile origins." But he quickly qualifies this by admitting that "this does not necessarily mean that such a mission is wrong, even though it has more often been pursued with zeal than with understanding." His conclusion is a modest effort to coordinate historical observations with ethical reflection: "What Paul hoped for has not happened, and no one can reproach the Jews for that. . . . There is no Jewish problem, but there is a Christian problem."[27]

J. Christiaan Beker's *Paul the Apostle* takes up this "problem" within the context of the thoroughly apocalyptic theology of the Apostle to the Gentiles. He defends Paul as the only New Testamant writer "who is passionately engaged with the Jews as the people of the promise and who, notwithstanding his radically different understanding of messianism, keeps his thought anchored in the Hebrew Scriptures and in the destiny of Israel as God's people."[28] The insistence of Paul on the priority of Israel in the divine plan of salvation must be understood within the context of his struggle for unity between Jewish and Gentile Christians. Beker contends that this unity "is undergirded by a theological principle: the faithfulness of God to his promises to Israel."[29] If the divine promises to Israel are abrogated, the justification and the inclusion of Gentiles lose their foundation. "The church of the Gentiles is an extension of the promises of God to Israel and not Israel's displacement."[30] Since the Jerusalem offering was designed in part to symbolize the spiritual indebtedness of the Gentile Christians to their Jewish origins, Beker notes how closely Paul's death was connected with this principle.

On the basis of Rom. 9—11, Beker contends that "Israel's strategic position in salvation-history is not confined to its past, as if Israel is now absorbed by the church. Israel remains a distinct entity in the future of God's purpose."[31] Thus when Paul referred to the "mystery" of Israel's salvation in Rom. 11:25, he wished to express the "undulating dynamic of God's salvation-history," in which successive periods of Jewish and Gentile disobedience and conversion would ultimately result in the conversion and unification of the world.[32] Within this framework, Beker insists that "Israel's salvation ('all Israel will be saved' [Rom. 11:26]) does not mean Israel's conversion as the result of Christian missions. 'All Israel' is not a designation for the Jewish-Christian church, because it points clearly to an eschatological event."[33] The apocalyptic framework allows Beker at this point to take up the tentative question of Dahl concerning the legitimacy of Christian missionizing of Jews, eliminating all equivocation. In connection with the insistence that the "priority" of the Jews remains intact, Beker repudiates Jewish conversion and calls for a renewed dialogue about the problems of apocalyptic messianism. The peculiarity of Paul's position was the "bifocal tension of his Christology. The Messiah has come, but without his kingdom."[34] That is, the fulfillment of the messianic promises is left to the future because Paul

refused the solution of later Christianity that identified the messianic fulfillment with the creation of the institutional church. On this modest—even
fragile—foundation, Beker calls for Christians to enter into respectful dialogue with their Jewish partners. While I remain skeptical about whether
Paul's expectation that "all Israel" would be saved was originally intended to
rule out Christian missionizing, I think Beker's portrayal of a central issue
for dialogue is sound.

There are some striking affinities both with Beker and Stendahl in the
recent essay by a German scholar, Pinchas Lapide. Acknowledging a measure of "ambivalence" in Paul's attitude toward the law, Lapide insists that
the encounter on the Damascus road implied "the great turning point of
God's plan of salvation, predestined since Abraham, which was to bring
about the reconciliation of Jews and Gentiles. The dawning of the new age
was regarded neither as a breakaway from the traditions of Israel nor as an
invasion into the Gentile world, and certainly not as the abolition of the
Torah."[35] In the interpretation of this modern Jewish scholar, Paul advocated two routes to salvation, one for Gentiles and another for Jews: "Jesus
became the Savior of the Gentiles *without* being the Messiah of Israel."[36] So
long as Pauline theology retains the ultimate unification of the human race
as a hope rather than an achievement, it will refrain from writing off "the
Jews as unbelieving, unsaved, and everlastingly obstinate."[37] Just as in
Beker's proposal, the basis of dialogue here is the messianic future. It therefore follows that Paul should be viewed as "neither an anti-Semite nor an
anti-Judaist."[38] I believe this conclusion is justified even if it remains unlikely that Paul's hope for the salvation of "all Israel" implied that Jews would
never accept Jesus as the Messiah.

In both of his books on Paul, E. P. Sanders has provided a bulwark against
an anti-Semitic interpretation.[39] His basic contention is that Paul's critique
of Judaism rests entirely on his Christian experience and thus has nothing to
do with the actual contours of Jewish practice in his time. To understand
Paul's counterposing of gospel against law as a polemic against an alleged
legalism in contemporary Judaism, following the mainstream of Pauline interpretation, is thus perceived to be a dangerous distortion. Starting from the
premise of faith in Jesus as the Christ, Paul's only criticism of Judaism was not
to accept this premise. Insisting on the single "entrance requirement" of faith
in Jesus Christ for both Jews and Gentiles, Paul established a kind of "third
race," the "true Israel" mentioned in Galatians and Romans.[40] The double
covenant theory favored by Lapide and others is therefore rejected by
Sanders: "The simplest reading of [Rom.] 11:13–36 seems to be this: the only
way to enter the body of those who will be saved is by faith in Christ."[41]

While Paul was perhaps not conscious of having broken with Judaism, his
thought remaining thoroughly grounded in Hebrew Scripture, Sanders nevertheless points to a denial of "two pillars common to all forms of Judaism:

the election of Israel and faithfulness to the Mosaic law."[42] This contention is somewhat problematic, in my view, because Paul explicitly affirms Israel's election in Rom. 3:1–2, 9:4–5, and 11:1–11, and defends the legitimacy of the Torah in Rom. 7:7, 9:4, and 13:8–10, and of Torah obedience among Christian believers in Rom. 14:1–15:6. Yet there is overwhelming evidence in support of Sanders's basic contention that Paul criticized Jewish religionists who rejected the gospel of Jesus as the Christ.

The most thoroughly revisionist perspectives currently available rest on the foundations prepared by Stendahl and Gaston. John G. Gager contends that Paul did not expect the conversion of Jews nor question the authenticity of Torah for them as a way of salvation.[43] Citing Rom. 3:30 that God "will justify the circumcised on the ground of their faith and the uncircumcised because of their faith," Gager argues that "Paul uses faith here not as the equivalent of faith in Christ but as a designation of the proper response to God's righteousness, whether for Israel in the Torah or for Gentiles in Christ."[44] Paul's main concern was to defend Christ as the means of salvation for the Gentiles. His "argument with the Jews" related to their "boast" in an exclusive relationship with God, excluding Gentiles. The polemic about the law was aimed at Christian Judaizers, not at non-Christian Jews. As Gager sees it, neither in Rom. 3 nor 10 does Paul "intimate that the failure of the Jews lies in their refusal to become Christians. What he does say is that their boasting and their failure to attain righteousness comes from a single cause, lack of *pistis*." So the reason the Jews were perceived to have "stumbled" was because they had not accepted the "legitimacy of Paul's gospel to and about the Gentiles."[45] When Paul decries the "unenlightened zeal" of the non-Christian Jews in Rom. 10, he is simply describing their refusal to accept the Gentile mission.[46] Norman Beck has recently accentuated this case by arguing that the most explicitly anti-Jewish passage of 1 Thess. 2:13–16 was interpolated[47] and the rest of the Pauline letters "are not virulently anti-Jewish."[48]

Despite its appeal as a basis for Jewish-Christian dialogue, the cogency of Gager's and Beck's case must be questioned at several points. For those who are skeptical about the rejection of the authenticity of 1 Thess. 2:13–16, it remains difficult to deny the degree to which it shares with Gal. 4:21–31 a polemical attitude not only toward Judaizers but toward non-Christian Jews. That Rom. 3:30 implies the possibility of justification through Torah obedience is contradicted by the thesis it was intended to prove, that "a person is justified by faith apart from works of law"(Rom. 3:28). And that "faith" in Romans involves acceptance of the Gentile mission rather than a relationship to Jesus as the Messiah rides roughshod over key passages such as Rom. 1:1–17, 3:21–26, and 10:5–13. Ed Sanders provides a more solid exegesis by insisting that Rom. 11:25–26 implies the acceptance by Jews of Jesus as the Christ. But Gager is on target in showing that Paul's argument does not entail a repudiation of the Torah or of the election of Israel. As Beker and others have shown, the authority of the Torah remains necessary to establish Paul's case about the justification of the ungodly in the earlier chapters of Romans.

It is appropriate that the final contribution to the discussion of Paul's view of the salvation of Israel should be that of Alan Segal, who offers a fair-minded and judicious evaluation of the evidence from a Jewish perspective. He finds it implausible that Paul offers "a double plan for salvation" in Rom. 9—11[49] and insists that "Paul argues that Jewish Christians (with faith) and gentile Christians (with faith) are equal, not that Jews and Christians are equal."[50] Segal admits that "as a believing Jew and a twentieth-century humanist," the interpretation suggested by Stendahl, Gaston, and Gager "makes more sense for today than does Paul's actual conclusion. It would have been easier for today's Christianity had Paul embraced cultural pluralism more fully."[51] Paul's perspective was forged out of his conversion, his successful mission to the Gentiles, and the largely unsuccessful mission to the Jews, but these factors tended to be overlooked in the traditional perspective that interpreted "Paul as opposing Judaism because it practiced self-salvation and volition."[52] Although committed to the Christ encountered in a mystical vision, Paul never "felt he had left Judaism."[53] He continued to respect the scripture and to leave room for the mysterious will of God. In this connection, Segal finds that "Paul's refusal to spell out the implications of his reasoning is extremely important," because "Paul obviously does not want to impinge on the sovereignty of God in spelling out how God intends to fulfill biblical promises."[54]

An important point needs to be remembered in this debate, namely that in his most important—and probably last—doctrinal statement in Romans, Paul defended the integrity of Jewish culture and of Jewish-Christians. In this letter Paul advances beyond the polemical stance of some of his earlier writings, particularly on the relation to Judaism. There is no doubt about his anguish for his fellow Jews expressed in Rom. 9:1–5; he defends the prerogatives shared by all Jews in Rom. 3:1–2 and insists on the acceptance of the Jewish Christians in Rom. 14:1–15:6. Their obedience to kosher food laws and celebration of Jewish festivals is not to be "despised," according to this passage. The integrity of both the "weak" and the "strong," both Jewish and Christian believers, is defended in principle, as pointed out in *Christian Tolerance*.[55] The consequence is that conversion to belief in Jesus as the Messiah does not entail the abolition of cultural distinctions or theological tendencies. This is a side of Paul's mature work that seems worth preserving when the precise expectations he had about Jewish conversion were not fulfilled. There is no justification in denying that Paul's hope in Rom. 11:26 did not materialize. The same could be said about his anticipation of the Parousia. In this connection, the insight of our Jewish colleagues Lapide and

Segal seems correct in stressing that Paul's vision of the "mystery" of Israel's conversion was followed by the paean to the inscrutable mind of God (Rom. 11:33–36). It is unlikely that Paul wished to exclude himself—or us—from the rhetorical question, "Who has known the mind of God?" In fact, as the evolution of Jewish-Christian relations over the past two thousand years has demonstrated, the answer is "No one!"

Paul's View of the Status of the Law

The most problematic issue in the relation between Jews and Christians is the status of the Torah. Several recent studies survey the entire range of Paul's use of the term "law."[56] Since there is no space here for an exhaustive survey, a discussion of the crucial text concerning Christ as the end or fulfillment of the law in Rom. 10:4 will suffice. The three basic positions that have been taken on the definition of *telos* (= end, goal) in this passage have very substantial implications for the relation between Jews and Christians. The view that *telos* means "end" in this verse is most characteristically advanced by Lutheran scholars, though its widespread appeal is visible in the translation of the RSV, "For Christ is the end of the law." The expression "the end of the law" is a famous title for European studies in Pauline theology.[57] It finds classic expression in Käsemann's Romans commentary, which rejects every connotation but "termination" as fatally flawed with un-Christian moralism. Paul understands law and gospel "as mutually exclusive antitheses" shaped by the apocalyptic "contrast and contradiction of the old and new aeons."[58] While Käsemann recognizes the semantic range of *telos*, he insists on the translation "end" because it embodies what is interpreted as Paul's anti-Judaistic theology in Romans.

> The Mosaic Torah comes to an end with Christ because man now renounces his own right in order to grant God his right (3:4). In the eschatological change the creature who wants to possess his own right is replaced by the Creator who has the right and who is acknowledged in the obedience of faith. Even for Israel no other possibility of salvation exists. Failing to understand the law, it falls into illusion and is overthrown. Christ exposes the illusion.[59]

The view favored by Calvinist interpreters and many others is that *telos* means "goal" or "fulfillment."[60] This perspective receives its most extensive defense among recent commentators in the work of British scholar C.E.B. Cranfield. Like his Lutheran counterparts, Cranfield rests his case not so much on the contextual details of the passage or a general consideration of the range of semantic possibilities as on the picture of Pauline theology as a whole. The fundamental conviction is rather defensive, "that there is no statement in any of Paul's epistles which, rightly understood, implies that Christ has abolished the law."[61] In an extensive concluding essay, Cranfield observes that the modern terms for "legalism" were not available in Paul's day. Thus he concedes that some of Paul's statements "which at first sight seem to disparage the law, were really directed not against the law itself but against that misunderstanding and misuse of it for which we now have a convenient terminology. In this very difficult terrain Paul was pioneering."[62] In drawing theological conclusions from this argument, the preference for a Calvinist rather than a Lutheran perspective comes through clearly. Cranfield insists that Pauline authority cannot be adduced for "the view that in law and gospel two different modes of God's action are manifested. . . . On the contrary, it is clear that we are true to Paul's teaching, when we say that *God's word in Scripture is one*."[63]

A more compelling presentation of this position is provided by American Paul W. Meyer, who disentangles it to some degree from theological biases. Observing that the "crucial decisions are made elsewhere and that this part of Paul's text is in fact and in practice understood within and from a wider whole,"[64] Meyer rests his case on an examination of the argumentative context. From Rom. 9:30 through 10:4 the metaphor of pursuing a goal is developed, with Israel pursuing "righteousness which is based on the law" but failing to achieve it because of a "false assumption with which the pursuit was undertaken (9:31f.).[65] This point is reiterated in Rom. 10:2–3 where zeal for the Torah is described as misguided, which is interpreted in the light of Rom. 7 where the capacity of sin to pervert the law is described. The proper sense of Rom. 10:4 in the context of this argument is "the intent and goal of the law, to lead to righteousness for everyone who believes, is (nothing different from) Christ."[66] Meyer observes that this interpretation "shows how unshakable his attachment to Torah . . . really was,"[67] which means that Paul should not be construed as "an apostate Jew."[68] In a similar vein, C. Thomas Rhyne alludes to the implication of this interpretation for the relation between the church and the synagogue:

> Therefore *in its witness to righteousness by faith, the law as the object of the synagogue's religious pursuits is upheld in the preaching and acceptance of the gospel in the church.* Though Pauline Christianity may not be continuous with the Judaism in which Paul had earlier so excelled, it is certainly continuous with Judaism to the degree that it finds its raison d'être in the law which witnesses to (and also promises) righteousness by faith.[69]

A third approach to the issue of interpreting *telos* in Rom. 10:4, the least defensible from the point of view of exegetical method, is to compromise between the two other positions. European commentators such as C. K.

Barrett, Otto Kuss, Franz Leenhardt, and F. F. Bruce argue that Paul intended telos to convey both the end and the goal of the law.[70] The most suc-
cinct statement of this argument is "the word 'end' (telos) has a double
sense; it may mean 'goal' or 'termination'. On the one hand, Christ is the
goal at which the law aimed in that He is the embodiment of perfect righteousness. . . . On the other hand (and this is the primary force of Paul's
words), Christ is the termination of the law in the sense that with Him the
old order . . . has been done away."[71] Typical of this effort to have one's
cake and eat it too is John W. Drane, who argues that Paul was "deliberately using the ambiguity of the word to cover up a subtle change in the
direction of his thought on the matter. . . . Paul seems to be implying that,
though the function of the Law has been radically altered by the coming of
Christ, it has not been altogether abolished."[72] This approach confuses the
interpretive alternatives developed in modern debate with the original
intentions of an ancient writer in a context lacking any hint of this particular ambiguity. As an unfortunate and unmethodical effort to gain the theological advantages of both the Lutheran and the Calvinist exegesis, it is the
least satisfactory approach to this passage.

There is an urgent need for new semantic and linguistic data to resolve
the impasse over the interpretation of telos in Rom. 10:4, eliminating the
necessity to decide the issue on the basis of theological preferences. An
important new dissertation by Robert Badenas, written at Andrews University in the United States, fills this need.[73] The original meaning of telos was
"highest point, turning point," and its primary associations were with the
ideas of intention and completion but never with temporal fulfillment or
cessation. The semantic range of the term thus encompassed (a) apex, (b)
aim, and (c) completion. Badenas provides an authoritative survey of philosophical usage, showing that in the New Testament period, telos is a technical term for final cause, goal, or purpose, a usage reflected in the verbal form
teleô in Rom. 2:27, "fulfill the law." After a thorough discussion of the
exegetical options, in which he rejects the polysemous compromise option
on methodological grounds, he shows that the argumentative context as
well as the linguistic possibilities favor the option of Christ as the goal of the
law. Two other American dissertations arrive at the same conclusion.[74]

One consequence of this resolution is that Romans provides a much less
polemical basis than otherwise for dialogue between Christians and Jews.
Paul's argument in 9:30–10:4 is that the ultimate purpose of the law was that
all persons, Jews and Gentiles alike, might find righteousness. If Christ is the
"goal of the law," the path of faith can be pursued without repudiating the
Torah. The crucial point is the avoidance of zealotism, the assumption that
conformity to a particular standard guarantees superiority over those who do
not conform. Such zealotism is a perversion possible to Jews as well as to
Christians.

Paul's Hope . . . for Our Time

When one takes the historical setting and argument of Romans into account, it is plausible to suggest that "all Israel will be saved" (Rom. 11:26) implied not simply the acceptance of Jesus as Messiah but concurrently, as the preceding argument in 10:1–13 indicated, a turn away from zealotism, and, as the succeeding argument in 14:1–15:13 shows, a turn toward tolerant coexistence between Jews and Gentiles. In the context of Romans, at least, being "saved" did not entail cultural or theological extinction. It involved preserving distinctive features of racial, cultural, and theological self-identity within the context of mutual acceptance.[75]

In none of these particulars was Paul's hope precisely fulfilled within his lifetime or the generations that followed. A militant minority within the Jewish community refused the message of this antizealot thinker and entered into a maelstrom of violence against the Gentile world. Paul himself was a victim of this violent campaign, his death resulting from the legal complications related to the riots in Jerusalem instigated by zealot opponents of his apostleship to the Gentiles. Succeeding decades witnessed the zealot uprisings in 66–73 C.E. (the Jewish-Roman War in Palestine), 115–17 (the Jewish revolt in Cyprus), and 132–35 (the Bar Kochba Revolt in Palestine), revealing the suicidally destructive capacity of the zealotism that Paul hoped would soon be ended.

After the first of these disastrous expressions of zealous crusading, Judaism turned away from this legacy under the leadership of the Jamnian rabbis, creating a nonnationalistic form of the Jewish faith. The long-term consequence was that Israel was in fact "saved." A remnant faithful to the Torah was preserved from zealotism, chauvinism, militarism, and violent apocalypticism. This salvation, to use Paul's term in Rom. 11:26, did not occur exactly as Paul had envisioned it. Yet some features of his program in Romans were embodied in the creation of Jewish institutions of education, legislation, and conflict resolution that were uniquely suited to the preservation of Jewish culture in a diaspora setting. By abandoning zealous violence as a means of bringing the messianic age, rabbinic Judaism was able to preserve the vision of international peace as part of a messianic future. A large measure of tolerant pluralism was created in the establishment of the canon of Hebrew Scripture and the subsequent development of the Mishna and Talmud where the contradictory voices of the sages were respectfully catalogued. An ethic of individual responsibility for the transformation of the secular world was crafted out of the same biblical resources that Paul used in Rom. 12—15, with striking similarities at almost every point. In view of the Pauline faith in the promises of God, it seems appropriate to value the remarkable development of Pharisaic Judaism and its creative, highly ethical contribution to world culture as evidence of the faithfulness and grace of God.

Insofar as Christian missionizing of Jews refuses to accept the divinely guided measures that were taken in the wake of the zealous wars, and insofar as such missionizing aims at destroying Jewish culture, self identity, and loyalty to the Torah, it runs counter to the mysterious and inscrutable will of God to which Paul gave his final allegiance in Rom. 11:33–36. To expect the fulfillment of Paul's hope that "all Israel will be saved" in the sense of accepting Gentile doctrine and self-identity is a misunderstanding of Paul's original vision of a pluralistic world community. The entire question of "saving" the Jews needs to be reconceived in light of what God has accomplished since Paul wrote Romans, inspiring and sustaining humane institutions of loyalty to divine law. But this does not mean that the critical resources of Pauline theology are irrelevant either for Jews or for Christian missionaries.

With the restoration of the national state in 1948, elements of zealous nationalism that had been opposed by the rabbis for generations began to predominate in Israeli self-identity. A similar virus of zealous nationalism has long infected Christian America, gaining in intensity during the later years of the Cold War.[76] Other nations have manifested these traits, as we are painfully reminded in the news from Eastern Europe. The Pauline hope of the unification of the world (Rom. 15:7–13) through the gospel of transforming love that produces respect between groups as diverse as the Jews and the Gentiles urgently needs to be placed on the agenda. Purged of all triumphalism and sobered by the recognition of the limitations of our own understanding, there is still a possibility of entering into the process of respectful dialogue, which is the direction the proper interpretation of Paul should impel us.

4. The Sexual Liberation of Paul and His Churches

For you are all children of God through faith in Christ Jesus.
　For as many of you who were baptized into Christ have put on
　　Christ.
There is neither Jew nor Greek;
　there is neither slave nor free;
　　there is no male and female.
For you are all one in Christ Jesus.[1]

(Galatians 3:26–28)

The debate over Paul's attitude toward women, pulled in one direction by the egalitarian caption above and in another direction by chauvinist elements in the tradition, is clear evidence of scholarship fruitfully responding to cultural trends. The questions thrown up by this debate show the inadequacy of previous views, especially those received from European exegesis,[2] and suggest the need for a new appraisal of Paul's development. The experience since the 1970s of gradually being sensitized to the moral and theological problems of an unacknowledged chauvinistic outlook raises the question of whether Paul himself was sexually liberated, to some extent, in the course of his career.

　Some of the studies written since the 1970s attempt to overcome the spiteful distortion of Paul's perspective.[3] Other investigations seek to relieve the conflicts by refuting the evidence concerning Paul's egalitarian attitude.[4] A series of revolutionary studies by Barre, Fiorenza, Meeks, Scroggs, Snyder, MacDonald, and Wire have changed the entire scope of the discussion.[5] Various hermeneutical theories have been applied to try to overcome the discrepancies that have come to light in the evidence.[6] The basic dilemma is that while some materials in Paul's letters are fully liberated, there are other passages pointing in a more chauvinistic direction, as Boucher, Pagels, Walker, and others have shown.[7] Feminist scholars have confronted this dilemma with particular directness: Munro posits a conflict "between patriarchy and charismatic community";[8] Pagels explains the apparent "ambivalence" as caused by Paul's eschatological reservation and his "fear of diversity" and "disorder";[9] Ruether speaks of the Pauline "contradiction between equality in the eschatological order and subjugation in the patriarchal order of nature";[10] Fiorenza describes the "double-edged" impact of Paul on feminine leadership, affirming their equality and freedom while subordinating "women's behavior in marriage and in the worship assembly to the interests of Christian mission."[11]

Light is thrown on our current situation when we take seriously the fact that at least one branch of early Christianity experienced very modern-sounding conflicts over gender roles in the first and second generations. The discrepancies in the evidence concerning the role of women in the church and the attitude toward female leadership reflect very real conflicts between groups and ideologies. In the Pauline churches in particular, such conflicts can be documented in some detail and an evolution can be traced from early to late stages of Paul's own development. Paul's own views of the role of women in the church and the language he used differ from his earlier to later letters. It is possible, in fact, to speak of a kind of "sexual liberation" in Pauline thought. A sketch of the major phases in this development, dealing with the evidence in sequence through Paul's career, is instructive.

The Earliest Evidence of Paul's Practice and Attitude

When one takes the chronological sequence of Paul's references to women into account, a remarkable evolution becomes visible.[12] The first stage of this evolution is prior to the writing of his first letter to the Thessalonians around 49 C.E. It is clear from references to Paul's missionary colleagues in periods prior to the writing of his first letter that there was a practical equality in mission between male and female, at least for Paul's branch of the church. One piece of evidence pointing in this direction is 1 Cor. 16:19, which refers to Prisca and Aquila, the married couple whom Paul met in Corinth and with whom he had close relations as a missionary colleague for a number of years. The fact that Prisca is usually mentioned first makes it fairly clear that she was the dominant partner, and some more recent studies of the sociology of early Christianity suggest that Paul probably worked under their patronage in Corinth. That is, they were patrons of the house church that they had founded prior to Paul's arrival. Paul refers in Rom. 16:3–4 to Prisca and Aquila as "co-workers," a technical term for early Christian missionaries.[13] It is clear that they are not in any sense subordinate to Paul. Paul views both of them as fully equal to himself in mission. This means that at least at the time of the beginning of the Corinthian ministry, that is, prior to the writing of 1 Thessalonians, Paul was working closely with at least one female leader in early Christianity.

We can push the evidence back even earlier than the Corinthian ministry on the basis of Paul's reference in Phil. 4:2–3 to two evangelistic colleagues Euodia and Syntyche. Paul refers to them as "laboring side by side in the gospel," using technical language that reflects early Christian missionary practice.[14] These two leaders are having a conflict at the time that Paul writes Philippians some years later, but on the basis of their importance for the congregation and the reference to their having worked with Paul while he was founding the mission, which took place in 48 and 49 C.E., there is clear evidence of a practice of equality in mission. This basic pattern is reflected in the various references to women in Rom. 16. The reference to Phoebe in Rom. 16:2 as a deacon and sponsor, or patron, of the church at Cenchraea probably reaches back to the time when the cities in the proximity of Corinth were being evangelized, that is, in 50–51 C.E. Phoebe is apparently a woman of independent wealth, and her traveling to Rome at the time of the Roman correspondence and Paul's request to give aid to her probably reveal that she was acting as a sponsor of Paul's mission to Rome. Paul refers to her having been a patron to himself in times past and also to other early Christian missionaries.[15] Four other women are mentioned in Rom. 16:6 and 12, and it appears they are also early Christian missionaries of some prominence whom Paul met in the eastern mission field prior to 56 C.E. and who are now back in Rome.

It is noteworthy in comparison with the transformation of Paul's theoretical approach to gender issues, that this pattern of equality in mission appears to remain constant. Earle Ellis's charting of all the references to Paul's co-workers reveals a remarkable cross section that uses the same terms for males as for females from the early to the late letters.[16] Moreover, in contrast to other areas of discrepancy between Acts and the Pauline letters, the witness to female leadership is mutually corroborating. Parvey appears to be on solid ground in suggesting a pattern that goes back to the leading women in Damascus (Acts 9:1–2), Joppa (Acts 9:36–43), Thessalonica (Acts 17:4), Beroea (Acts 17:10), and Caesarea (Acts 21:9). This pattern may well derive from the Hellenistic churches' perception of the meaning of the Pentecost promise that "your sons and your daughters shall prophesy."[17] Whatever the precise origin of the egalitarian pattern of leadership, it is at least clear that as far as the Pauline evidence is concerned the practice preceded the theorizing.

The evidence for equality in mission is all the more striking when one compares it with Paul's references to the issues of marriage and female roles in his earliest letter. When one looks at 1 Thess. 4:1–8, it is quite striking that Paul's language reflects the patriarchal tradition of his Jewish background rather than this egalitarian pattern of the early Christian mission whose evidence we have just sketched. Paul refers to the problem of marriage in Thessalonica as if it were a problem of male rights only. Women are referred to in the passage as the "vessel," which is a literal translation of the

Hebrew euphemism for a wife.[18] The ethical admonition in the passage is addressed to males only, "that each of you take a vessel for himself in holiness and honor," which reflects the Pharisaic and general Judaic marriage ideal in which it is the male's sexual rights that are in the forefront. The warning in 1 Thess. 4:6 not to "overreach and defraud" each other refers to respect for the marriage contracts of other people, in this case other males.[19] The commercial terminology employed in this verse is consistent with the terms used in rabbinic references to marriage. It seems to me quite striking that at this early stage Paul's language is patriarchal and highly traditional. One can only infer that nothing has stimulated the evolution of Paul's language at this point and that there is no evidence that he was conscious of the striking contradiction in language and outlook between the patriarchal tradition of Judaism and the egalitarian mission strategy of early Christianity in which Paul was a participant.

The Shift toward "Equality-in-Principle"

The next stage in the evolution of Paul's language is visible to us in a remarkable reference in 1 Cor. 7:1, which according to recent research is one-half of a proverb that Paul had apparently taught while he was in Corinth. It appears that this proverb, which reflects the traditional Judaic sexual ethic, ran something as follows: "It is well for a man not to touch a [strange] woman, lest he incur the wrath of God." The original intent of the proverb was to promote sexual responsibility, perhaps including a measure of "sexual asceticism."[20] Only the first portion of this saying is quoted in 1 Corinthians, but it is quite likely that Paul is being cited in this somewhat mutilated proverb and that the content of this sexual ethic is fully congruent with 1 Thess. 4:1–8, which was written during Paul's initial Corinthian ministry (50–51 C.E.). The proverb addresses males only and views women as sex objects. Its origin, terminology, and ideology are Judaic, and it clashes decisively with Paul's long-standing egalitarianism in missionary practice.

The evolution of Paul's perspective is evident in the materials written in the mid-fifties, after the writing of 1 Thessalonians in particular. Here we have an evolution toward "equality-in-principle," which may in all likelihood reflect conflicts over gender roles in Corinth. The first piece of evidence in this connection, chronologically speaking, is Gal. 3:28, the well-known reference to oneness in Christ between male and female. If Galatians was written in approximately 53 C.E. from Corinth, it seems quite likely that the effect of Corinthian Christianity and possibly the impact of Prisca and Aquila are visible here. The work on this verse that has been done in the past decade indicates quite clearly that we have a baptismal formula here that reflects Hellenistic Christianity and claims a transcendence over sexual, economic, and racial roles and expectations.[21] The elimination of subordinate status, of being minors under the law, which is the thrust of Paul's argument in Gal. 3, seems consistent with this perspective. It is interesting, however, that the closing greeting, both in Galatians and in the earlier Thessalonian letters, still retains the term "brethren" in its wording: "The grace of our Lord Jesus Christ be with your spirit, brethren. Amen" (Gal. 6:18).

The capstone in this evolution toward "equality-in-principle" between male and female in the church is 1 Cor. 11.[22] My reconstruction of the seven original portions of the Corinthian correspondence that were woven together to create 1 and 2 Corinthians suggests that this was the first letter in the series.[23] Agreeing with Murphy-O'Connor that the arguments for the non-Pauline character of this chapter do not "stand up to close analysis,"[24] I date the writing of this section of 1 Corinthians in the spring of 55, a few months after the Philippian letter. This passage responds to problems in the congregation concerning traditional gender roles. It is quite likely that the issue mistakenly translated as "veil" and "uncovered head" in fact relates to hairstyles[25] or the choice of a decorative hair covering.[26] It is probable that the debate was provoked by the emergence of androgynous impulses in the Corinthian congregation in which females were taking male hairstyles as a sign of their equality and/or their submerging themselves into an androgynous state on the basis of their early Christian experience.[27] Antoinette Wire affirms a portion of this explanation while stressing that the Corinthian female prophets are claiming the house church as their personal space where "they are no longer determined by shame through sexual subordination but are determined by honor through the spirit as persons who have put on Christ."[28] She drops any reference to androgyny in positing that female leaders were discarding the haircovering signifying their married state, thereby showing that "their freedom in Christ released them, at least temporarily, from symbolic attachment to their husband and their family."[29]

However one reconstructs the precise implications of the women's actions, Paul responds to this situation in a highly dialectical manner, insisting in vv. 11 and 12 on equality between male and female and the subordination both of male and female under God. This egalitarian line is held in tension with hierarchical role definitions, including the acceptance of traditional hairstyles for males and females, that one sees in 1 Cor. 11:3–7, 10, and 13–15. One thing is certain in this passage, however, that 1 Cor. 11:5 implies that women are leading early Christian worship services, which is consistent with the strategy of equality in mission evident in earlier letters. When one sums up the argument in 1 Cor. 11:2–16, it seems clear that Paul was attempting to maintain two seemingly contradictory points at the same time: sexual differentiation implying a measure of female subordination on the one hand and equality in honor and role on the other.

Paul Moves toward Consistent Equality

The later phases of the Corinthian correspondence show a further evolution of the egalitarian attitude toward what one might call "consistent equality." It surfaces in an early fragment of the Corinthian correspondence that is now embedded in 2 Cor. 6:14–7:1, which features an explicit alteration of an Old Testament citation to include the word "daughters" as well as "sons" among the prophetic members of the early church.[30] This reference in 2 Cor. 6:18 is a clear indication that Paul affirms a tradition of female leadership in the early church while at the same time resisting androgyny. Believers do not all become "sons of God," but rather "sons and daughters of God."

The very next section in this reconstructed Corinthian letter B continues a stress on sexual equality by dealing in 1 Cor. 6:12–20 with prostitution in a way that was completely unprecedented in the ancient world. In this passage Paul gives up the chauvinist language of his Judaic background and directs the ethic both to male and female members of the church. The theme that "you are not your own, so glorify God in your body" (1 Cor. 6:19–20) is addressed to both male and female. There is not a single allusion in this passage to the marriage contract, and there is no stereotyping of the female sexual partner as a "vessel." Instead the argument is conducted on the basis of male and female becoming "one flesh," based on Gen. 2:24. Paul claims in this passage that the body, which is the basis of personhood, is the "temple of the Holy Spirit" and that gender identity is therefore basic to personhood.[31] The final section of this letter includes a greeting that reflects this evolution toward a consistent view of equality. The greeting in 1 Cor. 16:23–24 is to "you all" rather than to the brethren as in Paul's earlier letters.[32]

In the next phase of the Corinthian correspondence the egalitarian ethic evolves into a full statement of conjugal rights between male and female. As we have seen, 1 Cor. 7:1b is a citation of the proverb that the radicals in Corinth had apparently mutilated in order to advocate an ascetic view of marriage.[33] The saying that "it is well for a man not to touch a woman," is what Paul counters throughout the entire chapter.[34] This citation indicates that a movement was under way in Corinth advocating platonic marriage and resisting the entrance into marriage contracts. This conclusion is confirmed by Barre's thorough study of the "marry-or-burn" saying of 1 Cor. 7:9. He shows that interpreters have added the term "cannot" where it is not warranted, implying that some Corinthians were incapable of resisting sexual temptation and hence should take the lower path of marriage.[35] Instead Paul states that if some *are not* controlling their sexual appetites, they should marry lest they suffer an eschatological penalty.

On the basis of these revolutionary studies, the antisexual stereotype that has constricted our understanding of 1 Cor. 7 can be removed. It is now clear that the reasons for Paul's personal preference for the unmarried condition were suitability for the eschatological situation and possession of a special gift, rather than a suspicion of sexuality or hostility toward women. It is now possible to grasp the remarkable premise of 1 Cor. 7:7b, that each person has a sexual charisma to which he or she should be responsive.[36] There is a remarkable connection between the sexual charisma theme in 1 Cor. 7:7b and the use of "have power over" in 7:4. If the marital desire for sexual fulfillment is viewed in a positive sense as a gift from God, then marriage is a mutual commitment to exercise that gift through union with one's partner. The very status that Paul found abhorrent in 1 Cor. 6:12 ("I will not be overpowered by anything" such as prostitution) is here viewed as appropriate in marriage. Sexual gift and sexual power are here linked in a new concept of somatic mutuality. When one takes the egalitarian transformation of traditional definitions of marital rights into account, Else Kähler is surely correct in affirming the "revolutionary" resonance of these lines.[37] It fits closely with Paul's elaborate effort to balance out the admonitions to males and females throughout 1 Cor. 7.[38] Here Paul explicitly places the male and the female on an equal basis, particularly extending the range of sexual rights from the male to the female: "For the wife does not rule over her own body but the husband does; likewise the husband does not rule over his own body but the wife does" (1 Cor. 7:4).[39] It is also clear that the free decisions both of males and females concerning marital partners in 7:12–24 are presupposed by Paul. Throughout this entire passage he refrains from viewing women as subordinate or as mere objects of the actions of others.

In view of the egalitarian high-water mark of 1 Cor. 7, the omission of the male-female theme from the baptismal allusions of 1 Cor. 12:12–13 is puzzling. Both passages originally belonged in the same portion of the Corinthian correspondence, so there is no possibility of an altered congregational situation to account for the difference. Scroggs makes a plausible case that the sexual categories were more likely deleted from 1 Cor. 12 than added to the baptismal declaration of Gal. 3:26–28,[40] and Cartlidge suggests the omission aimed "to avoid giving further aid to his opponents."[41] It could not have been motivated by a desire to undermine equality between males and females because the theme of charismatic equality is carried through in 1 Cor. 12:4–11; 14:26–32, and indeed throughout the three chapters that originally formed the climax of Corinthian Letter C. It appears more likely that the fear of encouraging androgyny led to this omission. In rejecting the intrinsic goodness of male and female characteristics, the Gnostic radicals in Corinth were violating the premise of 1 Cor. 12:12–14 that all who were given spiritual gifts were joined into one body. In Paul's view, the denial that sexual gifts were intrinsic to the identity of individual believers could contribute to the kind of devious comparisions between "heads" and "feet" that were plaguing the Corinthian church. The best guess is that Paul deleted the female-male reference in this context not to downplay equality but to maintain it in the face of androgynous threats.[42]

It is perhaps useful to wrap up our discussion of the Corinthian correspondence by noting that the greeting at the end of 2 Corinthians also lacks the reference to the "brethren." Verse 12 of 2 Cor. 13 refers to greeting "one another" with a holy kiss, and the final lines in verse 14 ask that "the grace of the Lord Jesus Christ . . . be with you all." This same egalitarian greeting is visible to us in Paul's later letter to the Romans. The greeting in Rom. 15:33 and the one in 16:20 have the kind of inclusive language that is consistent with the Corinthian correspondence.

There are several possible ways to explain this evolution in Paul's perspective, but the impact of the Corinthian ministry is the most likely answer. It is clear that there were major issues in Corinth concerning sexual roles and that the women leaders in Corinth had evolved toward an explicit liberation campaign of their own, adopting male hairstyles and behavioral patterns. I think it quite likely that the impact of this situation led to the evolution of Paul's own views.

Conflicts over Sexual Roles in Other Churches

We have referred already to the research showing that Gal. 3:28 is probably a quotation from an early baptismal formula implying that in Christ maleness and femaleness are overcome in a fundamental manner. Given the important role of androgyny in the ancient world, Wayne Meeks has made a significant assertion, which many current scholars have accepted, that the baptismal formula was understood as a unification formula by some branches of the Greek-speaking church.[43] In this context, Gal. 3:28 would have implied that sexual differentiation was in fact overcome and that females were incorporated once again into the original state, which in the imagination of the ancient world was, of course, a male state. The more recent work that has been done in 1 Cor. 7 seems to confirm this line of research that radical Christians who used the baptismal formula of Gal. 3:28 indeed believed that sexual differences were overcome in Christ. The difficulty that this Hellenistic conception caused in the early church we touched on already in reference to the debate over hairstyles in Corinth. The acceptance of male hairstyles by women as a sign of their having broken away from the subordinate status of women in the Greco-Roman world is most understandable with an androgynous hypothesis. There is evidence in several locations in the letters of early Christianity, even during Paul's lifetime, of social disruption caused by this rejection of traditional roles. I think in particular of the evidence in the Colossian letter of resistance against traditional gender roles that correlates with a pattern that begins to evolve in some of the later New Testament letters. The tendency is to insist on subordinate status for women, and this insistence, which emerges in the later New Testament letters, seems to reflect a perceived problem on the part of conservative leaders with the expression of the radical equality of early Christianity. The line that is quite visible by the end of the first century has been traced through the later period by Elaine Pagels.[44] The preference for God the Mother and the pattern of understanding salvation as incorporation into an androgynous state that transcends sexual differentiation was picked up in Gnostic Christianity and carried to its logical extreme. Part of the pattern that Pagels has noted is the dualism and the rejection of sexuality as such and the tendency toward asceticism and/or libertinism. The pattern toward the end of the first century and into the second century makes it quite clear that only one portion of the Pauline churches was able to keep the idea of radical equality intact, and they were able to do this only at the price of rejecting sexual differentiation as such. In this sense, the Gnostic theorists of the second and third century are a somewhat dubious resource for modern liberation movements since the equality was purchased at such a price.

While Paul's own evolution was in the direction of egalitarianism, there are numerous indications that many of his co-workers, even during his lifetime, tended in the direction of a larger measure of conformity with the gender stereotypes of the Greco-Roman world. While retaining equality in principle, the tendency was to limit it in practice. This pattern surfaces first in the Letter to the Colossians.

Eduard Schweizer has made a compelling case that Colossians was designed by Paul but drafted by one of his colleagues because of Paul's imprisonment at the time.[45] The Colossian letter has the first of the so-called "household tables" in chapter 3, in which the admonition "wives, be subject to your husbands" is found. The likelihood is that this acceptance of a traditional subordination pattern for women by one of Paul's co-workers was directed against a movement of radical equality of some type that rendered marriage and other family relationships questionable. James Crouch in his study of the subordination material in Colossians has made the case that the author is reacting against spiritual excesses by people who believed that traditional obligations "in the flesh" were now overcome.[46] Colossians thus reflects a development of "moderate subordination" because there is a strong emphasis in 3:19 on "husbands, love your wives and do not be harsh with them." Also it is important to take into account the fact that the closing greeting in Colossians is quite different from the greeting of a patriarchal letter such as 1 Thessalonians. The simple "grace be with you" in Col. 4:18 lacks any reference to the "brethren." It does not seem to me, therefore, that there is a full return to the culturally dominant pattern of the subordination of women in this writing.

A similar case, I believe, can be made concerning Ephesians, which appears to be the product of the next generation of the Pauline school. Once again there is a table of household rules, but it is qualified by the premise of mutual subordination in Eph. 5:21. "Be subject to one another out of reverence for Christ." This means that husbands are to be subject to wives as well as children are to be subject to parents and parents subject to children. This idea of mutual subordination is quite different from the chauvinistic pattern of patriarchy characteristic of Judaism in the ancient world and of much of the Greco-Roman world as well.[47] The sex ethic, however, just as in Colossians, articulates the admonitions differently for male and female and thus does not come up to the level of Paul's treatment in 1 Cor. 7, which was thoroughly egalitarian. It is also interesting to observe that the greeting at the end of Ephesians reverts to what was probably the traditional greeting of early Christianity, "Peace be to the brethren."

The Rejection of Equality in the Later Pauline Tradition

In the latter decades of the first century the stage is set for a full-blown conflict over the role of women in the church. It was unfortunate that the conflicts between conservatives and liberals produced such distorted approaches to female roles. The left wing of the Pauline churches, which was moving increasingly toward Gnosticism by the end of the first century, retained Paul's conception of equal roles for women but did so by denying the meaning of sexual identity. The conservative group reflected in the Pauline school toward the end of the first century moved toward traditional Judaic values and attitudes toward women and returned as well, at the same time, to the subordination patterns of much of the Greco-Roman world. One factor in this conflict between conservatives and liberals at the end of the first century was the arrival of immigrants from the conservative Jewish-Christian churches after the Jewish-Roman war that concluded in 70 C.E. But the consequence of this conflict was the virtual eradication of female leadership, at least in the orthodox branches of the early church.

Some of the earliest evidence about the trend toward sexual repression is visible from a study of the redaction of the Corinthian correspondence that apparently took place in the 80s or 90s. My study of the redactional process points to an early Catholic circle of the Pauline school that had chauvinistic attitudes toward women.[48] The most prominent evidence of this is the famous passage about women keeping silent in church (1 Cor. 14:33b–36).[49] This passage is so crucial for the discussion of the problem of gender roles in the Pauline churches that a case against the authenticity of these verses must be reviewed. That 1 Cor. 14:33b–36 is an interpolation that does not derive from Paul is evident first of all in the break of the flow of the argument. Verse 37 joins very neatly with v. 33a, providing a transition that is far superior to the transitions currently in the canonical text. One might note in this connection that most modern translations place awkward paragraph breaks, in the middle of v. 33 and after v. 36, indications of a strange transition that conservative commentators have tried their best to clarify.

The second argument in favor of the interpolation theory of 1 Cor. 14:33b–36 is the non-Pauline content. That women should "keep silence in the churches" (1 Cor. 14:34) was clearly not Paul's perspective, as we have seen. It contradicts 1 Cor. 11:5, which assumes that women are prophesying freely and openly in church services. It also contradicts the prominent role of women leaders in many other locations on the Pauline mission field. The language and reasoning of these verses is also non-Pauline with the term "permitted" in v. 34 used very uncharacteristically, and "the law" in v. 34 used in so absolute a manner as to exclude Paul's ordinary ethic. In this instance the reference is not to the precise wording of the Torah itself but rather to a tradition of early Judaism that interpreted Gen. 1—3 in a chauvinistic direction.[50] This construal of the law violates not only much of the Corinthian correspondence but also the central thrust of both Galatians and Romans. Paul's ethic is not legalistic, as this verse clearly implies. The reference to women being subordinate to men, speaking only "at home" (v. 35), contradicts the egalitarian ethic of 1 Cor. 7. Finally, in v. 36, the question about whether "the word of God" originated with you Corinthians or, by implication, in a Jewish-Christian setting has the argumentative force of making the pattern of female subordination favored by Jewish-Christian congregations normative for all congregations. The thrust of the argument in v. 36 is that a prominent female role in the church violates the original revelation of the gospel. This implies that Pauline churches are dependent on Jewish-Christian traditions for their ethic. This entire line of reasoning is contradicted by every Pauline letter written after 1 and 2 Thessalonians. Paul's concept of the spiritual integrity of Gentile Christianity is completely contrary to the authoritarian logic of this passage.

A third line of evidence that reveals an interpolation has to do with textual criticism. Some Latin versions and the Western text group place vv. 34–35 in another location in chapter 14. They place it after v. 40. There are other minor violations that have led several of the most prominent text critics to conclude that these verses were originally written in the margin and penetrated into the text at a later point in its evolution.[51]

It is particularly interesting to ask why these verses were inserted at the location in chapter 14 where we currently find them. It appears to be related to the wording of v. 32, that "the Spirits of prophets are subject to prophets." This basic principle is that all who share the prophetic gift should exercise that gift with autonomy and that they are under self-control when they do so. This principle clearly allows no room for sexual discrimination because there were both male and female prophets in the Pauline churches. With the insertion of vv. 33b–36, however, women are explicitly excluded from this role. This has an impact also on the interpretation of v. 37, in that the appeal to those who consider themselves "a prophet or spiritual" would now explicitly exclude females. The "command of the Lord" in this verse is thus not that they exercise their gifts responsibly, which had been the thrust of Paul's original argument, but that they be silent.

When one takes the location and content of this interpolation into account, the proximity both in ideology and language to the Pastoral Epistles is very prominent. Only in places like 1 Tim. 2:11–12; 5:13; and Titus 2:2 can one find a similarly explicit anxiety and irritation about the participation of articulate females in early Christian worship. This interpolation, therefore, links the redactor of 1 Corinthians very closely to the group responsible for the creation of the Pastoral Epistles.

The creation of the Pastoral Epistles by the Pauline school at the end of the first century or the very early part of the second century marks a climactic stage in the rise of sexual repression in early Christianity. Given the content of 1 and 2 Timothy and Titus, it seems clear that one of the primary goals of these letters, written in the name of Paul, was to stifle female roles in the church. First Timothy 2:8–15 limits public leadership in worship to men and insists that women should be modest and subordinate. Verse 11 is crucial, "Let a woman learn in silence with all submissiveness. I permit no woman to teach or to have authority over man; she is to keep silent" (1 Tim. 2:11–12). The proximity to the language of 1 Cor. 14:33b–36 is very striking in this instance. It contradicts Paul's line in 1 Cor. 7 by insisting that since Adam was formed first and Adam was not deceived that women should be subordinate. This pattern is also reflected in the rules and regulations for "widows" in chapter 5. The role of women in the Pauline churches is here defined as a matter of serving other people in the church, "washing the feet of the saints," and helping the poor. The role of women here is explicitly removed from the category of political leadership, and the qualifications of women to be supported by the church in carrying out even subordinate roles are sharply delineated and thay are placed under male jurisdiction.

In 2 Tim. 3:6 there is a negative allusion to women, reflecting the prominent role they were playing in the communities competitive with the early Catholic circles of the Pauline school. It is quite clear from Gnostic materials analyzed by Elaine Pagels and others that the pattern of female patron figures supporting the community of Christian Gnostics was probably carried over from the very first generation of the Pauline churches. There is a highly stereotyped implication in the polemical wording of 2 Tim. 3:6 that lists, among people to avoid, such heretics as "make their way into households and capture weak women, burdened by sins and swayed by various impulses." The wording of this verse reflects an attitude toward women strikingly different from the authentic Pauline letters. That women are simply "captured" because of their "weakness" is light-years removed from Paul's reference to the female missionary partners, colleagues, and patrons with whom he had worked during his lifetime.

A summary of the subordinationist ethic of the Pauline school is provided in the third of the letters that were written in his name. Titus 2:3–5 provides ethical guidelines for women that confirm their subordinate status. "Bid the older women likewise to be reverent in behavior, not to be slanderers or slaves to drink; they are to teach what is good, and so train the young women to love their husbands and children, to be sensible, chaste, domestic, kind, and submissive to their husbands, that the word of God may not be discredited." The reduction of the female role to housekeeping duties and the concern that prominent female leaders might look scandalous in the Greco-Roman world are characteristic here. This is the capstone of a subordinate definition of the feminine role that came to hold sway through most of Christian history.

Paul's Volatile Legacy

When one surveys the evidence of conflicts over gender roles in Pauline churches, the volatile quality of this legacy becomes apparent. Paul himself emphasized an equality of role between male and female, with gender identity retained and kept distinct between male and female. But this orientation that crystallized in the mature Pauline letters broke apart after his death. It seems quite clear that the left-wing branches of the Pauline churches retained the stress on equality between male and female and continued to encourage female leadership and sponsorship of congregations. But given the Greco-Roman tendency toward dualism in the first century and the affinity of these groups with Gnostic theology, the inevitable result was that the egalitarian tradition moved into androgyny. The positive appraisal of gender identity was dropped and the unspoken assumption of the recovery of an androgynous nature, especially for women, became dominant. The trends toward asceticism or libertinism, the opposite ends of the Gnostic sex ethic, remained characteristic of this tradition.

The conservative wing of the Pauline tradition, represented by the creators of the Pastoral Epistles, retained Paul's doctrine of sexual differentiation. They made excellent use of his arguments that women should retain different hairstyles than men, and so forth, but in the process they rejected the egalitarian legacy that he had laid down. They submerged the authentic references to equal male and female prophets with explicit commands written in Paul's name to eliminate leadership roles for women.

Several aspects of this volatile development bear on the contemporary discussion of the role of women in the Christian church. While Paul came from a chauvinistic Jewish tradition, he was evidently capable of moving in a liberationist direction, first in practice and then in theory. Several features of his theology could be mentioned as possibly encouraging an evolution in this direction. The idea of salvation by faith alone, evoked by a charismatic gift of grace, tends to transcend sexual and social differences. The stress on charismatic leadership in Pauline theology tends to undercut social stereotypes about who should exercise this kind of role. The emphasis on freedom from the law and the evolution of a charismatic ethic of love tends to relativize the social stereotypes that one finds in the legal tradition of Judaism. The apocalyptic urgency of Pauline theology, with its vision of a new age breaking into history, was correlated with an emphasis on a radically transformed community that would reflect the standards of the new age rather than the chauvinistic values of the old. Each of these theological commitments of Paul's own theology is consistent with an egalitarian structure of religious and family organization.

It is interesting to observe that a different set of theological principles emerged among the early Catholic heirs of the Pauline tradition. These principles were much less friendly to egalitarian ideals. In the Pastoral Epistles and the interpolation of 1 Cor. 14:33b–36 there emerged an authoritarian and chauvinistic kind of Christianity. In place of an emphasis on the Holy Spirit as the key to church leadership, there is a stress on apostolic succession and authority. Faith in these writings tends to be reinterpreted as a set of beliefs inculcated by tradition so that its socially transforming character is diminished. In place of a perfectionist ideal of a community reflecting the values of a new, egalitarian age, there is a tendency to urge conformity to societal expectations. In place of Paul's idea of charismatic gifts shared by all Christians, there is in these later New Testament writings a limitation of leadership gifts to male clergy, the bishops and elders. In place of freedom from the law, there arises an emphasis on the law of the Old Testament as the standard to be enforced in the church, with the result that male leadership is institutionalized.

In the evolution of early Christianity, none of the groups deriving from the Pauline tradition was able to preserve his legacy in its entirety by the end of the first century. The distinctive Pauline combination of gender equality with an affirmation of sexual differentiation fell apart because of a changed social environment and the loss of the charismatic, apocalyptic, perfectionist, and transformationist elements of Pauline theology. It seems to me that the challenge of the present moment is to recover this theological legacy and to provide the substantial underpinning of an egalitarian ethic toward which Paul was moving in the last decade of his life.

5. Slavery and the Tactful Revolution of the New Age

Were you a slave when you were called?
Don't worry about it,
although if you can gain your freedom, you'd better do so.
For a slave who has been called in the Lord is the Lord's freedman.
Likewise, a freedman who has been called is Christ's slave.
You were bought with a price: do not become slaves of human
masters.
Brothers, each person, in response to God, should live in accord
with his calling.

(1 Corinthians 7:21–24)[1]

Therefore, though I am bold enough in Christ to command you to
do what is fitting,
I would rather appeal on the basis of love,
and I, Paul, do so as an ambassador and also a prisoner of
Christ Jesus.
I appeal to you concerning my child,
whom I have begotten in my chains, Onesimus,
who was formerly useless to you,
but now is useful both to you and to me.
I am sending back to you this one who is my very heart.
I wanted to keep him with me,
so that he might serve me in your behalf during my imprisonment
for the gospel,
but I would not do anything without your consent,
in order that your good deed might not stem from compulsion
but from your own free will.
Perhaps this is the reason he has been separated from you for a
while,
so you might have him back forever,

no longer as a slave,
> but as one who is much more than a slave, a beloved brother,
especially to me, but now much more to you,
> both in the flesh and in the Lord.
So if you consider me your partner,
> welcome him as you would welcome me.

(Philemon 8–17)

The American cultural context has always been marked by the shadow of slavery. It was the shame of our early history, the root cause of the most traumatic war in our history, and a contributing factor to the racism that still marks our society—though to a substantially lesser degree than for most of the European or Asian countries from which our population emigrated. The awareness of the defense of slavery based on Paul's letters, especially Philemon, is a decisive factor in our hermeneutical tradition, reflected in the fact that a substantial number of our students with African American backgrounds reject fundamentalism because of the ambiguity of the biblical stance on slavery and their awareness of its human implications.[2] This kind of awareness needs to be awakened in the rest of American culture, leading to a critical reappraisal of Paul the Apostle to America.[3] We shall discover that when the authentic Pauline letters are separated from the later writings of the Pauline tradition and interpreted in the light of ancient cultural assumptions, Paul was in fact a revolutionary who struggled for the freedom of early church members in profound and successful ways.

Slavery in the Ancient World

The difficulty contemporary Americans have in assessing the significance of the references to slavery in 1 Corinthians and Philemon derives in part from the tendency to read modern conditions back into the ancient world. This is evident in the pattern of avoidance of the terms "slave" or "slavery" in English and American translations, reflecting the liberation interests of English-speaking culture since the nineteenth century. While these terms appear in the New Testament no less than 190 times, they are usually translated as "servant" or the like. There is a peril in modernizing the Bible so that its social and historical contexts are no longer visible.

One major difference between slavery in the Greco-Roman world and modern slavery in North and South America was the lack of a racial component. In place of a slave trade centered in Africa, there were five sources of slaves in Paul's time. The first and most important was warfare, which meant that the survivors of a Roman siege or campaign would be put on the block.[4] This also meant that slaves were something of a cross section of Mediterranean society. The other four sources of slavery were equally indiscriminate as far as race was concerned. The steadiest supply of slaves came from the children of slaves.[5] There were also persons who voluntarily sold themselves into slavery for economic reasons;[6] persons who fell into debt and forfeited their freedom, and certain classes of criminals whose punishment was enslavement.

The legal status of slaves was also more complicated than was the case in modern jurisprudence.[7] While both the ancient and the modern systems defined slaves as chattel and placed them under the absolute power of their masters, in the ancient world the rights of a slave could be defended by his owner or some other benefactor in the courts. Roman legislation shortly before Paul's time restricted the right of owners to use slaves in combat with animals in the colosseum and established the same trial procedures for slave criminals as for former slaves.[8] The courts also defined slaves as persons as well as things.[9] A different attitude from the modern is manifest in the fact that ancient writers disputed whether slavery was "natural" and whether inner freedom was possible for slaves,[10] but no one opposed the legal system of slavery as such.[11] Slave revolts in the Greco-Roman world aimed at reversing the status of slaves and masters. Apparently no one, including the slaves themselves, could imagine an economic system that was not based on slaves. The historian Zvi Yavetz summarizes the current scholarly consensus on this point: "In the Greek and Roman world slavery was an uncontestable fact and the idea of a slaveless society was inconceivable."[12] The sheer size of the slavery system may have had an effect at this point; one third of the population was slave; one third consisted of freed slaves; so that only one third of the population was nonslave, and even these could end up in slavery by a variety of means, as we have observed. Ferguson's figures are a little lower: 20 percent of the population were slaves in the city of Rome itself. A final difference from modern slavery is that the slave in Paul's time could expect to be manumitted after a certain number of years of service to his or her master.[13] There was a good chance of such manumission after slaves had served until they were thirty or forty years of age.[14] In some instances, particularly competent slaves were allowed to do work on the side and were able to buy their own freedom.

Dale Martin's recent analysis of the social status of slaves throws light on the complexity of the Greco-Roman system.[15] On the basis of literary and inscriptional evidence, he concludes that many slaves enjoyed "a certain degree of social stability, and therefore power,"[16] despite their vulnerability to the power of slavemasters. While most slaves held menial positions, he discovered striking evidence of slaves holding "managerial and administrative positions" in Greece, Macedonia, and Asia Minor where Paul's missionary activities were concentrated.[17] These "middle-level slaves" enjoyed a level of "independence, family life, financial abilities, and social power" that "belied their legal status as dispensable. They were by no means at the bottom end of the social pecking order," and insofar as they represented powerful owners, their status "would have appeared powerful, not weak."[18] Many of these slaves became upwardly mobile, "a recurring motif" within the popular novels and romances of the time so that voluntary enslavement became appealing for some with no other prospects.[19] But upper-class persons held such mobility in contempt, reflecting the significant disparities in the culture between upper and lower levels of the population. "The terminology of slavery meant different things for different people because the social institution of slavery functioned differently for different people."[20] These factors, rendering simplistic modern assessments implausible, have to be taken into account in evaluating Paul's unusual discussions of slavery.

When one thinks through what would have been involved in freeing a slave like Onesimus, the differences between the ancient and the modern systems becomes particularly significant. There were four legal components to a full writ of manumission for slaves, any one of which could be reserved to the owner, even in the interest of the well-being of the former slave. There was (1) the right to be a legal agent, which was sometimes less advisable than remaining under the protection of a powerful patron; (2) the right to nonseizure of person; (3) the right to choose one's own employment, which was a mixed blessing at times because of the economic vulnerability of freed slaves; and (4) freedom of movement.[21] Many instances have been discovered of slaves being disadvantaged by their manumission, in some cases being thrown into abject poverty.[22] In the cases of Paul's advice in 1 Cor. 7:21, and particularly in Philemon where Paul pleads for fair treatment of the slave Onesimus in so open-ended a manner, it might have been in the slaves' interest that some of these rights be postponed for a period of years until they had the means to support and protect themselves. The point is that most of the debate about whether Paul wanted slaves to be freed or not, and why Paul left so much open to discussion, unconsciously presupposes modern conditions and needs to be reformulated in a way that would have made sense to the ancient world.

Finally, the question of the punishment of runaway slaves is also hard to compare with American fugitive slave legislation or other modern examples. Recent studies make it plain that in general treatment of slaves in the Greco-Roman world was relatively humane, especially for those who had been part of a family system; conditions were much more harsh in the mines and galleys than for household slaves such as Onesimus. There was also the institution of asylum, effective in the Greek cities, in which an abused slave could appeal to a priest who was in a position to intercede for better conditions before the slave returned. Some have suggested Paul was involved in this case in a kind of Christian asylum system, but the *amicus domini* ("friend of the master") regulations in Roman law appear more relevant now. But as far as the law was concerned, any punishment for runaways was legal, including even execution, which was characteristically done by crucifixion to serve as a warning for others. The smoldering hostility between slaves and masters was a fixed reality in the culture, expressed in the popular proverb, "as many enemies as slaves."[23] Owners retained absolute power of life or death over their slaves, which helps us understand the urgency of Paul's advice both in 1 Corinthians and in the letter to Philemon.

The Corinthian Admonition Concerning Slavery

The discussion of slavery in 1 Cor. 7:21–24 is an illustration of Paul's preference for Christians to remain in their sexual and cultural status[24] since the end of time was expected quickly and the dawn of the new age in Christ had already fundamentally equalized such status anyway.[25] His premise was that "in one spirit we were all baptized into one body—Jews and Greeks, slaves or free" (1 Cor. 12:13). A liberation movement in Corinth, described in chapter 4 above, sought to alter such societal relations, principally in the sexual arena, in order to more fully embody this oneness in Christ. A "theology of exaltation" in terms of charismatic freedom from the law was probably being promoted by the radicals in Corinth, leading some to think that all bodily and legal obligations were null and void.[26] While Paul is willing to grant a large role to individual judgment in this chapter, Paul's basic advice is to remain in the situation one was in when called to be a Christian because "that situation itself is taken up in the call and thus sanctified to him or her."[27] One can serve others out of love in Christ and function as a crucial member of a church whether as slave or free. The Christ-event relativizes all human relationships and transforms every social role. In a surprising manner, Paul can even portray himself "as a slave of Christ and a slave of all," thus challenging the patriarchal leadership model and placing himself on the side of the slave members of the congregation.[28]

When Paul's basic position set forth in 1 Cor. 1:1–4:21 and 7:17 is taken into account, his opening admonition concerning slavery in 1 Cor. 7:21 sounds much less "conservative" than it has usually been taken to be: "Were you a slave when you were called? Don't worry about it, although if you can gain your freedom, you'd better do so." Not to "worry" or become "concerned" reflects the premise that "your calling in Christ eclipses such conditions, but thereby also transforms them into situations where you may live out your Christian 'calling.'"[29] He is "not calling for Stoic indifference"[30] or implying that slavery is unburdensome. In fact, Paul turns immediately to the possibility of manumission and the most likely construal of the ambiguous phrase that follows is "by all means make use of it," or in my translation, "you'd better do so."[31]

The opposite situation is reflected in 1 Cor. 7:23 where Paul uses the metaphor of purchasing slaves to the work of Christ; since Christ has bought you, do not voluntarily "become slaves of human masters." In view of the practice of selling oneself into slavery either temporarily or permanently in order to deal with financial exigencies, Paul's counsel seems very unambiguous. Scott Bartchy's construal is preferable at this point to the commentators[32] who prefer to make this admonition into a vague metaphor: "Your total somatic existence belongs to God. Therefore do not sell yourselves into slavery."[33] While Paul argues that Christ transforms all roles and relationships, there is no doubt that the status of being free of a human master is perceived as fundamentally consistent with being under the Lordship of Christ. It is worth observing, however, that this argument could not be grasped so long as scholars believed Paul was the author of Colossians, Ephesians, and 1 Timothy, which directly admonish slaves to be obedient to masters, strongly implying that their condition is willed by God. The stance of the historical Paul was that when Christians have a choice in the matter, they should neither prostitute themselves (1 Cor. 6:12–20) or enter into human bondage (1 Cor. 7:23).[34] This provides an essential premise to understand the most extensive and subtle discussion of the matter in Paul's authentic letter to Philemon.

The Historical Setting of Philemon

Some New Testament introductions do not take much time for Philemon, giving the impression that this little letter does not have great theological or ethical significance. The standard textbook by David Barr does a more adequate job than most although he does suggest that it expresses Pauline "whimsey."[35] A counter thesis suggests that Philemon is a supreme example of Paul's pastoral skill and moral diplomacy. It is one of the most subtle letters in world history, an expression of Paul's "ambassadorial style." There is even a possibility that the Greek term for ambassador is used in the letter. Since the words for "old man" and "ambassador" would have been pronounced the same, many modern translators and commentators follow the conjecture first made by Bentley, that Paul's dictation originally intended the word "ambassador," which makes far better sense in Philem. 9. Whatever one does with this translation, the fact remains that Philemon is a polished diamond, whose refraction throws light on Paul's pastoral strategy, the ethical issue of slavery, and the problem of transforming Christians into persons of genuine equality.

It is clear from v. 13 that Philemon was written during one of Paul's imprisonments, probably during the period of Paul's "affliction in Asia" mentioned in 2 Cor. 1:8, which my chronology places in the winter of

55–56 C.E.[36] Several reconstructions of the relationship between Onesimus and Paul have been developed in the past thirty years, resulting in a likely basis of our reconstruction here. The well-known study by Edgar J. Good-speed makes the intriguing suggestion that the runaway slave Onesimus was the same person as the later bishop Onesimus of Ephesus, and that he was responsible for the creation of the Pauline letter corpus that includes this piece of private correspondence that meant so much to his later life.[37] John Knox works on the correlation between Philemon and Colossians, suggest-ing that the "service" requested of Archippus in Col. 4:17 was the freeing of the slave, Onesimus, so he could serve Paul's missionary activities.[38] This means that Archippus rather than Philemon would have to be viewed as the primary recipient of the letter.[39] Since Archippus is only mentioned after Philemon and Appia, however, most scholars have found this implausible. Norman Petersen presents the more widely accepted view that Onesimus the slave belonged to Philemon, and that Paul seeks his freedom by writing the letter. He shows how "Paul's story about Philemon is constructed around the themes of indebtedness and repayment as these occur within the broth-erhood of Christ, and that these themes, however literal or metaphorical, raise the fundamental issue of the economy, the integrity, of the brother-hood."[40] After a careful analysis of the social relations and structures implic-it in the letter and the symbolic universe implicit in the story of the runaway slave, his conversion, and return, Petersen describes the ironic interplay between the two domains of indebtedness in which Philemon is shown to stand:

> On the one hand, Onesimus's conversion is the occasion for the repay-ment and canceling of his worldly debt, while Philemon's conversion is the occasion for his incurring of a debt to Paul in the domain of the church. On the other hand, Paul pays Onesimus's worldly debt in the cur-rency of the world, and Philemon must pay his own debt in the domain of the church in the church's currency. The irony here is that the church's currency is Philemon's freeing of his own slave.[41]

What remains unclear in Petersen's brilliant analysis is why Onesimus should have come to Paul in the first place, especially in prison, and on what legal basis Paul could have appealed to Philemon.

Several recent studies have developed a compelling new answer to these puzzling questions about Onesimus's relation to Paul, suggesting that Paul was the *amicus domini* of Philemon, the slaveowner.[42] In Roman law there was an arrangement under which estranged slaves could appeal to a friend of the owner to intercede and thus to resolve the difficulties between the slave and the owner. This theory was confirmed by Scott Bartchy in the 1991 annual meeting of the Society of Biblical Literature, quoting from Proculus that slaves were not liable to punishment if they fled to an *amicus domini*. Thus Onesimus was not a "runaway slave" but an alienated slave who appealed to Paul for help. This explains why Onesimus should have taken the seemingly dangerous course of seeking out Paul even within a Roman prison where he otherwise might easily have been apprehended by the authorities.

The Transformational Rhetoric of Philemon

The subtle brilliance of Philemon has been uncovered by the application of rhetorical criticism, with a major advance being made by American scholar Forrester Church in 1978.[43] That Paul uses deliberative or advisory rhetoric in this letter means that the traditional motivations of "honor" and "advantage" would have made sense to everyone. "Honor" appears in the appeals to Philemon's free will in vv. 12–14 and in the refusal of Paul to dishonor him by ordering him about. "Advantage" appears in the brilliant play on the name "Onesimus," meaning "useful" or "profitable," with Paul suggesting that while Onesimus had actually been useless as an apparently dissatisfied slave, now he can be useful not only to Philemon but also to the church. The motif of "providence" is found in vv. 15–16.

A key theme in Church's analysis is the word *splachna*, translated as "very heart" in the caption of this chapter. This word "is introduced three times during the course of Paul's appeal, once each in the exordium, proof, and peroration. Taken together they constitute a syllogism that is itself the touchstone of Paul's argument: if Philemon refreshes the very hearts of the saints (v. 7); and, if Onesimus is Saint Paul's very heart (v. 12); then, to refresh Paul's very heart, Philemon must refresh Onesimus (v. 20)." This term *splachna*—literally "bowels, heart, or as we might say today, guts"—is used in such a way as to convey the deep personal attachment Paul has to this runaway slave. In dealing with him, Philemon, therefore, has Paul's heart in his hands. This powerful expression of partnership (v. 17) and affection (v. 10) is closely bound up with Paul's request that Onesimus be accepted back in the community, "no longer as a slave, but one who is much more than a slave, a beloved brother" (v. 16).

Paul's choice of words leads me to go further than Forrester Church, who concludes that Paul is simply using the return of Onesimus to teach a general lesson about practical "Christian love." The letter clearly implies some level of actual freedom for Onesimus, either now or in the future. To welcome Onesimus as Philemon would welcome Paul (v. 17) implies receiving him as an equal partner in every sense of the term. As Lloyd A. Lewis remarks on the basis of the extensive use of familial language in this letter, "Onesimus thus stands on a par with both Paul and his former master."[44] To tell Philemon that he is "confident of your obedience, I am writing to you in the knowledge that you will do ever more than I say" (v. 21) implies that the logic of equality in Christ is to be carried out in some direct manner. As G. B. Caird remarks, the wording of this verse "is the nearest he comes to hinting at emancipation."[45] The level of manumission is left open for obvious reasons. But there can be no doubt for those who follow the rhetoric of Philemon that Paul is making a powerful case for liberation.

The Relation of Philemon to Liberation

The tendency to read modern conditions back into Philemon and to draw false conclusions from its subtle argument is visible in what Larry Morrison identified as the "Pauline Mandate," the early American defense of slavery.[46] He concludes that "as far as the New Testament was concerned, the major passage Southerners found which accepted, indeed justified, slavery was the Epistle of St. Paul to Philemon, sometimes referred to as the Pauline Mandate."[47] The definitive study by H. Shelton Smith confirms that "defenders of human bondage" in the pre-Civil War south "felt much more at home in the letters of Paul than they did in the teachings of Jesus, because those documents contained specific instructions on the duties of masters and slaves. In fact, virtually every proslavery tract of any consequence explored the Pauline epistles far more exhaustively than any other portion of the New Testament."[48] Among the authentic Pauline letters, such tracts cited 1 Cor. 7:21–24 and Philem. 10–18, which are ambiguous in their support of slavery, but they are interpreted in the light of the much more specific references in the deutero-Pauline writings of Eph. 6:5–9; Col. 3:22, 4:1; and 1 Tim. 6:1–2. Smith found two major emphases drawn from these scriptural references. First, the admonitions that slaves should obey their masters in the deutero-Pauline letters presuppose that slavery is approved by Paul. With regard to Philemon, if Paul "had really felt that slaveholding was a sin, Paul would not have returned his newly won convert, Onesimus, to his owner, Philemon, without making this fact absolutely clear. Yet far from censuring his 'beloved fellow worker,' Paul, according to . . . a prominent Methodist preacher of Georgia and a slaveowner, recognized that Philemon's lawful authority over Onesimus was 'of a character too sacred to be interfered with.'"[49] Second, the proslavery interpreters point out that slaveholders like Philemon were prominent church members who had apparently not been required to repent of this before becoming Christians. So slavery was evidently not considered a sin by the early church. Conveniently overlooked in this assessment, it appears, are passages like Gal. 3:28 and 1 Cor. 12:13 where the equality of slaves is clearly stated. Smith observes that southern churchmen wanted "to push the Bible argument continually, drive abolitionism to the wall, to compel it to assume an anti-Christian position," thus forcing northern churchmen to support them.[50] There is evidence that this was successful to some degree because Lincoln had a secret poll taken of the churchmen around Springfield, Illinois, prior to the presidential election of 1860 and was chagrined to find that the overwhelming majority were planning to support proslavery candidates. "I do not so read the scripture," he told his colleague Herndon sadly. On the basis of what we now know about the real position of the Apostle Paul, Lincoln was far ahead of the theologians of his time in this assessment.

To defend the brutal and racially discriminatory modern American system of slavery by citing Philemon is as great a misunderstanding as the tradition of Pauline conservatism that says that since Paul did not demand the abolition of slavery, or specify how Onesimus was to be freed, he must have wished to conserve the system. Both sides of this argument remind me of the student who commented after a discussion of the route and tedious schedule of Paul's travels, "What I can't understand is, why didn't he take the bus?" As we now know, the abolition of slavery was not even a possibility in people's minds, so to draw inferences from this is absurd. The fact remains that Paul appeals not only for the protection but also for some level of freedom for Onesimus. But he does so in a persuasive way that reflects a "more fundamental revolution" than traditional conservatives or liberals have conceived. He goes far beyond the usual parameters of European exegesis, which assumes the freedom of the new age is present only "in principle" and that no concrete social embodiment of such freedom could be sought with regard to slaves or other persons in a subordinate status.

My grasp of the ethical implications of Paul's position is dependent on dialogues with a theological student from Zimbabwe who argued that if Paul on his own authority had simply demanded the freedom of Onesimus, he would have been retaining the domination system on which slavery rested. Slavery is a system of bossing people around. If Paul had bossed Philemon, the slavemaster might submit and grudgingly free Onesimus, but the principle of domination would still be intact. And slavery would spring up again, inside the church, in more ways than one. Instead, Paul subverts the entire system of domination by appealing to Philemon's free decision, to act in a manner consistent with the equality and love between brothers and sisters in Christ. Paul is the tactful revolutionary of the new community, leading it to act in a manner consistent with *koinônia*, the fellowship and sharing of believers in the new age.

This is why one must note the crucial role of rhetorical "persuasion" in Paul's pastoral work. In v. 14 Paul insists that he wants "nothing by compulsion" from Philemon, "nothing without your consent." Rather than using apostolic authority to force him to decisions that might be inappropriate, Paul seeks to persuade an equal brother in Christ to act in a way consistent with the transforming event of Christ.[51] It is a marvelous model for ministry, consistent with what modern hermeneutics can teach us about the ongoing revelation of God's word. We need to be honest both about the original circumstances of Philemon, and about our own situation, testing the adequacy of our interpretation through public discussion and criticism along the way. But Paul is a model for the most profound revolution of history, the tactful revolution of the new age of grace. It works by persuasion rather than by force. It counters the impulse of zealots and fanatics whose strident demands for conformity to their policies leave the principles of domination and exploitation of the old age untouched. Paul's letter to Philemon is addressed to the whole church, urging that it act as the vanguard of a new creation, embodying the revolutionary new principle of fellowships and equality. If Philemon treats Onesimus with the same thoughtful respect that he himself has experienced in this letter, a new world begins to dawn. But if he refuses, the weight of the church and of the apostle will come down on the side of liberation: "Yes, brother, let me have this joy from you in the Lord! Refresh my very heart in Christ. Confident of your obedience, I am writing to you knowing that you will do more than I say. At the same time, prepare a guest room for me, for I am hoping through your prayers to be restored to you" (vv. 20–22). This is what one might call "gentle persuasion": gentle, realistic, but firm at the same time. Paul will not take No for an answer. The tactful revolution of grace is tough, persistent, and resourceful, and it rests on personal bonds of love and solidarity that extend powerfully across space and time. Philemon had better not mess with Paul's *splachna*, his very heart—the slave Onesimus! This is the tactful revolution of the new age, a model for creative transformation, not just of the slave but also of the slaveowner.

Paul's letters could support an ethic of extraordinary relevance for the United States of America, a country whose main theme has been "freedom" but whose major flaw has been the incapacity to link such freedom with concrete issues such as slavery, prejudice, economic subordination, and the lack of mutuality. Pauline theology has a yet-undiscovered relevance for the ongoing debate about whether freedom in this country is anything more than the "aristocratic idea of freedom as an inherited quality of the individual—expressed through power over others in a hierarchical, paternalistic order."[52] These words of Orlando Patterson express his effort to connect freedom with the Puritan ideal of a commonwealth, a covenanted society that now should include its alienated minorities, including former slaves. In Philemon's case, it was the free slaveholder who as a "slave of Christ" had the obligation to work toward the liberation of his own slave while both were bound together in the new family of the church, the vanguard of a new age. That tactful revolution could be ours as well.

PART 2

NEW PAULINE RESOURCES FOR THE AMERICAN FUTURE

6. Tenement Churches and Pauline Love Feasts

Now concerning brotherly love you have no need [for someone] to
      write to you,
  for you yourselves are God-taught to love one another;
    for you also do this to all the brothers in the whole of
      Macedonia.
But we urge you, brothers, to abound more and more,
  to aspire to live quietly,
    and to work with your own hands as we exhorted you,
  in order that you [all] may behave fittingly toward outsiders
    and that you [all] might not be in want.
                         (1 Thessalonians 4:9–12)

For even when we were with you, we gave you this command,
  "If anyone does not want to work, let [him/her] not eat!"
                         (2 Thessalonians 3:10)

The only quotation from the Bible in the constitution of the former Union of Soviet Socialist Republics is the famous line about not being fed without working. It is curious that it played a larger role in a communist state than it has in mainline churches around the world, where it is occasionally cited as a warning against laziness but is never included in the founding instruction of church members as indicated by 2 Thess. 3:10. Could this and other passages in the Pauline letters disclose a tradition of voluntary communalism that has been buried by our dominant interpretive tradition? Why is this question never raised in the standard studies of the Thessalonian correspondence?[1] What implications might this have for our understanding of the setting and common life of early Pauline congregations and of American church life?

73

Coming to Terms with the Resistance against Communalism

The consideration of these questions must begin with the observation that only one model is currently available to define the congregational life of early Pauline churches. Mainstream biblical scholarship, conforming to its Euro-centric perspective, tends to view the early church as defined by hierarchical-ly organized house churches. In such churches, it is assumed, patrons were in charge, and they provided the space and provisions for the Lord's Supper. Even passages like the captions above are interpreted in the light of such a premise although a communal situation of shared resources, involving eating together regularly and relying on the support of members rather than on a patron would seem to fit the wording of these two passages more naturally. One might expect a reference to early Christian Love Feasts, or at least an allusion to the Lord's Supper, in explaining these passages. However, none of these possibilities is even mentioned in the standard commentaries on 1 and 2 Thessalonians,[2] which reflect the hostililty toward communalism in all of its forms that is characteristic of European and American biblical scholarship. Arising from the struggle against various forms of sectarian communalism in the European Reformation, this hostility was reinforced by twentieth-century atrocities in creating collective farms on the graves of peasant farmers and by enforcing industrial communism through Gulag Archipelagoes.

Similarly, mainline scholarship on the Lord's Supper normally avoids any reference to early Christian groups actually sharing their daily meals togeth-er or any consideration of a link between the Lord's Supper and the Love Feast. That the eating in 2 Thess. 3:10 might refer to the Lord's Supper, embedded in a practice of communal meals, is never considered. The purely symbolic meal of modern Christianity, restricted to a bite of bread and a sip of wine or juice, is tacitly presupposed for the early church, an assumption so preposterous that it is never articulated or acknowledged.

The strange constriction of mainline interpretations concerning the Lord's Supper, the Love Feast, and various forms of eating meals together results in euphemistic explanations of the communal terms strewn throughout the Pauline letters. They are tacitly recontextualized to fit the polite circum-stances of modern churches where members live in private homes and gather infrequently for worship in church buildings. Hence in the passage above, *philadelphia* is translated literally as "brotherly love," which in contemporary usage implies positive feelings of "affection"[3] toward neighbors or other distant church members. It certainly does not suggest the presence of extended fami-lies where caring for one another could take concrete communal form. The reference to *ta agapan allēlous* is translated "to love one another," which for modern interpreters implies "mutual love for fellow Christians"[4] who are understood to be distant persons with whom one should get along harmo-niously at infrequent meetings. So love is reduced to the willingness to be agreeable, losing any connection to sharing resources or eating together, which in this passage is suggested by the reference to the "work of your hands." This reference to handwork is understood to be an admonition to some modern form of middle-class self-reliance aimed "against slackers who will not work"[5] and who therefore "of necessity must have been economically dependent on others."[6] Paul's goal is thus seen to promote "economic self-sufficiency,"[7] which for the modern interpreter and reader seems to imply a capitalistic economy where each family unit should take care of itself. The possibility that Paul's language might imply communal sharing of the proceeds of the "work of your hands" to provide for a Love Feast is not even considered.

The reference at the end of 1 Thess. 4:9–12 cited above to *mêdenos chreian echête* is translated by the New Revised Standard Version in a manner consistent with this middle-class orientation of mainline commentaries as "be dependent on no one." This translation implies individual self-sufficiency in the economic sphere, which is far removed from the literal concern Paul expresses that the community "might not be in want."[8] Similarly the references in other letters to "sharing what you have" and being "generous" are construed in terms of occasionally giving alms to the poor, understood to be separate from one's own self-sufficient family. The term *koinônia*, the technical expression in Greek for sharing things in common,[9] is reduced to "fellowship,"[10] which in modern churchly use implies friendly discourse between distant church members who actually have a minimal level of interdependence. This euphemistic tradition prevents modern readers from questioning whether the early Pauline Christians were as individualistic and politely distant as mainline Christians in the modern era, or whether their ways of expressing a transformed life may have contained communal elements suppressed by standardized interpretation.

Interpreters in the North American context should find it natural to raise such questions because communes have so frequently been established here. Mark Holloway[11] traces the impact of the Pilgrims at Plymouth; the Anabaptists; the Mennonites; the Amish; the Labadists; various Bohemian, Moravian, and Baptist experiments; the Quakers and the Shakers; the Rappites and Zoarites; Owen's New Harmony colony; Alcott's Brook Farm; Noyes's Oneida community; the Fourier communities; the Amanites; and the Hutterites. The last-mentioned group began among peasants and the urban poor in and around Zurich during the Reformation, fled to Moravia, then to Russia, and finally to North America in the 1870s where they have expanded to around four hundred agricultural communes, thus constituting the longest lasting communal organization in modern times. Their worship centers in the remembrance of the martyrdom of their early members in Europe.[12] Many of the other utopian groups began in Europe and found they could not flourish there because of official harassment that lasted through the nineteenth century.[13] The cultural environment remains somewhat hostile to communal ideas down to the present; aside from monasteries, convents, and deaconess homes associated with mainstream churches,[14] there were relatively few Christian communes in Europe until the modest flowering of house churches and base communities beginning in the 1960s.[15]

Marguerite Bouvard described her visits to some of the religious, rural, and behaviorist communes that arose in great numbers in the 1960s and 1970s, showing how they inherited "the problems as well as the visions of their forebears."[16] An account of intentional Christian communities and house churches within Roman Catholic parishes emerging since the 1970s is provided by Bernard J. Lee and Michael A. Cowan.[17] They describe this movement as an "earthquake" that is shaking the foundations of traditional church life and providing a "creative transformation" of church life in the United States.[18] Frances FitzGerald offers a penetrating analysis of four utopian experiments in contemporary America in *Cities on a Hill*.[19] Groups as diverse as the gay liberationists in the Castro district of San Francisco; a retirement community in Sun City, Arizona; Jerry Falwell's church and college in Lynchburg, Virginia; and the Rajneeshpuram community near Madras, Oregon, shared the idea that "they could start all over again from scratch . . . and if necessary reinvent themselves."[20] She notes the peculiarity of this "quintessentially American" utopianism from the perspective of Europeans.[21] In the current American context, there are communal systems in every part of the country, ranging from house churches, Hutterite colonies, secular or religious rural communes, Branch Davidian or Mormon settlements to traditional monastic communities.[22] In addition there are numerous monuments to the communal experiments of the past.

Our culture has also witnessed vital analogues to the common eating patterns that seem similar to the eating together of the early church. Many churches still practice some form of the Love Feast or common meal as part of their regular church life. One also thinks of the day-long "Brush Arbor" and "Cane Break" services with picnic meals shared communally by black Christians during slavery times; of the extended periods of eating and living together during open-air revivals during the Second Great Awakening; of eating together at barn raisings or Sunday school picnics or ice cream socials; of the occasional but traditional potluck dinners in churches all over the country. The difference from the older European practice is evident in every town in America because churches here tend to have fellowship halls with kitchens. European churches do not. Another distinctive American development is the creation of huge church campuses with recreational and educational facilities and a wide range of social services and programs that allow members to live virtually separately from the outside world.

I think it is time that American scholars begin to wonder whether the communal forms flourishing all around them, often explicitly derived from what religious leaders thought were New Testament precedents, may not in fact have their historical as well as their ideological origins in early Christianity. Could texts like these from 1 and 2 Thessalonians reflect communal forms of church life? Is the model of a house church, with its hierarchical structure and its reliance on philanthropy rather than mutual sharing, really adequate to account for all the data in the Pauline letters? Could the creation of communal church structures account in part for the extraordinary appeal that Christianity held out to the urban underclass in the Greco-Roman world?

Tenement Churches Alongside House Churches

There is indisputable evidence for the traditional picture of house churches in early Christianity, starting with references to the "church in the house" of particular patrons.[23] Although the word *oikos* can refer to the atrium of a Roman villa, a "Peristyl" Greek house, a Hellenistic style of building with rooms around a central courtyard, or even an apartment in a tenement building,[24] most studies of house churches assume a building owned by a patron, somewhat analogous to the situation of middle- or upper-class housing in contemporary Europe or North America.[25] Jerome Murphy-O'Connor's calculation of the maximum size of thirty to forty members for a house church congregation rests on the premise of a free-standing villa.[26] His more recent work considers the possibility that the shop space on the ground floor of a tenement building might be used for a "house church" such as Prisca and Aquila sponsored in Corinth, Ephesus, and Rome; it might accommodate a group of ten to twenty believers.[27]

The model of a house church presupposes a patron who owns or rents the space used by the Christian community. A number of such persons are mentioned in the Pauline letters including Phoebe, Erastus, Crispus, Stephanas, Gaius, Philemon, Appia, and Nympha. A house church is thus assimilated into the hierarchical social structure of the Greco-Roman world, in which heads of houses exercise legal and familial domination over their relatives and slaves.[28] In the words of Wayne Meeks, "The head of the household, by normal expectations of the society, would exercise some authority over the group and would have some legal responsibility for it. The structure of the *oikos* was hierarchical, and contemporary political and moral thought regarding the structure of superior and inferior roles as basic to the well-being of the whole society."[29] This model of a house church has led to the widely accepted theory of Gerd Theissen that such churches were marked by "love-patriarchalism" in which the hierarchical social order is retained while mutual respect and love are being fostered by patrons serving as leaders of the congregations in their houses.[30]

Studies of the evidence in Thessalonians and Romans began to raise questions in my mind whether the house church model was adequate to explain all of the evidence about church life in the Pauline letters. I was particularly impressed by the study of Roman Christianity by Peter Lampe,[31] which identifies the precise districts in the city where Christianity got its start. Using a topographic method based on the coincidence between five different types of archeological and literary evidence, Lampe showed that two of the most likely areas for early Christian churches were in Trastevere and the section on the Appian Way around the Porta Capena, both inhabited by immigrants. In neither area was the situation conducive to the development of "house churches."

Both Trastevere and the district around the Porta Capena were swampy areas where the poorest population of Rome lived. "Trastevere was the harbor and worker quarter; it contained harbor workers . . . , laborers in the many warehouses, seamen and brick and tile workers. . . . potters . . . millers working with imported grain . . . tanners and leatherworkers."[32] Roman statistics indicate that Trastevere was the most densely populated section of the city with the highest proportion of high-rise slum dwellings in the city. Lampe also investigated the statistics concerning bakeries and found that Trastevere had the lowest number per square kilometer of any section of Rome, indicating very low socioeconomic conditions. Trastevere was full of immigrants out of the East and was the site of mystery religion shrines and temples. This section, which lay across the Tiber from the rest of Rome, was left untouched by the Roman fire, which may account in part for the later scapegoating of Christians by Nero.[33]

The area around the Porta Capena was a damp valley with heavy traffic into the city. Lampe provides this description: "The quarter is populated by traders, handworkers and transport workers. . . .Transport work is night work in Rome. . . . An indication of the social status of transport workers, donkey drivers, and carriers is indicated by the fact that hardly a cemetery inscription refers to such a profession."[34] To summarize, "In the two regions of Trastevere and Appian Way/Porta Capena the lowest population lived, so that an inference about the Christians living there is easy."[35]

Corresponding to the description of these slum districts where the bulk of the early Christians lived is Lampe's analysis of the social background of the names of persons greeted in Rom. 16. Two-thirds of the names indicate Greek rather than Latin background and hence confirm their immigrant status. After a careful and rather conservative estimate, he also concludes that "of the 13 persons about whom something definite can be said, more than two-thirds point with great certainty to slave origins."[36] Here as elsewhere in the early church, the bulk of the members were slaves and former slaves, with the rest coming largely from lower-class handworkers.

An even more compelling set of inferences can be made when one analyzes the lists of members or leaders in two of the five groupings Paul identifies in Romans. In Rom. 16:14 Paul refers to "the brothers," who are together with five persons:[37] Asyncritus, Phlegon, Hermes, Patrobas, and Hermas. These names indicate a thoroughly Gentile membership and ethos, with a mix of slave, freedmen, and Greek immigrants evident. As Heikki Solin has shown, persons with Greek names in Rome reflect a social background that was almost exclusively slave or former slave.[38] Since all five names are Greek and associated with slavery, it is likely that this church consisted entirely of persons with low social status. This status gives it a high likelihood of being located in one of the tenements of Trastevere or Porta Capena. Since none of the five names appears to be playing the role of patron for the group, the social structure probably differed from that of the traditional house church. The selection of the title "brothers" for this group indicates an egalitarian ethos, which would be appropriate for a group without a patron.

Romans 16:15 refers to another Christian cell that also falls outside the traditional model of a house church under the supervision of a patron. It is identified with the title "the saints," perhaps indicating an affinity with the moral legacy of conservative Jewish Christianity. The names of its leaders or major participants, however, are Greek: Philologus, Julia, Nereus, Nereus's sister, and Olympas. All five appear to be either slaves or former slaves, so that this group would also be an excellent prospect for placement in the slums of Trastevere or Porta Capena.

When one considers the housing situation in the slum districts of Rome and other urban centers during the first century, the plausibility of the house church model for such groupings as the "saints" and "brethren" of Rom. 16:14–15 is further diminished. It is now clear that the majority of early Christian converts lived in the apartment buildings called *insulae* in the inner cities rather than in private villas.[39] The studies by Frier and Packer show that 90 percent of the free population and an even higher percentage of the slave population in the cities of the empire lived in the upper floors of *insula* buildings.[40] The upper portions of the four- and five-story apartment blocks typically contained tiny cubicles of about ten square meters in which one family lived. A kind of vertical zoning was characteristic, with larger apartments for upper- or middle-class renters on lower floors and slaves or freedmen crowded into the upper floors.[41] These slum buildings contained no central heating, no running water, and no toilet facilities. Occupants were often fed from a common kitchen;[42] others cooked on charcoal braziers in their rooms. The population density in these districts is difficult for moderns to imagine. John Stambaugh has estimated a population density of 300 per acre for the residential areas of the city of Rome,[43] almost two-and-a-half times higher than twentieth-century Calcutta and three times higher than Manhattan Island.[44]

The question that I have begun to ask is whether church groups consisting entirely of members living in tenement buildings and lacking the sponsorship of a patron may have conducted their services within the *insula* itself, either using one of the workshop areas on the ground floor or using space rented by Christian neighbors in upper floors, clearing away the temporary partitions between cubicles to create room for the meeting. In either case the church would not be meeting in space provided by a patron but rather in rented or shared space provided by the members themselves.[45] I propose we begin thinking about the possibility of "tenement churches," in addition to the traditional concept of "house churches," as forms of early Christian communities. On the basis of the evidence in Romans, one would infer that the class structure of tenement churches was monodimensional. In contrast to house churches that have an upper- or middle-class patron along with his or her slaves, family, friends, and others, the tenement churches consisted entirely of the urban underclass, primarily slaves and former slaves. Lacking a patron who would function as a leader, the pattern of leadership appears to have been charismatic and egalitarian. Each of the groups greeted in Romans has five persons named, who were probably the charismatic leaders of the community. If the persons named are the renters of family living spaces in the tenement building rather than charismatic leaders of the group, the social pattern still appears to be egalitarian. No one of the five appears to have a position of prominence over the others. The leadership pattern appears to be collective rather than hierarchical. So who provides the economic support, the resources for the Lord's Supper, and the means for hospitality and charity characteristic of early Christianity in such a community? The system of love-patriarchalism would certainly not be relevant in a group of slaves and former slaves residing in a densely packed tenement building. Since similar circumstances are implicit in the Galatian, Thessalonian, and Philippian letters, this question cannot be restricted to peculiar conditions within Roman Christianity. Some other system must be implicit in these letters, perhaps one that has been overlooked by an interpretive tradition that, as we have seen, is instinctively hostile to communalism and thus inclined to a euphemistic construal of the relevant terms.

The Pauline Love Feast as a Communal Meal

The path toward an alternative to the concept of love-patriarchalism in early churches has been available since 1951. Bo Reicke's classic study of the early Christian systems of diaconal service and the Love Feast showed that the eucharist was celebrated in the context of a common meal by a broad stream of early Christianity through the fourth century.[46] The direct references to the "Agape" in John 13:1; Jude 12; Ignatius, *Smyrna* 6:2; 7:1; and 8:2, as well as the discussions of common meals in Acts 2:44–47 and 1 Cor. 11:17–34, show that the eucharistic liturgy was combined with diaconal service, understood as serving meals in celebration with the faith community. Whereas researchers have often attempted to separate the sacramental celebration from the common meal, Reicke showed that early Christian sources, beginning with the biblical evidence, point toward the "single Christian sacrament of table fellowship."[47] The evidence justifies calling all such celebrations in the early church "Love Feasts." Such meals were marked by eschatological joy at the presence of a new age and of a Master who had triumphed over the principalities and powers. This joy was treated with ambivalence by early Christian writers because it tended toward excesses of zealous impatience with the continuation of a fallen world and sometimes resulted in licentious behavior. At times an overly realized eschatology in some of the Agape meals led to Christian forms of the Saturnalia in Thessalonica[48] and to Gnostic excesses in Corinth.[49] Reicke observes, in fact, that the only New Testament passage that refers to such joyous celebrations as completely unambiguous is Acts 2:46. All other passages express criticism of excessive behavior in connection with these celebrative Love Feasts.

The close association between *agape* and the communal meal documented by Reicke leads me to wonder whether the frequent admonitions "to love the brethren" in the Pauline letters may not have been intended to encourage support and participation in the sacramental celebration. In groups organized as house churches, the primary admonition would obviously be to the patrons, encouraging their involvement in love-patriarchalism. But in the context of groups organized as tenement churches, to whom would these admonitions of love be directed? Certainly not to patrons because they are not present within the community itself. I think we should consider developing a second interpretive category to be used alongside "love-patriarchalism," namely "love-communalism." If one prefers to avoid the awkwardness of this Germanic sounding expression, perhaps it would be better to speak of "aga-paic communalism" as the ethical framework suitable for the early Pauline tenement churches. The provisions for the meal in that context would have to come from the sharing of the members. But this is all quite theoretical. Is there direct evidence anywhere in the Pauline letters for this kind of communal support for the Love Feast?

There is in fact a passage in 2 Thessalonians that could provide such evidence: the verse cited in the Soviet Constitution. I believe a case can be made that the form, content, and background of this verse, "If anyone does not want to work, let [him/her] not eat" (2 Thess. 3:10b), point in the direction of a communally supported system of Love Feasts in the church at Thessalonica.[50] But in addition to the hostility against communalism, the lack of a form-critical analysis of 2 Thess. 3:10b in standard commentaries or in specialized investigations of New Testament forms has kept scholars from considering such implications.[51] The discussions of this verse in commentaries and other investigations tend to understand it as a general admonition to maintain a modern-sounding system of individual self-support.[52] A recent study even argues that the author wishes to "wean such persons from the welfare syndrome" of relying on a patron for economic support.[53] Such comments ignore the distinctive form and function of this saying as well as the relevant communal parallels in the ancient world.

The form of 2 Thess. 3:10 is a typical example of casuistic law,[54] found in various settings in the ancient world.[55] The first half of the saying describes the nature of the offense and the second half provides the legal remedy or consequence.[56] Modified versions of this form are found elsewhere in the Pauline letters, setting forth general rules for congregational behavior (Rom. 14:15; 15:27; 1 Cor. 7:13, 15, 21; 8:13; 9:11; 11:6),[57] but there are no exact parallels in the letters to this classic legal form in which the offense is described in the conditional clause and the sanction in the second clause. Since the sanction implies communal discipline rather than some judicial punishment enacted by an official agency, this saying should be classified as a community regulation.

Instructive parallels to the content of this particular regulation have been found in the Qumran scrolls where the sanctions for violating the rules of the community include exclusion from the table of the "pure," the reduction of food allotments, or excommunication from the community.[58] The regulations of Hellenistic and Greco-Roman guilds also prescribe penalties of exclusion from the common meal or from the guild itself for certain offenses, though the payment of fines is a more usual punishment.[59] Deprivation of food was also used in boarding schools to enforce proper academic performance.[60] I find it significant that all of these parallels to 2 Thess. 3:10 reflect settings in which communities are eating their meals together. Other examples sustain the generalization that social coercion through deprivation of food in the ancient world presupposed a communal system of some kind.[61] None of the parallels reflects the premise of independent self-support of individuals and families that dominates the interpretation of this verse in mainline churches and standard investigations.

The content of the offense in 2 Thess. 3:10b relates to an unwillingness to work, not to one's ability to work or the availability of employment.[62] The verb "want" in this context implies conscious refusal to accept employment.[63] The sanction is described with a two-word imperative: *mēde esthietō* ("let not eat!"), implying that deprivation of food as such is in view, not temporary exclusion from a particular meal. The form-critical method leads to the question of the type of social setting implicit in the sanction because the sanction must be enforceable for the regulation to be effective. This means that the community must have had jurisdiction over the regular eating of its members, which would only have been possible if the community was participating in eating together on an ongoing basis. This inference is confirmed by the parallels from Qumran and the Greco-Roman world, all of which presuppose a situation of common meals organized by the community. It would be impossible to enforce this sanction if the members of the congregation ate all their meals in their own private homes or tenement spaces. The reference to eating in the absolute would also be overstated if the sanction merely related to exclusion from occasional sacramental celebrations. The formulation of this community regulation thus demands a Love Feast system organized on a regular, frequent basis.

Form-critical method seeks the *Sitz-im-Leben* of particular forms of social discourse on the assumption that literary forms reflect specific types of settings.[64] In this instance the creation as well as the enforcement of this community regulation require very specific conditions. The form-critical analysis of casuistic law in the Old Testament and the Ancient Near East indicates that the creation of such rules is the result of corporate jurisprudence rather than individual literary ingenuity.[65] Such sentences are abstracted and reformulated to make them universally valid. "These casuistic principles are therefore not, by origin, laws deliberately composed; their authority rests on tradition and custom; they are common law."[66] These considerations make it appear unlikely that the author of 2 Thessalonians composed this community regulation *ex nihilo*. If Paul was the author of 2 Thessalonians, an even stronger case can be made that he did not create the regulation. As noted above, the form of his policy advice on community issues never otherwise follows the precise casuistic form of a communal regulation. This particular casuistic regulation probably arose out of previous conflicts of a very specific type. The creation of the regulation required communities that were regularly eating meals together, for which the willingness or unwillingness to work was a factor of sufficient importance to require regulation, and in which the power to deprive members of food was in fact present. The same three conditions would be required for the author of 2 Thessalonians to advance this regulation in the particular context of conflicts in the Thessalonian churches. The form and content of this community rule, therefore, indicates the existence of such conditions both in earlier congregations and in the audience to which 2 Thessalonians was addressed—whether written by Paul in the early 50s or by a deutero-Pauline writer in the 90s. A system of Christian communes was required in which meals were being shared on a regular basis and for which the refusal to work posed a significant threat.

Given the references to "brotherly love" (1 Thess. 4:9) and "well doing" (2 Thess. 3:13) in close proximity to the discussion of labor for bread, it appears likely that the food for the Love Feasts in Thessalonica was being provided by community members rather than by patrons. If the meals were being provided by patrons, it would be relatively immaterial whether particular guests were gainfully employed or not. Another social structure is implied by the form of this regulation, one in which food was being contributed by the members. In that kind of structure, the conscious refusal of able-bodied persons to add what they could to the common meal would present a morale problem of such a scale as to jeopardize the entire system. The form-critical assessment of the community rule thus points to the social structure of a "tenement church" rather than to the traditional "house church," not only in Thessalonica but in those other early Christian communities where the regulation was formed into "common law."

The social importance of the regulation for the Thessalonian community is confirmed by the introductory comments in 2 Thess. 3:10: "For when we were with you, we used to give you this command." The imperfect verbs point to repetitive instruction,[67] which would have been appropriate only if the instruction were actually crucial to the life of the community. If 2 Thessalonians is a pseudonymous letter, its author apparently wished to present this command as foundational in early Christian catechism. The introductory comments assume an even larger significance if Paul was in fact the author of 2 Thessalonians, because the founding visit was cut off unexpectedly before the formation of the congregation was deemed complete. This community regulation must have been of primary relevance for the daily life of the congregation if it had been repeatedly stressed during so short a founding visit (1 Thess. 2:17). In either case a tenement church structure in which communal meals were being provided by the members themselves is the only form of early Christian congregational life for which such instruction could actually be considered absolutely essential.

Additional Evidence of a Love Feast System

Both 1 and 2 Thessalonians reflect a Love Feast system that is being supported by the contributions of church members. The caption at the head of this chapter from 1 Thess. 4:9–12 deals with "brotherly love," which is primarily a familial category[68] implying that Christians are in some sense living together as a new fictive family, replacing their families of origin.[69] The extraordinary weight Paul gives to the bond between members of the new Christian family is somewhat disguised by the traditional translation used by the NRSV: "for you yourselves have been taught by God to love one another." Paul actually refers to their being *theodidaktoi* ("God-taught") in such love. There is a broad consensus that this term was coined by Paul since it appears nowhere else in the pre-Christian period.[70] The term contrasts, as Abraham Malherbe points out, with being "self-taught," which was the claim of the philosopher Epicurus. In this instance, the purpose of being "God-taught" was *philadelphia* in 4:9, used only one other time by Paul in Rom. 12:13. In both cases, as Malherbe hints, Paul intends a mild critique of Epicurianism as well as "a practical concern for the material needs of members of the church."[71] Calvin Roetzel suggests a link to Hellenistic Jewish usage of "self-taught," with the intent of promoting "social responsibilities" in Thessalonica.[72] While pointing out the absence of explicit polemic at this point in the letter and the lack of evidence concerning a knowledge of Hellenistic Judaism in the Thessalonian environment, John Kloppenborg has recently lifted up the prominence of *philadelphia* in Greco-Roman celebrations of the mythical twin brothers who excelled in mutual devotion, Pollux and Castor.[73] It is certain that the congregation knew this tradition because Thessalonian coins struck in the first century feature the twins mounted on horses; the brothers were also prominently featured in the western gate of the city.[74] It seems significant that the only public ritual associated with the brothers was a seasonal feast provided to the poor by the rich,[75] but it does not seem plausible that Paul coined the word "God-taught" to avoid a direct allusion to these mythical deities who taught *philadelphia*.[76] There is nothing disparaging in this reference, which if anything is extraordinarily grandiose; the God teaching the Thessalonians is clearly the "living and true God" who in 1 Thess. 1:9 has saved them from idols like Castor and Pollux.

I think it is more likely that Paul exploited categories associated with the local environment in order to sustain the distinctive form of common life that marked early Christian congregations, namely the Love Feast that replaced the pagan festivals. The sharing of resources and feeding of the poor is being accomplished here by a Christian form of brotherly love. The God who instructs the Thessalonian Christians about performing this kind of love is clearly the parent of Jesus Christ (1 Thess. 1:10), understood to be the Lord of the Feast. Since the passage goes on to discuss the necessity of working "with your own hands" and thus avoiding "want" in the community (1 Thess. 4:11–12), a contextual construal would suggest that "brotherly love" = members of the new Christian family contributing their fair share to the Love Feast, signifying the transformation brought by Christ.

The same linkage between handwork, eating, earning bread for the community, and brotherhood is found in 2 Thess. 3:6–13, which includes the rule about not feeding persons who refuse to work and ends with the admonition, "brothers, do not be weary in doing good." The good in this instance is not some euphemism about general responsibility;[77] in this context, it refers to supporting a community whose life centers in a Love Feast dependent on the contributions of each member. The translation of this passage needs to be carefully rendered so as to remove the individualistic and capitalistic slant that disguises the link to the communal meal. For instance, the admonition in the NRSV that the members should "do their work quietly and earn their own living" (2 Thess. 3:12) actually should read "working with quietness, they eat their own bread."[78] There is no implication in the Greek text that each person or family should be economically independent or eat separately but rather that the community as a whole should avoid dependency. The way to do so is for each person to continue doing the "good" of contributing to the common meal.

I believe these and other Pauline churches were devising various ways to continue the communalism of the original Jesus movement and of the experiment of *koinônia* in Acts 2. Some churches provided resources through patronage and others through sharing, but in each case there was a sense that a new age had dawned and that Jesus was present in the feast. In his recent book on the historical Jesus, John Dominic Crossan writes about "the heart of the original Jesus movement, a shared egalitarianism of spiritual and material resources." He insists "that its materiality and spirituality, its facticity and symbolism cannot be separated."[79] I think the same could be said for the Pauline Love Feasts in their various forms. They fused sacramental life with regular sharing of material resources in the context of celebrative meals. They joined ecstatic joy at the presence of a new age by forming new families of brothers and sisters to cope with poverty and alienation in the slums of the inner cities. They united care for the poor with worshipful celebration of Christ as the Lord of the Banquet.

Concluding Reflections on the American Scene

The robust development of Pauline tenement churches constitutes one of what Lee and Cowan have termed the "dangerous memories" of Christian solidarity that could help us cope with the isolating maladies in this country: "the Christian ethos demands that we challenge any form of individualism that would tolerate inequitable distribution of the world's goods. Such a challenge is a redemption of the individualism that violates the web of relationships which sustains us, that fragments the body of Christ."[80] The Pauline Love Feast could stimulate the contemporary church to develop viable forms of economic cooperation, new ways to integrate the sacraments into revitalized forms of potluck meals,[81] and new strategies for the "underclass" in American cities to begin coping together since the patronage system of governmental aid has become so alienating and unreliable. It could lead current church leaders to retrieve the impulses of American communalism and discover new ways to integrate them into the now faltering "mainstream" of congregational life.[82] It could help us recapture Josiah Royce's vision of "a community of those who are artists in some form of cooperation,"[83] whose labor embodies the awareness that both in the church and in the society, "we are all one loving and beloved community."[84]

7. Discharged from the Law of Consumerism

> While we were in the flesh, our passions that were sinful because
> of the law
>   were at work in our members to bear fruit with respect to death.
> But now we are discharged from the law, having died to that
>   in which we were being held down,
>   so that we might be slaves in newness of spirit and not
>   in the obsolete letter.
> What then shall we say?
>   Is the law sin?
>   By no means!
> But I did not know sin except through law.
>   For I was unaware of coveting except that the law said,
>   "You shall not covet."
> But finding a foothold through the commandment,
>   the sin worked in me all covetings,
>   for without the law sin is dead.[1]
>
> (Romans 7:5–8)

One of the areas of Pauline theology that seems most limited by the European legacy is the doctrine of the law. The traditional line of interpretation is well known: Christ frees us from legalism and its attendant self-righteousness because we are saved solely by grace, not by performance of the law. There are several major problems with this line of interpretation. From the beginning it tended to pit what some call the "Catholic Substance" of doctrine and morals against the "Protestant Principle" of salvation by faith alone. From the time of Luther this interpretation of the law resulted in polemics against Catholic moral teachings as new and pernicious forms of the law from which true faith ought to free every Christian. Later polemical targets included Calvinists and Pietists, who were perceived to be soft on the doctrine of freedom from the law. This style of polemical interpretation had

the delightful advantage of revealing the sin to be entirely resident in someone else's house, but it is hardly defensible in our ecumenical atmosphere
today. But the more difficult barrier to this line of interpretation is that the
so-called Catholic Substance of moral certainties has substantially evaporat-
ed from a broad stream of culture in the United States. In this relativistic
age, millions of Americans, even of the church-attending population, seem
no longer to be afflicted by the burden of conformity to biblical law.

At the same time, however, new laws that do not originate in religious
systems have arisen to dominate the behavior of thoroughly secularized
North Americans—the laws of the consumer society, promoted by advertise-
ments in the most powerful media of our time. It is to bring what Paul wrote
in Rom. 7:5–8 into this new arena that you are invited to share in a tongue-
in-cheek exploration. Bear with me in a little fun at the expense of some of
the sillier phenomena of American life.

Soon after we moved to the Chicago area in 1980, I began hearing about
alligators invading the U.S.A. I noticed tiny alligators sewn on sport shirts
and even saw bumper stickers that seemed to express resentment against
those who wear such things: "Save an alligator, kill a preppie!" So I inquired
of some of our seminary students working with youth groups in the Chicago
area and received extensive reports about dress styles, codes of behavior, and
rituals of prestige that marked the classes in our public schools. Then to
inform myself more fully, I decided to see if I could find a copy of *The Official Preppie Handbook*.[2] Thereafter I borrowed a copy of *The Yuppie
Handbook*[3] so that my research—if it deserves the name!—would be complete. I am ready to report on a new phase of the interpretation of Paul.
Since both of these handbooks are now sufficiently passè that we can smile
about them, they can be seen as typical expressions of the larger and contin-
uing phenomenon of American consumerism. I would like to show how Paul
the Apostle to America proposes to free our culture from the plague of alligators.

Paul and the Law of Conformity

At first glance Paul's message about being "discharged from the law" may
seem many worlds removed from the rituals of consumption and behavior in
modern society. For hundreds of years interpreters have assumed that the law
from which Christians were to be freed was that of the Old Testament,[4]
amplified in oral form by the Pharisees.[5] That was a law with a pretty serious
texture: regulations about moral and cultic behavior, allegedly designed to
render humans acceptable before God. For a long time we interpreters
assumed that law in this sense had always been too complicated to obey, that
it evoked guilt feelings because even the most strenuous efforts to obey would

fall short of the high demand. Sabatier described Saul's Pharisaic conscience in the following terms: "In vain would he have sought to satisfy it with a partial righteousness; it demanded nothing less than perfect holiness . . . and with this law his conscience entered into an incessant and unequal struggle, in which it was always and inevitably worsted. Every fresh effort resulted, of necessity, in a more humiliating defeat."[6] To be saved by grace, according to this usual interpretation, was to be forgiven for such inevitable failures. Since the law in this traditional sense functions mainly by showing where we have failed,[7] it would seem to have little to do with feeling obligated to wear the proper sports shoes or the latest style of pinstripe suit.

Several things have come together in recent years to force Pauline scholars to revise this long-standing interpretation. One is the discovery of what Krister Stendahl calls the "robust conscience" of the apostle Paul.[8] When Paul describes his previous life in Judaism, it is clear that he felt he had been entirely successful at obeying the law. "As to righteousness under the law," Paul reports that he had been "blameless" (Phil. 3:6). No one could say this honestly if he were plagued with the "introspective conscience" that has marked Western Christians since the times of Augustine and Luther. Paul apparently felt that the Jewish law, with all its complication, was perfectly capable of being fulfilled. This realization has been driven home in studies by E. P. Sanders and others.[9] This means that since Paul's shouldering of the yoke of the law at the age of thirteen when he went through an ancient form of the Bar Mitzvah, he had not failed a single time.[10] This is so mind-boggling for guilt-ridden Western Christians that it has taken us quite a while to rethink what the law really meant for Paul.

What is clear to leading scholars today is that our understanding of Paul's conversion and of the place of guilt in the scheme of salvation need to be revised. It was not Paul's inability to perform the law that led to his conversion but just the opposite: his perfect conformity to the law. What we need to be relieved of, in other words, is not a guilty conscience about noncompliance with the law but rather from conformity itself.

Well now, this suddenly seems to place Americans on pretty familiar territory. If the problem of the human race is too much conformity, then there must be a simple solution: nonconformity. This is where Americans excel. Have we not conveyed to the entire world a taste for blue jeans as a sign of the nonconformity and freedom of the Western hero? Is not our popular music with its message of love and independence and rebellion the rage of nonconformist youth the world over? And what could be more typical of the mainstream of our liberal religion as well as of our dress codes than nonconformity? Turning back in the past thirty years to read Thoreau's *Walden Pond*, a whole generation of Americans has learned to "march to a different drummer." The "basic reading list" in *The Preppie Handbook*[11] includes books such as Salinger's *The Catcher in the Rye* and Anderson's *Tea and Sympathy*, vintage statements of achieving self-identity through nonconformity. As a consequence, we have prided ourselves on becoming the most nonconformist zealots in the world in a way—wearing blue jeans to the symphony and Adidas to the prom. We demonstrate in countless ways that we think of ourselves as "discharged from the law," to use Paul's expression from Romans.

Yet there is an oddity in the nonconformity of Americans, as most of us are aware. The preppie and yuppie handbooks provide page after page of detailed instructions about how to look nonconformist and how to distinguish yourself from the rest of society. Reading through these details brings one face-to-face with a strange and passionate new conformity. Rejecting earlier ideas of color coordination, for example, the *Preppie Handbook* says that "primary colors and brilliant pastels are worn indiscriminately by men and women alike, in preposterous combinations. In some subcultures, hot pink on men might be considered a little peculiar; preppies take it for granted."[12] One demonstrates nonconformity by style and color combinations that defy traditional tastes and prove one's uniqueness. The "Yuppie ten commandments" begin with "Thou shalt have no other gods before thyself" and "Thou shalt take unto thee only designer labels."[13] Yet the oddity is that a designer label type of uniformity thereby arises. Despite their passionate quest for nonconformity, all preppies were immediately recognizable in any American school. And to make the oddity even more striking, those who opposed the preppie style and made every effort to refuse to conform to it, ended up looking like other like-minded nonpreppies.

Now, this was a little disquieting to teachers and parents who assumed that the American tradition of nonconformity would encourage the emergence of an "inner-directed" generation. The "law," to use Paul's term, has a strange way of reappearing where we least expect it. Having liberated our youth from the dress codes and supervised behavior that marked public schools in an earlier era, we were surprised to find that they imposed much more stringent codes upon themselves. And those enforcing the new codes of behavior and dress that are visible at every level in our society are not stern teachers or preachers but even more tyrannical forces—our friends, our colleagues, and we ourselves. About a decade ago, I found a delightful cartoon that embodies this insight, depicting a first-grader heading off to school. The caption reads as follows:

> First-grader dressed in Dukes of Hazzard jeans, Smurf sneakers, E.T. t-shirt, carrying Hulk lunchbox with Superman peanut butter sandwich, Snoopy schoolbag with He-man pencils and sharpener, Star Wars writing paper, who has just taken his Flintstones vitamins and eaten Pac-Man cereal, ready for school to develop his "individual potential."[14]

Let me put the dilemma of the law in a nutshell: if conformity to the law is the human problem, then nonconformity would appear to be the obvious solution. But if there is as much conformity in nonconformity as in conformity itself, something deeper must be wrong beneath the surface that our liberal educational system has overlooked.

The Passion of Coveteousness

The reason Paul may be relevant to the seemingly silly phenomena of preppies and yuppies, of Nikes and Boondockers, is that he understands and explains the deeper dimensions of our human motivations. In Rom. 7:5–8 Paul describes how the "passions that were sinful because of the law" lead humans to "death." Paul goes on to explain how sin invades and corrupts the law. "I did not know sin except through law. For I was unaware of coveting except that the law said, 'You shall not covet.' But finding foothold through the commandment, the sin worked in me all covetings" (Rom. 7:7–8).

In other words, it is not the law of wearing alligator pins that causes our bondage, but "our sinful passions" that motivate such behavior. It is what we hope to get out of conforming or nonconforming that counts. That is why Paul refers to coveting as the essence of sin.[15] The insatiable desire to possess and wear and display precisely the properly impressive things is related to "sin," the prideful desire to stand alone at the center of the universe. As Barrett observes, covetousness "means precisely that exaltation of the *ego* which we have seen to be the essence of sin. . . . Regardless of his place in creation . . . man desires, and his desire becomes the law of his being. He, rather than God, becomes Lord."[16]

The preppie and yuppie phenomena reveal that recent Americans have hoped to deal with the threats of the world by conforming to its standards. It is to assuage our fear of being unacceptable that we work so frantically to earn acceptance and fall so deeply into despair when we do not measure up. Feeling threatened every time we fall behind in the search for status and prestige, we act in such a way as to get ahead of others and to keep constantly ahead. The definition of a yuppie, according to Piesman and Hartley, involves someone who "lives on aspirations of glory, prestige, recognition, fame, social status, power, money or any and all combinations of the above."[17] The sin in all of this is the aggressive placement of ourselves at the center of the world,[18] which involves crowding others out, and even in the final analysis usurping the central place of God.

The picaresque hero of Saul Bellow's novel, *Henderson the Rain King*, embodies this kind of anxious centering on oneself in language reminiscent of Paul's terms, "sinful passion" and "covetousness." Gene Henderson, the six-foot-five brawler and fornicator introduces himself from the opening pages of the novel as a person who "behaved like a bum." Despite the wealth of his family and some personal abilities, he was unable to find himself in life because there was "a disturbance in my heart, a voice that spoke there and said, *I want, I want, I want!* It happened every afternoon and when I tried to suppress it, it got even stronger. It only said one thing, *I want, I want!*" Henderson tried various things to get this voice to let up. He even took up violin playing after the death of his father, cradling the magnificent Guinarius instrument in his huge hands and screeching without a great deal of success to try to match his father's expectations. But nothing helped. The voice continued to say, "*I want, I want, I want, I want!*"[19]

It is the "I want" of covetousness that keeps Americans from acknowledging our limits, that leads us to continue clawing each other to get ahead. This is what makes the cycle of conformity and nonconformity so compelling. Michael Kinsley dealt with this peculiar issue of stylistic conformity in an article that explained why he and his friend would actually pay more for a shirt without the preppie symbol.

> My friend and I come from similar backgrounds, have similar tastes and a similar view of the world, and neither of us owns any shirts with alligators on them. Why not? It is tempting to say that we are free from such petty snobbery, and would rather save a dollar or two than gain whatever status is available from displaying an alligator on the chest. On reflection, however, the truth is different. If offered two shirts, one with an alligator and one without, I, at least—and he too, I think he would admit—would pay at least a dollar or two *more* if necessary for the shirt without the alligator.[20]

Kinsley sorts through the motivations that might lead to such seemingly irrational behavior and then "by process of elimination, then, the awful truth: we feel superior to people who wear alligators. We are snobs."[21] What Kinsley calls "reverse snobbery" is by far the most prevalent kind "in the slice of American society occupied by people who worry professionally about things like snobbery and social class," he writes. But since it requires the same energy to avoid conforming to the nonconformity of others that conformity itself would consume, he admits "the game . . . is exhausting, but probably unavoidable."[22]

What Kinsley writes is certainly correct so long as the Pauline insight is overlooked. The cycle of conformity is "unavoidable" so long as its underlying cause is unrecognized. That cause is our lingering feeling of vulnerability that sets the entire mechanism of coveting off in the first place. Without getting at the root cause, the serious consequences of our exhausting games of conformity and nonconformity will continue on and on.

But it is not simply the rituals of consumption that are at stake here. Kinsley reports that the "nastiest feud" he ever had was with a friend who claimed identity as a member of the nonconformist "proletariat" although he actually belonged "in the top 10 percent of income distribution in America. He virtually called me a bounder and challenged me to a duel," Kinsley reports.[23]

A similar vehemence was expressed in the strangely hostile bumper sticker, "Save an alligator, kill a preppie!" In the early 1980s it was sometimes seen on older model cars with bumpers that also had stickers about "Save the whales!" and "Support the nuclear freeze!" The vehemence was odd: wearing J. C. Penney slacks in place of Calvin Kleins may or may not be suitable to your taste or budget, but why speak of killing in support of your preference? A similar kind of vehemence is often found in the high-toned ads in our classy magazines. While I was lecturing on this topic in an elegant American suburb, a member of the audience was reminded of an ad for the Aston Martin Lagonda. Its text is as follows:

> It's one thing to trundle by in a Bentley, Jaguar, Mercedes or the like. Everyone in your neighborhood has one of these. It's quite another thing to come in for a landing in your Lagonda. . . . We build the Lagonda at the rate of three a week. Twenty-four are designated for the United States market each year. That's about as fast and as many as we can manage. Should your neighbors ask you as you glide by, what kind of car the Lagonda is, by all means tell them. Should they ask where they can get one, tell them they probably can't. That should do it.

The ad is entitled "Demoralize Thy Neighbor."[24]

Robin Scroggs has tried to explain the mysterious vehemence of coveting in his book *Paul for a New Day.* "Covetousness is a primary expression of aggression—the attempt to possess, control, seize from another, and metaphorically at least, to kill."[25] Scroggs understands this in light of the Freudian dynamic of the superego that resists and simultaneously internalizes parental authority. There is murderous Oedipal energy in coveting. Whether this Freudian explanation is on track or not, Paul's own experience and the current hostilities in our society suggest the serious effects of what Paul called "our sinful passions" that invade every arena of law, no matter how liberated or up-to-date. This leads us to the very heart of Paul's gospel about being "discharged from the law."

Conformity to the Law and Paul's Conversion

When Paul speaks in our passage about actually being "discharged from the law, having died to that in which we were being held down," he is talking about the effect of Christ as he had experienced it. Paul's conversion was directly related to his own conformity to the cultural and religious laws of his tradition.

Paul had pursued a first-century form of the admonition to "Save an alligator, kill a Christian!" because he was full of unacknowledged hostility. Paul was convinced that the followers of the martyr Stephen who had broken free from the law should be tortured and killed. The price of their nonconformity should be made visible to everyone as a warning. He was acting out of the zealous ideology that gripped a portion of Judaism in the period before the Jewish-Roman War, in which the heroic model of Phinehas in Num. 25 inspired lynching strategies to cope with evil-doers.[26] As Beverly Gaventa suggests, Paul's description of his former life in Judaism in Gal. 1:11–17 "connects him with the zealous Jews of the Maccabbean period. He saw himself as following in the tradition of those who acted forcefully to defend that which is proper in Judaism."[27]

Paul opposed the Jesus movement because it liberated people from conformity to the law and because its leader Jesus of Nazareth had been executed as a lawbreaker and a public threat.[28] His persecution of the church was in direct proportion to the passion with which he maintained his own conformity to the law. In this view, Paul was a kind of first-century Ayatollah Khomeini.

What Paul discovered in his conversion was that Jesus the Sabbath breaker was Jesus the Messiah. His appearance to Paul proved that he was indeed resurrected, as the disciples were claiming. This caused what Gaventa has termed a drastic "shift in cognition," a "transformation" in that "what had seemed unthinkable—a crucified messiah—becomes a revelation."[29] The resurrection meant that everything Jesus taught and lived and died for was confirmed by God.[30] In an instant, full of grace and judgment, Paul suddenly discovered the truth about himself, and about all conformity everywhere, from the Jewish law down to *The Yuppie Handbook*.

This encounter on the way to Damascus had a series of transforming consequences. Paul discovered his own hostility against God, for in his zeal for the law he had ended up supporting the crucifixion of the Messiah and the persecution of his followers. There is an unconscious level of sin buried at the heart of religious observance, he discovered. As Karl Barth commented on this passage in Romans, "Religion is the working capital of sin; its fulcrum; the means by which men are removed from direct union with God and thrust into disunion."[31] This was a level and depth of sin that no religious thinker in the Orthodox Jewish tradition up to this point had imagined. It implies a far more pervasive plight for humans than was perceived by any of the Greco-Roman writers that he might have encountered or studied in Tarsus.[32]

Paul also discovered the murderous consequences of the law when it was corrupted by the human energy of coveting. He discovered in a sense that the "I want, I want, I want!" that marked his observance of the law was directly related to the violence of his life. While he had assumed that such violence was ordained by God, he suddenly discovered the true dimension of his activity. He was involved in murder.

Yet at the same time and in the same experience Paul discovered the forgiveness of Christ and the restoration of a proper relationship with God. At the deepest level of his motivations, driven by anxiety about pleasing God and the rest of the world, he was set free by unconditional love. He discovered something that Saul Bellow's Gene Henderson wanted from the beginning. Gene once read in a book the words "the forgiveness of sins is perpetual and righteousness first is not required." But he forgot where the book was placed in his father's gigantic library, and every time he got in trouble later in his life he rifled through the books trying to find that quote again. "But I never found that statement about forgiveness."[33] Not until the end of the novel, after he had traveled to Africa and come under the influence of a profoundly religious African chief did Gene discover forgiveness for himself. He returned home and decided that he would enter the medical profession to serve humanity. He discovered that "whatever gains I ever made were always due to love and nothing else."[34]

In a similar way, Paul discovered his own calling through a conversion that led him to become a missionary to the Gentiles, the nonpreppies of the human race.[35] Paul became convinced that the good news about the grace of God, rather than conformity to a single code, was the means by which the world could be transformed and reunited. As Stendahl describes it, "the center of gravity in Paul's theological work is related to the fact that he knew himself to be the Apostle to the Gentiles, an Apostle of the one God who is Creator of both Jews and Gentiles (cf. Rom. 3:30)."[36]

When we go back to Paul's conversion and understand it not as the relief of a guilty and introspective conscience but as a revelation of the depth of human sin and the power of divine love to overcome that sin, then we are in a position to grasp what being "discharged from the law" means. It is the grace of God that sets us free from the law of the yuppie and the postyuppie handbooks. Even though we remain vulnerable, we are declared to be okay. For the first time in our lives, we can accept ourselves exactly as we are because Christ has opened up the festering boil of the human heart. Its poison drove Jesus to the cross, and by that death we were healed, loved, transformed, and set free. "We are discharged from the law" of conformity! This is good news for persons shaped by contemporary culture in the U.S.A.

Freedom in the Spirit

But this is not quite the end. Our text needs to be taken in its entirety. Rom. 7:6 reads as follows: "But now we are discharged from the law, having died to that in which we were being held down, so that we might be slaves in newness of spirit and not in the obsolete letter." The premise here is that all of us are slaves. None is absolutely free. Liberation from conformity to a particular law never leaves us neutral,[37] for as we observed earlier, the belief that we are simply nonconformists leads us into another form of bondage. At this point Pauline theology corrects a crucial illusion in the American view of freedom. So the question of life is whom shall we serve? Which Lord shall be our mistress?

The alternatives that Paul describes are to serve the "obsolete letter" or to live "in newness of spirit." The obsolete code[38] could be the Old Testament or the Pharisees' oral law or the mores of our society. In our cultural situation, the obsolete code can be represented by the latest mode of fashion promoted by the elite magazines. For others, the code is provided by television ads featuring well-known luminaries who prescribe the consumption of the right products. But such codes are always obsolete, no matter how new they appear to be on the surface. They are constantly shifting and being replaced by newer fashions. No matter how sophisticated you are, there will always be someone somewhere in Paris or New York or San Francisco or Chicago capable and smug enough to show you how far out of it you really are. There will always be a new product touted by the knowledgeable as superior to what you are currently using to eliminate the yellow waxy buildup from your kitchen floor.

True freedom is to be found in "newness of spirit," in which we are bound to others, called to serve others rather than to be served.[39] The "fruits of the spirit" are manifest in a community of "love, joy, peace, patience, kindness, goodness, faithfulness, gentleness, self-control" (Gal. 5:22–23). These fruits of humane mutuality replace the culturally conditioned products of prestige. "Yuppies don't love their lovers," *The Yuppie Handbook* declares. "They love Vivaldi, their new apartments and the color of the ocean off St. Thomas in January."[40] When people are set free from the spirit of consumerism, they become capable for the first time of sustaining genuine relationships. The spirit of Christ constantly conveys to our fearful hearts that we are beloved whether we conform or not. The spirit makes us know from day to day that we are acceptable and can call God our "Abba," our accepting parent (Rom. 8:15–17). The alienating struggle for acceptability is rendered obsolete. This is why Paul did not intend for this "newness of spirit" to be understood individualistically and competitively. When moved by the Spirit, the early Christians were to recognize themselves collectively as legitimate "children of God" (Rom. 8:16). Whether they had warts or not, whether fat or slim, slow or bright, liberal or conservative, they were "fellow heirs with Christ" (Rom. 8:17).

In the confidence that only Christ can provide, Paul would suggest that the latter-day heirs of the Spirit are even free to buy alligator shirts and their current equivalents: to wear them without self-consciousness if it happens to fit their taste; to wear them, and to pass on the love and acceptance they feel both to alligators and to preppies. Discharged from the law, they can finally be themselves and let others do likewise in a new life together in the Spirit. To use the silly lingo of *The Yuppie Handbook* for one last time, this humane and committed style of "personal interfacing"[41] could become the positive expression of being discharged from the law of the consumer society.

8. Truth and Dark Mirrors: The Opening of the American Mind

Love never fails.
> But where there are prophecies,
> > they will pass away;
> where there are tongues,
> > they will be silenced;
> where there is knowledge,
> > it will pass away.

For we know in part
> and we prophesy in part,

but when that which is perfect comes,
> what is in part will pass away. . . .

For now we see in a mirror darkly,
> but then face to face.

Now I know in part;
> then I shall fully know,
> > even as I am fully known.[1]
> > > (1 Corinthians 13:8–10, 12)

There is a metaphor for approaching the truth in 1 Corinthians that addresses a key issue in the future of American higher education. Paul acknowledges that he and other Christians "see through a glass darkly"; or as another translation renders it, "now we see in a mirror dimly, but then we shall see face to face." I would like to explore the interpretation of this provocative metaphor and relate it to perception theory, to modern scientific and hermeneutical methods, to the center of Paul's theology, and finally to the problems of higher education in an era of relativism as articulated by Allan Bloom in *The Closing of the American Mind*.[2] I believe the Apostle to America offers a more promising approach than Plato, whom Bloom advocates as the antidote to relativism but who in actuality would undermine any effort to open the American mind to truth in the context of cultural pluralism.

The Struggle to Interpret the Mirror Metaphor

In 1 Cor. 13 Paul provides a memorable and provocative set of images that could provide significant resources for the future debate over the role of higher education. The traditional interpretation of Paul's metaphor of the "mirror" (*to esoptron*) in 1 Cor. 13:12 had only a partial bearing on this discussion because it stressed only the negative implications. Humans have access to truth only in reflected form, through mirrors that are far from satisfactory. The context of Paul's discussion is rather clear. He was contending with early Christians who were uncritically trusting prophetic visions and ecstatic insights. Messages coming from glossolalia—ecstatic speaking in tongues—were perceived by some of the Corinthians to provide direct access to the angelic realm of truth. The entire thrust of 1 Cor. 13 serves to relativize such claims: "Our knowledge is imperfect and our prophecy is imperfect," Paul insists, "but when the perfect comes, the imperfect will pass away" (1 Cor. 13:9f.). In place of the arrogance that comes from the claims of direct and final access to truth, Paul urges the primacy of love as the appropriate requirement for living in a world of limited vision.

This interpretation has characteristically been supported in the commentaries by speculations about the inadequacies of ancient mirrors. A prominent German commentator suggested that compared with modern mirrors, ancient reflecting devices were "often made of imperfect material" whose images lacked "clarity." "God's being is visible to us only in the unclear reflection of his creation and rule and therefore remains obscure to us."[3] A famous English commentary echoes this theme: "Ancient mirrors were of polished metal, and the Corinthian mirrors were famous; but the best of them would give an imperfect and somewhat distorted reflexion. . . . To see a friend's face in a cheap mirror would be very different from looking at the friend."[4] There is an unfortunate premise in such interpretations: that the ancients shared our ability to compare ancient with modern mirrors. From this perspective the "dark mirror" was understood as a strictly negative metaphor, expressing an inability to grasp the truth in any direct way.

This strictly negative approach appeared to express Greco-Roman skepticism about whether truth was accessible to humans. One thinks of Seneca's dictum that "what is revealed does not exist in a mirror."[5] What humans see in the mirror should never be confused with the truth that remains finally beyond our grasp. In an era of moral and political corruption, the Stoic dream of the world as the mirror of the divine had faded. If this is what Paul had in mind, there would be little support in these verses to unite "truth" and "vital piety"!

The opposite view of Paul's metaphor of the mirror is found in the definitive study by Norbert Hugedé,[6] which points out the pride of ancient writers and craftsmen in their mirrors. He discovered that nowhere in the ancient

world is there a reference to the opinion expressed by modern commentators, that ancient mirrors offered only faint and unsatisfactory images of reality and that mirrors themselves were responsible for distortion. Ancient
writers refer instead to the capacity of mirrors to provide reliable guides to
self-reflection and accurate reflections of other objects seen from angles otherwise inaccessible. Hugedé's study was followed up by an appreciative article by Frederick W. Danker, who argued for an entirely positive use of the
mirror image in 1 Cor. 13:12.[7] Even the Greek term translated "dark," the
Greek origin of our modern term "enigma," is treated as a positive expression of an appropriate example or symbol of truth. Hence Danker concludes
that "the inadequacy of the vision in 1 Cor. 13:12, then, is not due to any
haziness in the reflecting medium. The imperfection consists rather in this,
that we now see the eternal splendors indirectly. But what we do see now
through the eye of faith we see quite clearly, for the thought of unclear spiritual vision is foreign to the apostle's thought, observes Hugudé. The apostle
knows in whom he has believed!"[8]

With this positive approach, Hugedé links 1 Cor. 13:12 with 2 Cor. 3:18:
"And we all, with unveiled face, beholding the glory of the Lord, are being
changed into his likeness from one degree of glory to another." In Christ, we
see the reflection of the glory of God, and in contemplating and emulating
Christ we are transformed. Danker adds the further connection with 2 Cor.
5:7, "We walk by faith, not by sight." To see ultimate truth is to have direct
access to the real object, but Paul maintains we have only indirect access
through faith. For Danker this is enough because the mirror image is so
exact a copy of reality itself.

The problem I have with the Hugedé-Danker perspective is that it takes
insufficient account of the balance between the positive and negative elements in Paul's rhetoric.[9] We see this critical balance in the very verse
Danker cites from 2 Cor. 5: "by faith, not by sight," which is clearly antithetical in its formulation. Paul is downplaying vision in favor of faith. The
same antithetical emphasis is visible in 1 Cor. 13. Here we find a critique of
the illusion that angelic tongues and prophetic visions provide an absolutely
reliable grasp of ultimate reality. Listen to the wording of Paul's argument
after the reference to the "sounding brass and tinkling cymbal":

> If I have prophetic powers, and understand all mysteries and all knowl-
> edge, and if I have all faith, so as to remove mountains, but have not love,
> I am nothing. . . . Love never ends; as for prophecy, it will pass away; as for
> tongues, they will cease; as for knowledge, it will pass away. For our
> knowledge is imperfect and our prophecy is imperfect; but when the per-
> fect comes, the imperfect will pass away. . . . For now we see in a mirror
> darkly, but then face to face. Now I know in part; then I shall understand
> fully, even as I have been fully understood (1 Cor. 13:2, 9, 12).

Both "knowledge" and "prophecy" are indirect, partial, and enigmatic, Paul argues. Philosopher Paul Gooch concludes that Paul is viewing "our present knowledge of God as partial because imperfect. It suffers the imperfections of childish experience, of indirect vision, and of puzzles requiring solution; and in each of these characterizations Paul can make sense of his claim that the partial will be made useless when full face-to-face knowledge of God is enjoyed in the life to come."[10] I believe it is likely that Paul's argument provides a critique of overly credulous attitudes encouraged by early Christian Gnosticism and prophetism. One thinks of the credulous Gnosticism later expressed in the *Odes of Solomon:* "Behold! the Lord is our mirror: Open your eyes and see them [your eyes] in Him; and learn the manner of your face."[11] In the face of proto-Gnostics who were certain that they perceived the divine spark in the reflection of their own visages, Paul insists that he knows only "in part." The mirror of our perception is "dark," enigmatic. This was a stunning admission for an early Christian apostle whose authority was so widely respected. Paul does have knowledge, but as the mirror metaphor implies, it is indirect, reflected. Not until history comes to an end and persons enter into the realm of the next life will knowledge become complete.[12]

The comparison with Plato's theory of knowledge is worth developing at this point because of the crucial role Plato plays in the educational rationale presented by Allan Bloom, to be discussed below. Both Plato and Paul "locate full reality beyond the physical world and make that reality the object of complete knowledge."[13] In the *Republic* (7:514–19), a vision of the forms of knowledge is accessible to the philosopher gazing in the cave, provided there has been an adequate striving to define and follow what is good and beautiful. Whereas Plato taught that "our awareness of the world can have only the status of belief," which is necessarily fragmentary and distorted by the burden of temporality, the cave vision offers "the apprehension of unchanging realities." In contrast, "for Paul, there is no ascent in this life, no privileged knowledge of god for the few."[14]

It is precisely the Pauline dialectic between reflected knowledge in its various sources and the perfect forms of such knowledge that is essential for the maintenance of a scientific spirit and a healthy form of religion.[15] Paul's theology takes both sides of the dialectic with equal seriousness, which provides a viable contribution to contemporary theorizing about perception and education. People *do* see an impressive measure of truth through reflection: the face in the mirror *is* their own. The natural world *is* largely accessible through the application of the various reflecting devices provided by the scientific method. We *do* have some access to historical truth through reflections in documents and the archeological record. In a sense one could say that science is a methodical approach to reflected truth. It uses techniques and equipment, symbolized by the ancient technology of mirror making, to grasp what is otherwise inaccessible. The achievements of modern methods are sufficiently impressive that we have as much reason to be confident as the ancients were of their polished mirrors.

Yet the opposite insight is equally correct, and humans neglect it at their peril: no human being has direct access to absolute truth in any field, whether it be science or theology. Heisenberg's "principle of uncertainty" is as true for the science of New Testament studies as for modern physics. You can perceive this in my account of the checkered path of the scholarly interpretation of a single verse from 1 Corinthians. It reminds one of Jacob Bronowski's words in "The Principle of Tolerance": "All knowledge, all information between human beings, can be exchanged only within a play of tolerance. And that is true whether the exchange is in science, or in literature, or in religion, or in politics, or even in any form of thought that aspires to dogma."[16] When we overlook this element of uncertainty, confusing the image for reality, we inevitably fall into distortions, and the quest for new truth is misdirected.

To put this in other terms, the indirect knowledge gained through scientific observation always contains a degree of subjectivity. We are as conscious of this in modern social science and humanities as natural scientists have become. Modern interpretive theory speaks of the hermeneutical circle, the degree to which the way we put questions and seek for answers determines the shape of those answers. A portion of our own face is always in the mirror, so to speak.[17] Paul seems to refer to this in 1 Cor. 13:11, alluding to childish naïveté and mature acknowledgment of limits. "When I was a child, I spoke like a child, I thought like a child, I reasoned like a child; when I became a man, I gave up childish ways."

As we know through modern science, every measurement inevitably distorts the reality being studied. Paul seems to have had an aspect of this insight in mind when he inserts the element of time into the process of seeing reflections: 1 Cor. 13:12, "now . . . then; now . . . then." Our basic finitude—our time-bound natures as humans—requires the acknowledgment of the reflected quality of all truth. We all see in mirrors, more or less darkly.

The Pauline metaphor thus embodies the peculiar tension between the first and second commandments that stands at the heart of genuine biblical faith.[18] If one were to hold only the first commandment about having "no other gods before me," it would breed fanaticism. But if one held only the second commandment about not worshiping "graven images," this would produce relativism. Each sickens when held apart from the other. When held in creative tension, the quest for truth continues, and tolerance is preserved. This is the stance of genuine "faith." We live by faith that the reflected images to which we have access contain a measure of truth, but we can never be absolutely certain. In every arena of knowledge we are forced to live by faith, not by direct sight. To state this in the words of Bronowski, "There is no absolute knowledge. And those who claim it, whether they are scientists or dogmatists, open the door to tragedy. All information is imperfect. We have to treat it with humility. That is the human condition, and that is what quantum physics says. I mean that literally."[19] These insights lead us straight into the central message of Paul.

The Mirror and the Problem of Self-Deception

The idea that even the most profound religious knowledge remains a matter of seeing in a glass darkly reaches beyond epistemology. It has implications beyond the scientific and interpretive methods used in the liberal arts and in various fields of scientific research. It is related to Paul's central teaching of sin and salvation in his last and most extensive letter. Romans was written fairly soon after the Corinthian correspondence, presenting some of the same ideas in powerful new formulations.

Paul relates perception and misperception of the truth to the universal plight of the human race in Romans 1:18–32. All human beings, he argues, have an innate capacity to recognize God in the created order, but we "suppress" this truth (Rom. 1:18) and worship ourselves instead. In other words, we begin to worship the mirrors we have made, rather than the transcendent realities they reflect. We worship the techniques we have developed and the images they afford. We exchange "the truth about God for a lie and worship and serve the creature rather than the Creator" (Rom. 1:25). When this occurs, Paul contends, the human capacity to acknowledge uncomfortable dimensions of truth is crippled. "So they are without excuse," Paul writes, "for although they knew God they did not honor him as God or give thanks to him, but they became futile in their thinking and their senseless minds were darkened. Claiming to be wise, they became fools" (Rom. 1:20–21). Whenever humans idolize their techniques and partial truths, they inevitably begin to lie about it, trying to suppress the realization of what they have done. They begin to deceive themselves, pretending to be something they are not (see 1 Cor. 3:18; Gal. 6:3).

An important breakthrough in understanding this theme was achieved by Dan O. Via, Jr., who analyzed a number of Pauline passages on the basis of insights derived from modern psychological and literary studies of self-deception.[20] Whereas a person knows the truth, nevertheless he or she "believes the opposing cover story. . . . The real story causes the man to ignore the evidence for itself or to look for evidence for the cover story. . . . The concept of self-deception demands that the person remain aware of the evidence for the unwelcome real story, for that is what motivates his effort to rid himself of the awareness of it."[21] In Paul's view, we humans "conceal the truth from ourselves, do not spell it out, because we want to be blameless in our own eyes, want to be justified, on the basis of an effort that is our own

(Rom. 10:2–3; Phil 3:3–9)."[22] Via sees the law as involved in this process of deception because its original purpose is subverted by the human desire for self-reliance. "The law's deception of me (Rom. 7:10) engenders an ignorance (Rom. 10:2–3), hardness of mind (2 Cor. 3:14), and blindness (2 Cor. 4:4) in which I mistakenly believe that my own righteousness of the law is the equivalent of the righteousness of God (Phil. 3:9) rather than its opposite."[23] In order to account for the deceptive as well as the positive functions of the law in Pauline theology, Via suggests that the former describes the law "ontically, what it is under the actual conditions of fallen existence," whereas the more positive function refers to "God's creative intention. . . . The law intends faith and life, but humankind as flesh subverts this intention so that the result of the law is sin."[24] Paul has a grasp of the complex causes of this self-deception, which are both psychological and social: "self-deception is not a posture that is simply freely chosen but is a condition into which also I am seduced by a personified transcendent power—the law. . . .The law deceives me in and through my deception of myself."[25] Paul uses terms like "principalities" and "powers" to describe the array of social forces that align themselves with this corruption of human law into a means of distortion, making it clear that "human beings are victimized by other personalized powers—sin, law, flesh—as well as by the consequences of Adam's sin (Romans 5)."[26]

The recent survey of research into the psychology of self-deception by Daniel Goleman provides further insight into what is a well-nigh universal problem.[27] Confirmation is emerging from this research of the cogency of Paul's insights. Goleman writes that the "roots of self-deception seem to lie in the mind's ability to allay anxiety by distorting awareness. Denial soothes."[28] Studies of perception bring modern psychologists close to Paul's view of the power of idolatrous images to prevent a vision of the truth. Our judgment of the relevance of information is determined by what psychologists are now calling "schemas" in the human mind that lead us to suppress contrary information.[29] As we can see in connection with the mirror metaphor, some of the most powerful schemas involve religious insights. The measure of the pious reputation one can achieve is determined by adhering to these schemas. This requires that humans suppress the disclosure of details that counter their image of virtue and piety. Goleman describes "the urgent need for compelling antidotes to self-deception," not only for individuals but also for groups. "The new research reveals a natural bent toward self-deception so great that the need for counterbalancing forces within the mind and society as a whole— forces such as insight and respect for truth—becomes more apparent than ever."[30] The problem is that psychology appears near the end of its resources in searching for truly effective counterbalances for this human habit of suppression. The relevance of Pauline thought to this research, it seems to me, is not only its clear prescience of the basic cause of the dilemma but also its clear grasp of a powerful antidote.

Paul had discovered the shocking reality of self-deception at his conversion. Prior to this, Paul had been worshiping the mirror of the religious law. This led him to oppose Christianity. The encounter with the resurrected Christ revealed the reality of the dark mirrors of Paul's life. For when truth revealed itself in a new and unexpected manner, in an iconoclastic peasant from Galilee, Paul had opposed it with all his might. The schemas he had struggled to preserve as a Pharisee would have to be abandoned if Jesus were really risen from the dead. So the appearance of the risen Christ meant that Paul had to admit he had been looking at life in a distorted manner. But Christ's appearance meant something else as well. Paul discovered that the unconditional love of sinners that Jesus had taught and embodied was available even to someone at war against God. He discovered that if God loves us unconditionally, we can live with cracked mirrors. Since "love never fails" (1 Cor. 13:8), since it rests on the love of God shown in the Christ-event,[31] we can face the uncertainties of our schemas. By recognizing Christ in faith as the image of God, conveying the essence of divine love to a fallen world, Paul learned to accept himself as a limited creature whose knowledge and prophecy were "in part." He was reconciled to what Bronowski called "the human condition."

Paul was therefore willing to grant an extraordinary role to collective evaluation by members of communities shaped by the Christ-event. With regard to the inspired utterances of prophets and the ecstatic speakers in tongues, he insists on the need for interpretation, on orderly communication with one person speaking at a time, and on public accountability: "Let two or three prophets speak, and let the others weigh what is said" (1 Cor. 14:29). Here he encourages the faith community consisting largely of uneducated slaves and handworkers to engage in the evaluation of presumably inspired utterances, which in the view of most of the Greco-Roman world would have been considered beyond evaluation. This remarkable reliance on accountability to a pluralistic, democratic community is visible in Paul's earliest letter, where he urges the church as a whole: "Do not quench the spirit. Do not despise prophecy, but test everything; hold fast to what is good and abstain from every form of evil" (1 Thess. 5:19–21). Similarly in his great letter to the Romans, probably his last writing, Paul urges that the members of the varied house and tenement churches should "ascertain what is the will of God—the good and acceptable and perfect" (Rom. 12:2).[32] Even if God's will is glimpsed by inspired prophets or seers, it needs to be weighed by the rank and file, relying on their own moral and spiritual standards. The discipline of dark mirrors requires collective assessments rather than the authority of experts to detect the virus of self-deception that always distorts the truth. This is consistent with Josiah Royce's insistence that "interpretation is a conversation, and not a lonely enterprise."[33] The same principle is visible in many sections of the Pauline letters where ethical and theological advice is offered. In the words of philosopher Paul Gooch, "Paul's counseled obedience requires the judgment of the believer, not an unquestioned acceptance of rules."[34] This leads us to the heart of the current dilemma in American education.

The Problem of Relativism: Plato Versus Paul

Allan Bloom argues that the quest for truth in any form has largely been abandoned in the contemporary American university, that the dogma of cultural relativism has "extinguished the real motive of education, the search for the good life."[35] There are two kinds of openness, he contends:

> the openness of indifference—promoted with the twin purposes of humbling our intellectual pride and letting us be whatever we want to be, just as long as we don't want to be knowers—and the openness that invites us to the quest for knowledge and certitude. . . . This second kind of openness encourages the desire that animates and makes interesting every serious student . . . while the former stunts that desire.[36]

The source of the profound relativism that hobbles the quest for truth and reifies irrational personal preference is what Bloom calls "*the* most important and most astonishing phenomenon of our time."[37] This is the triumph in America of the European theory of "value relativism" advanced by Frederick Nietzsche and Max Weber. Rather than distinguishing between good and evil, as in classical philosophy and traditional theism, they argued that no one can move beyond whatever people may arbitrarily choose to value, whether it be true or good or whatever. This radically undermines the role of reason and opens the door to a vapid subjectivism that finally undercuts the ideals of the enlightenment on which American democracy and education rest. Bloom has nothing but contempt for this triumph of irrational European thought:

> Who in 1920 would have believed that Max Weber's technical sociological terminology would someday be the everyday language of the United States. . . . The self-understanding of hippies, yippies, yuppies, panthers, prelates and presidents has unconsciously been formed by German thought of a half-century earlier . . . and the new American life-style has become a Disneyland version of the Weimar Republic.[38]

Given the tragic outcome of the Weimar Republic, Bloom leaves no doubt about the irrational passions and antidemocratic destructiveness that such value relativism brings in its wake. But the further consequences are that it lames the quest for truth and discredits the central task of education in leading students to participate in the enjoyment of whatever is truly good.

Bloom advocates a liberal education based on the "great books" of Western culture whose classic philosophy, theology, and literature hold to the accessibility and immutability of truth. He is particularly enamored with Plato, who advocates the shared quest for the eternal truth by friends committed to dialogue concerning the good life. "Throughout the book," Bloom admits, Plato's *Republic* is presented as "*the* book on education, because it really explains to me . . . the real community of man . . . is the community of those who seek the truth. But in fact this includes only a few, the true friends, as Plato was to Aristotle at the very moment they were disagreeing about the nature of the good."[39] The classical premise, of course, was that the realm of ideas provided direct access into ultimate reality and that humans could participate in this ultimate realm so long as they were capable of sophisticated forms of reason and possessed the requisite virtue. But as Karl Popper has shown, this capability was restricted to an elite group of leaders, while all others in the ideal "Republic" would be forced to remain in their subordinate status.[40] In contrast to Socrates's ideal of the philosopher, the Philosopher King "is no longer the modest seeker, he is the proud possessor of truth. A trained dialectician, he is capable of intellectual intuition, i.e. of seeing, and of communicating with the eternal, the heavenly Forms or Ideas. Placed high above all ordinary men, he is 'god-like, if not . . . divine,' both in his wisdom and his power."[41] The exercise of absolute authority by such persons is justified by Plato's definition of justice as achieving the "interest of the best state" by requiring everyone to do the work "for which his nature is naturally best fitted." This would mean, in Popper's words, that "the state is just if the ruler rules, if the worker works, and if the slave slaves."[42] It goes without saying that since such a philosopher is capable of perceiving divine truth, his definition of the Forms lies beyond rational refutation or communal evaluation.

Bloom's orientation to this classical tradition entails a claim of the final superiority of the Western tradition of philosophy[43] and a resistance against broadening the classical curriculum to include the viewpoints of other racial groups[44] or of women.[45] If Karl Popper is right, this overbearing tendency is consistent with Plato, who proposed a method of breeding the master race of future Philosopher Kings so as to separate them permanently and absolutely from the lower classes,[46] who argued that barbarians and slaves were fundamentally inferior and incapable of responding to the good,[47] and who rejected all forms of egalitarianism on principle.[48] The necessity of all lower classes to submit to the master race was justified by Plato's dictum that "the greatest principle of all is that nobody, whether male or female, should ever be without a leader. Nor should the mind of anybody be habituated to letting him do anything at all on his own initiative, neither out of zeal, nor even playfully. But in war and in the midst of peace—to his leader he shall direct his eye, and follow him faithfully. . . . In a word, he should teach his soul, by long habit, never to dream of acting independently, and to become utterly incapable of it."[49] This is one of the most elaborate cases ever made, by the most brilliant philosopher in history, in favor of an elitist monopoly on truth that avoids even a hint of dark mirrors.

Bloom and Plato are forthright reactionaries, wishing to anchor our culture to the past by chains of iron, whereas Paul the Apostle is oriented toward the future. Responding to the rapid social change in the ancient world, Plato's philosophy rests on the premise that "all social change is corruption or decay or degeneration," in Popper's words.[50] The search for eternal forms of truth, accessible through a rational process controlled by an elite group of Philosopher Kings, could produce a refuge for a society against the ravages of time. Repudiating the messy politics of democracy in Athens, he yearned to return to archaic kingship, where a ruling class had indisputable authority because of religious sanction. He hoped for "the coming of a great law-giver whose powers of reasoning and whose moral will are capable of bringing this period of political decay to a close. . . . He certainly believed . . . in the possibility that we may stop further corruption in the political field by *arresting all political change*."[51] This is why "acting independently" is such a threat, to be stamped out with ruthless efficiency in Plato's Republic. This is why the educational system he favored was "based upon an authoritarian view of learning—upon the authority of the learned expert, and 'the man of proven probity,' who turns out to be none other than the dutiful advocate of Plato's reactionary vision."[52]

One of the most shocking consequences of Plato's vision is his advocacy of propaganda to convince the lower classes of the correctness and inevitability of this expert knowledge of the eternal forms, requiring the abandonment of the structures of a democratic society. He proposed the creation of a fraudulent myth to prove that "God . . . has put gold into those who are capable of ruling, silver into the auxiliaries, and iron and copper into the peasants and the other producing classes."[53] Since any mixture of these metals allegedly causes degeneracy, it follows that a wise eugenics should aim at allowing the upper class to breed only with similarly golden types in order to preserve the order of the state.[54] Beyond this, the Philosopher King should be prepared "to administer a great many lies and deceptions" for the benefit of the state. Such myths must be believed as true, he argued, "since anything that serves the interest of my state must be believed and therefore must be called 'true'; and there must be no other criterion of truth."[55] In the end Plato advocates a propagandistic use of dark mirrors not as an acknowledgment of the fragility of all human knowledge but in the guise of clear lenses into absolute, timeless truths controlled by an elite that serve to sustain a totalitarian system.

I believe that the honesty of Paul provides a way to avoid these reactionary, chauvinistic, and totalitarian implications because it is based on a more realistic sense of the radical twistedness of all human knowing as revealed in the cross of Christ. Hence the Pauline dialectic can provide a more responsible base for maintaining the need for the quest for truth, while acknowledging the brokenness of all human definitions thereof. His orientation is toward the future rather than the past, believing that communities of faith are granted insights that move beyond culturally perverted dogmas but that even these insights require evaluation because they necessarily fall short of the perfect knowledge that will be available only at the end of time. Thus Paul is a more reliable basis for an American educational theory than Plato, who would sustain a static myth of cultural superiority and also encourage an elitist conflict with the innovative, critical impulses of popular culture in all of its forms. The popular poets and musicians remain a danger to Plato's and Bloom's republics,[56] but they are the natural conversation partners of Paul the Apostle to America. His metaphorical thinking, his resistance against elitism in every form, his acknowledgment of the failure of traditional culture, his skill in preserving the health and growth of small countercultural groups, his reliance on shared experiences of encountering revelation, his reliance on the collective, critical judgment of common people, his patience with ambiguity, and his apocalyptic urgency about a dawning new age invite dialogue with the countercultural visionaries of our time. That dialogue is likely to be the most decisive arena where the commitments and values of future Americans will be formed.

Higher Education and the Discipline of Dark Mirrors

A panel of leaders in higher education met recently to think about the next quarter century, concluding that "American higher education faces circumstances that, if not confronted courageously, could prove fatal to our system."[57] Among other challenges, they express concern that "America's crisis of values and ethics will deepen the difficulty of creating a sense of community in a changed world."[58] This is related to the larger crisis in carrying forward the Enlightenment ideals of seeking knowledge through the use of critical methods, through the technology of mirrors, so to speak. As recent as well as past experiences have shown, "knowledge is distorted when it, wittingly or unwittingly, serves unscrupulous social powers, when it violates the concreteness and complexity of things, or when it abandons the wisdom of the past."[59] These words of theologian Edward Farley support his contention that "knowledge serves a desire that cannot, it seems, be finally satisfied. Elusiveness, frustration, and fragility are features that knowledge shares with other fundamental human desires, all of which take place in the context of the general fragility of human existence."[60] This fragility is intensified in a period like our own, when rapid social change affects everything, and when social pluralism becomes more and more dominant and unsettling. Minority voices, long silenced by a dominant culture, begin to produce what appears to be a threatening cacophony of countervailing claims of truth. If one begins with an authoritarian expectation of harmony, based on anything approaching Plato's educational ideal, the creation of a unified community seems to be out of reach.

In this era of cultural pluralism, relativism, and moral confusion, Paul the Apostle to America challenges educators to consider the discipline of dark mirrors within the context of what Henry Young calls "an organic pluralism" that overcomes the assumption of the cultural normativeness of dominant groups and affirms the interdependence of multiple cultures and methods.[61] In a time when the fanatics claim 20/20 vision into the truth and the relativists affirm no truth at all, there is a need for faithful people who continue in the task of seeking self-critical forms of holistic knowledge that include insights from a variety of sources and communities. This critical faithfulness is as necessary for citizens as for scientists, for church members as for social workers and health care personnel; for musicians, poets, and artists in all media of expression. We not only need this kind of balance for ourselves as individuals but should seek to support it and even insist upon it in our educational and religious institutions. The need is for critical loyalty, conscious of the shortcomings of our theologies and methods and institutions but loyal to the vision of the truth that has been partially embodied therein.[62] But in every intellectual context, without a critical perspective concerning the partiality of all knowledge, loyalty to particular traditions of truth can all too easily degenerate into sectarianism.

The issue of maintaining critical loyalty to the truth is particularly acute in an era when leaders have called for the recovery of teaching moral and ethical values in all of the schools of this country.[63] The Jewish scholar Norman Lamm, president of Yeshiva University, advocates values derived from the same Judaic heritage that influenced Paul. The particular danger Lamm sees is "value-agnosticism," taking the critical impulse without its counterbalance of loyalty to shared values.

> To be value-neutral means to abandon the very premise on which the search for and transmission of knowledge is pursued. If the university does not teach the moral superiority of education as opposed to ignorance, of reason over impulse, of discipline over slovenliness, of integrity as against cheating—then its very foundations begin to crumble.[64]

Paul would echo these insights while calling for a continuation of the quest for truth as seen in the dark mirrors that are available to all persons of faith.

Paul would thus provide some common ground between conservatives and progressives in educational theory, affirming both pluralism and the ongoing quest for truth in a democratic context.[65] He would insist that current advocates of the "essentialist" tradition in education[66] should remain critical of their foundations and aware of the structures of self-deception that afflict knowledge in every field and culture. He would encourage the advocates of "educational progressivism"[67] to rebuild the foundations of the quest for truth by leading students into a critical appreciation of the older as well as the newer classics of our pluralistic culture.

I believe a case can be made that Pauline thought would support a constructive approach to the educational task and that this heritage could provide a viable counterbalance to some of the trends in contemporary higher education. It could reconnect us with the legacy of Josiah Royce who sought to "remain true to the deepest spirit of his Pauline Christianity, despite the vast masses of ancient imagery and of legend which he must learn to view as mere symbols of deeper truth," holding fast in the end to "the Pauline doctrine of the presence of the redeeming divine spirit in the living Church,"[68] which consists not so much in a particular denomination as in the universal "Beloved Community" that values insights from all of its varied members.[69] After all the clanging cymbals die down and the fierce debates burn low, Paul's conviction is worth commending: that faith, hope, and love will endure, and that future discoveries are required to rectify our partial knowledge in every field.

9. Paul and the Democratic Prospect

Now there are varieties of charismatic gifts,
    but the same Spirit;
and varieties of services,
    but the same Lord;
and there are varieties of activities,
    but the same God who works in all within all.
To each is given a manifestation of the Spirit for the common good.
                    (1 Corinthians 12:4–7)

What then, brethren? When you come together,
    each one has a psalm,
      has a teaching,
        has a revelation,
          has a tongue,
            has an interpretation.
Let all things be done for building up. . . .
Let two or three prophets speak,
    and let the others weigh what is said.
If a revelation is made to someone else sitting by,
    let the first person be quiet. . . .
The spirits of prophets are also subject to the prophets,
    for God is not of disorder but of peace.
             (1 Corinthians 14:26, 29–30, 32)

Brethren, the desire of my heart and the prayer to God for them is
        for salvation.
    For I bear them witness that they have zeal of God,
        but not according to understanding.
                    (Romans 10:1–2)

Although Paul did not intend to do more than provide advice for early house and tenement churches, his theology had wide-ranging consequences for later times. It provided some of the foundations for a democratic, egalitarian society as well as insights into its most lethal danger. Paul's recommendations for a radical democratization of early Christian worship provided the inspiration for the Protestant dissenters who advocated democratic reform in Great Britain and America, thus becoming an important source of our ideals of freedom, equality, and democratic process. Similar ideas were developed by continental Protestants of Anabaptist persuasion. These various groups practiced varieties of democratic church order based on the Pauline letters for more than two centuries before a secular form of such order could be embodied in the American constitution. Some years ago church historian James Hastings Nichols pointed out that Americans seem "quite unaware of the fact that the moral dynamic of their democracy was the creation of one very specific Protestant ethical tradition."[1] Most contemporary Americans remain unaware of Paul's contribution, tending to view him as an authoritarian personality opposed to equality and democracy. Most American churches remain similarly unclear about the most decisive contribution they could make to American democracy: not just by involving themselves in political issues and campaigns but by maintaining the Pauline legacy in their own organizations, thus nourishing democracy's roots.

Paul's insight about the threat of zeal surfaced at a decisive moment in the joint congressional hearings on the Iran-Contra affair in 1987. Senator Paul S. Sarbanes cited the words engraved in the United States Capitol: "The greatest dangers to liberty lurk in insidious encroachment by men of zeal, well-meaning but without understanding."[2] Sarbanes gave no indication that he recognized the ultimate Pauline source of this idea, which the famous Jewish Supreme Court Justice Louis D. Brandeis embodied in the dissenting opinion he wrote in 1928 limiting the power of the government to wiretap telephone conversations:

> Experience should teach us to be most on our guard to protect liberty when the Government's purposes are beneficent. Men born to freedom are naturally alert to repel invasion of their liberty by evil-minded rulers. The greatest dangers to liberty lurk in insidious encroachment by men of zeal, well-meaning but without understanding.[3]

The abuse of power by idealistic and well-meaning agents of the government that Brandeis resisted is similar in its motivation and consequences to Paul's understanding of his former life as a Jewish zealot, thus providing a deeper grasp of an issue that perennially arises in American culture. I would like to show that Paul's insights are crucial for the prospect of American democracy.

Paul's Critique of Zealotism

Paul's reference to "zeal without understanding" stands in a passage that begins in v. 30 of chapter 9, in which Paul takes up the puzzle that Israel failed to respond to the revelation of divine righteousness in the Christ-event. In the opening verse of chapter 10, Paul describes his anguish that fellow Jews had not all accepted Jesus of Nazareth as the Christ. He goes on to acknowledge the sincerity and vehemence of Jewish faith: "They have zeal for God" (Rom. 10:2). That is, they are honest in their passionate commitment to Yahweh's law. Zeal in this instance is a technical term for an intensified form of religious devotion that came into particular prominence in the period from the Maccabbean Revolt to the Jewish-Roman War. In the belief that "God will punish the whole nation" for violations of the law "unless someone acts on behalf of God . . . to kill or root out the offenders," zealous violence was "motivated by the jealous desire to protect one's self, group, space, or time against violations."[4] Such zeal intensifies the sole loyalty due to God into a kind of cultural fanaticism.

The problem with such zeal, as the end of v. 2 states it, is that uncompromising devotion is "without understanding." The intensified form of zeal that Paul had earlier embodied in his persecution of the church and which some of the extremists of his time were harboring was misguided and thus counterproductive. When a person is passionately committed to a false cause or to a destructive end, then no amount of sincerity can prevent evil consequences. In the context of the argument of Romans, this lack of understanding has two dimensions. The first has to do with the transforming impact of the Christ-event on this intensified kind of zeal for the law. A widespread theory in first-century Judaism was that if all Israel were devoted to the law and to the high principles of the oneness of God with sufficient passion, the messiah would appear and all Israel's troubles as a colony of Rome would disappear. Some segments of the revolutionary movement believed that passionate zeal for God required absolute repudiation of any other earthly king and hence called for resistance against Roman rule.[5] Following the example of Phinehas and the Maccabees, these passionate religionists "showed the same readiness to take the law into their own hands and even to use violent means to preserve the integrity of God's law and his sanctuary, often sacrificing their own lives in the process."[6] Zeal in this context was "an eschatological intensification of the Torah" requiring violence against transgressors and expecting divine intervention in an apocalyptic framework.[7] David Rhoads concludes that the revolutionaries, although splintered into various factions, "fought with the common hope that God would bring a decisive victory. . . .The Jews believed they could count on God's decisive aid because they were supporting their commitment to him by aggressive military actions."[8]

Jesus had rejected such zeal, calling instead for love and understanding of the enemy and submission to Rome.[9] He died in place of the zealot Barabbas, having refused to play the role of the militant messiah and to call for the legion of warrior angels when captured or to respond to the messianic taunts to come down from the cross. His resurrection meant that God had confirmed that this nonviolent one was indeed the promised Messiah and that the method of bringing the messiah through zealous violence was obsolete. So to persist in the tradition of extremist zeal was in Paul's view to lack "understanding" of this pivotal event in Israel's messianic history. Christ reveals the ultimate purpose of Israel's law, which is that Israel should live in harmony with its circumstances and not destroy itself and the surrounding world in a zealous crusade, which for some was linked with the desire to become the most powerful nation on earth, embodying the rule of God.

The second aspect of this lack of knowledge or understanding has to do with the enforcement of cultural conformity. The earlier argument of Romans was that no one is made right by conformity to the law because humans tend to make their obedience into a means of proving their superiority over others. This theme is explicitly stated in Rom. 12:2, "Do not be conformed to this world, but be transformed by the renewal of the mind." Zeal in its extreme form can be understood as passionate conformity to a particular aspect of the world. We would speak today of "cultural conformity," making oneself precisely match the expectations and laws of a particular group. We recognize this dimension more clearly in others than in ourselves, of course. We readily identify Islamic terrorists as zealots who conform without reservation to the teachings of the Ayatollah Khomeini or some other fundamentalist authority. Paul was making a similar point about his former zealotism and some of the other extremist zealots of his day: they were conforming in a mindless, uncritical way to the values and models of their culture. To use the language of earlier chapters of Romans, they were in bondage to the law but failed to understand their motivations or the implications of their actions. To use the wording of Rom. 10:3, "seeking to establish their own righteousness, they did not submit to the righteousness of God" when it appeared in the form of Jesus. Their real motivation was competitive, to be more zealous than others so as to gain prestige. The ultimate purpose of divine righteousness is thus lost from sight as one becomes so zealous as to be willing to risk the very world the law was intended to preserve. "Zeal without knowledge" in the Pauline sense is thus destructive and counterproductive. It ends up destroying the very values and communities it seeks to preserve.

It is important to remember that Paul is speaking from experience in these words. He had been a violent member of a radical branch of the Pharisee party, sincerely and unreservedly devoted to the cause of bringing the messiah through conformity to the Jewish law. His record prior to conversion was plain: "as to the law, a Pharisee; as to zeal, a persecutor of the church; as to righteousness under the law, blameless" (Phil. 3:5–6). He had conformed to the values of his religious tradition out of competition, claiming at one point to have "advanced in Judaism beyond many of my own age among my people, so extremely zealous was I for the traditions of my fathers" (Gal. 1:14). There was no doubt about his sincerity or his ability to pursue the high cause: he persecuted heretics such as the Christians without reservation (Gal. 1:13). But he had lacked understanding, either of his own deeper motivations or of the self-destructive aspects of fanatical zeal itself.

When Paul encountered the risen Christ, he had to admit that Jesus was being confirmed by God as the promised Messiah and that his entire zealous campaign had been on the wrong track. He discovered that the kingdom of God is not going to be brought by violence. Paul discovered the unconditional love of Christ, conveyed even to someone like himself who had persecuted the Christians. So he no longer had to remain rigidly committed to establishing his own righteousness through conformity to the law; he was accepted by Christ just as he was and thus was set free from a destructive bondage to "zeal without understanding." He no longer felt the necessity to suppress others in order to ward off the wrath of God. Without such freedom, Paul's development of egalitarian, cross-cultural, democratic methods of group life would have been impossible.

The Radical Democratization of Pauline Churches

In 1 Cor. 12—14, Paul is dealing with the chaotic conditions of early Christian worship, marked by the simultaneous expression of charismatic gifts of prophecy and glossolalia, by a competitive atmosphere where many were expressing themselves rather than listening, and by an inattention to the need for understandable discourse and public discussion. Some of the radicals in Corinth apparently construed their abililty to speak in tongues as an indication of their superior spiritual status as Gnostics, capable of divine, angelic speech understandable only to themselves and God. They believed themselves to be in a kind of trance state, under the power of a divine force when engaged in such charismatic activities, and thus incapable of controlling themselves or listening to others. The ecstatic precedents of Greco-Roman religion such as the Bacchanalia, with its orgiastic dancing, singing, and carousing were apparently being followed in Corinth, on the premise that the charismatic spirit received by congregational members was amoral and asocial.

If Paul had favored an authoritarian path, it would have been simple to place strong leaders in charge who had the power to bring this situation under control by stamping out excessive freedom. This is the route most frequently taken in subsequent Christian history, when excitable revivals of the Spirit have repeatedly erupted. But Paul took another path, developing a revolutionary approach to group life. He legitimates the "varieties of charismatic gifts . . . services . . . activities" but insists that the same Lord is present in all (1 Cor. 12:4–6). If this Lord is Jesus, which 1 Cor. 12:3 had reiterated, and which the proto-Gnostics in Corinth would have acknowledged, then his standards of love and accountability must guide the exercise of the charismatic gifts. Paul's argument allows the congregation to see that the irrational, amoral, orgiastic exercise of the gifts tacitly presupposed that the pagan spirit was still active in Christian believers. But if it is Jesus Christ who manifests himself in these charismatic activities, their aim is "the common good" (1 Cor. 12:7). This opening gambit offers profound resources for the democratic organization of church life because it explicitly claims that God's Spirit is active in each and every member of the group, not just in the authorized leaders or particularly gifted prophets or charismatics. To use the words of an Anabaptist commentator on these verses, the "real gift of the Spirit comes to all. It lies at the heart of the faith and holds the body together."[10] Moreover, Paul places each member of the group in a position of discernment and accountability: if the gift is being exercised without reference to the common good, following the guidelines of love that Jesus advocated, then it is a pagan spirit and should be resisted. By addressing this requirement to every member of the congregation rather than just to leaders or specially trained theologians, Paul is establishing the principle of a broadly based sense of responsibility that lies at the root of egalitarian, democratic consciousness.

Paul's description of worship at Corinth in 1 Cor. 14:16 presupposes egalitarian participation but one that was apparently lacking in this crucial element of responsibility. He lists the inspired contributions that "each" Corinthian brings: a new hymn, a revelation, or a new interpretation. The diversity of contributions and the insistence on "each" makes clear that every man, woman, and child in a small house church was expected to participate. The modern expression "participatory democracy" is an apt description of this Pauline congregation.

The innovation in Paul's advice begins with the insistence that if each such gift is exercised in accordance with the love of Christ, it will be done for "building up" the congregation. The idea of "building up" is probably related to the premise of the church as the temple of the Holy Spirit (1 Cor. 3:16–17), and it is used throughout the Pauline letters to describe both Paul's work of founding and nourishing congregations and the work of individual congregational members.[11] There is an extraordinary measure of communal responsibility in Paul's use of this idea, similar to the proverbial Mennonite barn raising in which the entire community participates. The way charismatic gifts can produce such upbuilding is to make them publicly accessible and understandable. Thus Paul insists that in place of the simultaneous exercise of gifts in Corinth, the congregational members should take turns: "Let two or three prophets speak." In the case of glossolalia, Paul advises similarly that "only two or at the most three; and each in turn" should speak (1 Cor. 14:27).

Several important assumptions surface here. The communal relevance of each contribution is presupposed. No matter how uneducated a congregational member may be, his or her contribution is to be heard. This was a revolutionary premise, for Paul's time as well as for ours because the religious expert always tends to be given precedence. The insistence on having an interpreter present whenever there is glossolalia, along with the rule that speakers in tongues should remain silent if no one interprets (1 Cor. 14:28), has a similarly radical egalitarian implication. Persons with special levels of spiritual development, making them capable of understanding the significance of glossolalia, are not given precedence here because the process of interpretation makes the message publicly accessible. This also implies that every member of the community needs to hear because his or her growth is essential for the vitality of the temple as a whole. The class-bound, educated premises of the Greco-Roman world are being systematically undermined by these new democratic arrangements.

Another important assumption in Paul's approach is less transparent to current readers who may not share the notion that religion is an involuntary, irrational experience, as was widely assumed in the Greco-Roman world. Paul's assumption that the prophets and glossolalists could control their behavior was not shared by his culture and was emphatically not shared in the Corinthian church. They apparently felt that ecstasy was a matter of the divine Spirit "driving them" (1 Cor. 12:2), so it would be impossible to say no to it, to alter its flow, or to be responsible for its outcome. David Aune concludes from his definitive study of prophecy in the ancient world that the "basic assumption" of Greco-Roman tradition "was that if a god was actually speaking through an individual, that person's own mind must become inactive in order that his speech organs might become instruments of the divinity."[12] Paul insists, however, that the prophets and ecstatics can not only take turns but that "if a revelation is made to someone else sitting by, let the first person be quiet" (1 Cor. 14:30). He calls for an unprecedented measure of conscious responsibility, an awareness of the needs of the congregation and of the state of other congregational members as compared with the ecstatic traditions of the ancient world. The high point of this line of argument is the claim that "the spirits of prophets are also subject to the prophets" (1 Cor. 14:32). As Robertson and Plummer observe in their classic commentary, "The spirits of sibyls and pythonesses were not under their control; utterance continued till the impulse ceased. But this is not the case with one who is inspired by God; a preacher without self-control is no true prophet; and uncontrolled religious feeling is sure to lead to evil."[13] On the premise that God's nature is "not disorder but peace"

(1 Cor. 14:32), the implication is that prophets know when God wants them to speak and when to be silent, all for the upbuilding of the community. If more than one is speaking at a time, one must be faking it if the God manifesting himself/herself in prophecy is the God of loving order.

The implications for this theory of congregational life are strikingly democratic and egalitarian. Rather than placing someone in charge of the prophets and ecstatics, Paul urges that each should learn to follow the voice of God responsibly. The principle of control is within each member, not in some hierarchical structure in the congregation. A supreme role is afforded here to individual responsibility, acting out of love on behalf of the community. The community regulations suggested by Paul are flexible and dependent upon the mature responsibility of the congregational members. They are rules for democratic discourse, aimed at giving each person an opportunity to make his or her contribution and ensuring that such contributions are valued and heeded.

Perhaps the most surprising feature of Paul's suggestions from the perspective of the traditional view of Paul as the sole authority in his churches is at the end of 14:29: "and let the others weigh what is said." It is clear from the formulation that the evaluation is made by the congregation as a whole, not by its leaders or its skilled theologians.[14] This was clearly a characteristic approach for Paul to take because there is a more elaborate form of this admonition in 1 Thess. 5:19–22 and Rom. 12:1–2. His trust in the collective judgment of common members of house and tenement churches, consisting largely of uneducated slaves and freedmen, is an extraordinary measure of his democratic ethos. Furthermore, Paul is clearly countering in these passages the widely shared premise of Greco-Roman culture that prophecy was necessarily obscure and enigmatic, requiring interpretation but remaining essentially beyond rebuttal.[15] For Paul, the prophetic oracles and ecstatic experiences and messages of various sorts may be translated into ordinary language, weighed, evaluated, and then acted upon in light of the community's experience of the Spirit, the Christ-event, and the situation.

The Use of Paul in American Democratic Theory

So far as I can tell, Paul's ideas concerning radical democracy had a more direct effect on the British Reformation than the continental one. Although Mennonites, Brethren, Hutterites, and Moravians developed many components of an egalitarian church order, they tended to rely on the Jesus tradition. Perhaps the brutal weight of Rom. 13, which was used to justify their persecution and execution by mainline Protestants and Catholics alike in the sixteenth and seventeenth centuries, led them to avoid reliance on Paul's letters. At any event, when seeking the origins of the American tradition of democracy, scholars have looked primarily to the Baptist, Congregational, Quaker, and other dissenting groups within British Protestantism. These groups experimented with the Protestant doctrine of the priesthood of all believers and used the Bible as their guide to church life, often becoming quite intolerant of those who rejected these views. Christopher Hill begins his quest for the intellectual origins of the democratic revolution in England by noting that the "Bible, especially the Geneva Bible with its highly political marginal notes, came near to being a revolutionists' handbook. . . . John Lilburne had the Bible in one hand, the writings of Sir Edward Coke in the other."[16] The most explicitly democratic—and hence revolutionary—portions of the Bible from the perspective of these groups were the authentic Pauline letters.

While Calvinism in general sustained the idea of limited government, it was the various forms of British Puritanism that created the basis for modern liberal democracy. The left-wing Puritans, in particular, derived their view of the church from Paul's letters and thus opposed the rule of bishops and demanded the right to conduct congregational life in accordance with the democratic principles discovered therein. As Ralph Barton Perry writes, these early Congregationalists, Baptists, and Quakers were "saturated with democratic feeling." He cites a pamphlet of John Lilburne, the leader of the Levelers, which proclaims the equality of men and women, upper and lower classes, which appears to be influenced by Paul's ideas in Gal. 3:28. He traces the influences of these democratic ideas to the American colonies, particularly in the political system devised for Connecticut following a sermon by Thomas Hooker.[17] The Protestant radicals gained the ear of the Parliamentary army in the mid-1640s, and there are some who claim that "modern democracy was born in June, 1647, when at Newmarket and Triploe Heath the Army covenanted not to disband until its rights and liberties were assured."[18] Nichols quotes from A. D. Lindsay's description of the British Baptists, Independents, Congregationalists, and Quakers who took this radically democratic position because they "had practical and indeed daily experience of a fellowship united in a common purpose beyond themselves, to which purpose each and every member was found to have something to contribute."[19] The language of 1 Cor. 14 is evident in this formulation, and the idea of a social contract was the political equivalent of this idea of a voluntary church. "In these matters John Locke, the classic theorist of Anglo-American democracy, showed himself a true son of the Puritan Independents."[20]

Both in England and the American colonies, these groups developed from Paul's letters and other New Testament passages an emphasis on the guidance of the Spirit in the decision making of the church, a habit of "entering into discussion, the submission of diverse views to mutual criticism,"[21] derived from 1 Corinthians and 1 Thessalonians. But before these ideas could fully flourish, the freeing of the church from the civil authority, sought by the Levelers in England and by Roger Williams in America, had to be achieved. But once these radical ideas began to be practiced by local congregations, producing an invigorating transformation of individuals and groups, parallel freedoms were demanded for the society as a whole. In this way, democratic theory arose out of democratic practice within the congregations themselves. Praxis preceded theory. And this practice was based on Paul more than any other single source. A case could thus be made that Paul the Apostle to America was one of the decisive sources for the impulses toward democracy and egalitarianism that have marked our culture since its beginnings as a British colony.

The Peril of Zealous Extremism in American Democracy

Paul's warning about the peril of zeal was not directly coordinated with his congregational theory, and it has been much less widely understood in our culture, which has often tended toward zealous extremes. I traced the forms of zeal through American culture in *The Captain America Complex,* showing their roots in Puritan adaptations of the holy-war materials of the Old and New Testaments, and suggesting their expression in widely shared forms of popular culture. Paul's warning fits the more realistic side of American civil religion, the tradition of "prophetic realism" found in a figure such as Abraham Lincoln.[22] There is in fact a double warning in Lincoln's first political speech that resonates with Paul's language. In his address before the Young Men's Lyceum in Springfield, Illinois, in 1838, Lincoln responded to the episodes of "mobocracy" related to agitation over slavery by showing its lethal threat against the rule of law in a democratic government: "Whenever the vicious portion of the population shall be permitted to gather in bands of hundreds and thousands, and burn churches, ravage and rob provision-stores, throw printing presses into rivers, shoot editors, and burn obnoxious persons . . . with impunity; depend upon it, this Government cannot last."[23] The second warning concerns a zealous leader of towering ability and charisma who might take it upon himself to win fame by thwarting majority rule and the constitution:

> But new reapers will arise, and *they*, too, will seek a field. . . . Many great and good men . . . would aspire to nothing beyond a seat in Congress, a gubernatorial or a presidential chair; *but such belong not to the family of the lion, or the tribe of the eagle.* What! think you these places would satisfy an Alexander, a Caesar, or a Napoleon?—Never! Towering genius disdains a beaten path. . . . It scorns to tread in the footsteps of *any* predecessor, however illustrious. It thirsts and burns for distinction; and, if possible, it

will have it, whether at the expense of emancipating slaves, or enslaving freemen. . . . And when such a one does, it will require the people to be united with each other, attached to the government and laws, and generally intelligent, to successfully frustrate his designs.[24]

As historian Harry Jaffa remarks in his extensive discussion of this speech, "Lincoln knew that both Caesar and Napoleon had overthrown republics by posing as their defenders, preserving republican forms until there was no power in the republics to resist them."[25] What he feared was someone marked by zeal without understanding, so to speak, willing to violate the law in order to achieve his ends and thus to subvert a constitutional society. He viewed this as one of the two perennial threats to the American prospect.

A paradigmatic expression of the "insidious encroachment by men of zeal" surfaced in one of the most popular figures to emerge out of recent political developments. The appearance of Oliver North before the joint House-Senate hearings on the Iran-Contra affair was an extraordinary revelation of zealous extremism. The country gathered in front of television sets as millions of enthralled Americans responded to "Jimmy Stewart cast in 'Rambo Goes to Washington,'" as *Newsweek* described it.[26] This is an apt allusion to the classic 1939 film, *Mr. Smith Goes to Washington*, starring Jimmy Stewart as the selfless superhero who kept his integrity in the wicked capitol. As Jonathan Alter observed, "North has Stewart's cracking voice and patriotic gaze down pat; the nobility of the common man shines through, particularly when set off against big-city lawyers. . . . The difference, for those who have trouble discerning it, is that Jimmy Stewart triumphed in the end by telling the truth. Oliver North has triumphed by defiantly admitting lies."[27] The political system for whose integrity Stewart struggled is viewed by North and his supporters as the source of corruption, with congressional lawyers playing the villainous role that Claude Raines had acted with such malevolence in *Mr. Smith Goes to Washington*.

The fusion of these heroic images into militant zeal was evident in North's military appearance. Although he had not worn a uniform while in the White House, North displayed it proudly at the hearings, the rows of medals reminding the audience of soldierly prowess and bravery in Vietnam. At one point in the hearings, he virtually cited a line from one of the Rambo films about that war they were not "allowed to win."[28] Like Rambo, his soldierly exploits were reportedly on the superheroic level; a fellow officer said admiringly that "Ollie could fight his way through a regiment of North Vietnamese regulars armed with nothing but a plastic fork." But the exploits that most captivated the public were efforts to gain the release of Americans held hostage in Lebanon. The accounts of North's risky journeys, the threats against his life, and his willingness to die to avoid revealing secrets under torture led Cheryl Lavin to gush in the *Chicago Tribune*:

He came across as a hero. Not a phony Hollywood hero. A real hero. In his first week as a witness, North was dazzling. . . . This wasn't Sylvester Stallone or Arnold Schwarzenegger fighting a play war with catsup blood. This man fought real wars. He dripped real blood. His war didn't end when the cameras stopped turning. His enemies pursue him into his home. Right this minute they're after him. And face to face with the scariest terrorist in the world, he doesn't blink. Any time, any place, he told Abu Nidal. Man to man. One on one. You and me. The country watched transfixed.[29]

Although a career officer and a highly efficient bureaucrat, Oliver North also expressed contempt for constitutional process. The code name for the State Department in North's memos was "Wimp." He blamed Congress for being "fickle, vacillating, unpredictable" in its policy toward the Contras, thus justifying his illegal secret operations. He repeatedly expressed scorn for Congress's various attempts to act as a check and balance against executive power in foreign policy. North admitted but never apologized for the fact that he lied to governmental officials both inside and outside of the Reagan administration, that he shredded vital documents in the very presence of his investigators, and that he participated in falsifying governmental records. Feisty and tough, proud and humble at the same time, loyal to God and country, "the marine spoke in the language of the zealot," as R. W. Apple, Jr., observed."[30]

The task of the zealot to take the law into his own hands to purge Communists and rescue the innocent was expressed in Lt. Col. North's elaborate efforts to circumvent congressional restrictions through secret operations to aid the Nicaraguan Contras by profits earned in the illicit sale of arms to Iran. His lawless stance was continued in the destruction of documents and lies to investigators. He openly acknowledged a plan to create a "self-sustaining, stand-alone entity" that could carry out such activities "free from normal Congressional oversight and control."[31] The stunning feature of North's testimony was that these revelations were made without the slightest sense of shame. So long as the American superhero is devoted to the higher cause, crimes committed in the course of redemptive crusades are incidental and irrelevant. As Jonathan Alter observed, "The instant North resolutely admitted to having lied and falsified documents, many viewers thought it unfair to hold him accountable for it. Confession became salvation before the hearings broke for lunch."[32]

The appeal of lawless, superheroic attempts to restore national honor and symbolically win a lost war surfaced in the outpouring of public support for Ollie North. Among the 120,000 supportive telegrams received during the course of North's testimony, many referred to the restoration of patriotism and pride. USA Today ran an Ollie hot line and received 58,863 calls advocating another medal for his efforts; only 1,756 calls said he deserved a jail sentence instead.[33] A woman from Beaver Island, Michigan, reported that people "would like to elect Ollie president, just as soon as he's out of jail."[34] After examining the astounding public response to North's testimony, Wayne King concluded: "Alone, Colonel North appears to have transmuted the psychic tenor of the nation from cynicism and suspicion to patriotism and belief."[35]

North continues to receive huge fees to popularize "zeal without understanding" as the appropriate form of American patriotism, retaining his stature as a figure of national significance. Many people expect him to seek a future political role. Although his supporters lost the presidency in the election of 1992, they are now close to controlling one of the major political parties in this country, and their story is far from over. The present interlude is therefore a crucial time for Americans to think through the underlying issue of zeal that Paul the Apostle to America throws in such sharp relief.

Zealotism as a Threat to American Democracy

A number of sensitive observers in the past decade have lifted up the threat posed to a constitutional democracy by zealous extremism. The cultural significance of the North episode is that agents inside and on the fringe of the United States government in recent decades have followed these principles to enact what Justice Brandeis most feared. Wade Huntley has recently pointed to the significance of this trend while weighing the "spiritual" cost of the cold war, which the United States presumably has won. He cites "the cynicism of secret CIA-sponsored coups of elected regimes, the breached trust of Watergate, the duplicity of the Iran-Contra affair . . . secret Bush Administration policies, rooted in cold-war logic, contributed to the military buildup of Iraq. . . . Too often both our leaders and the public were willing to compromise American principles and ideals (not to mention laws) in the name of fighting Communism."[36] William Pfaff observed that "Casey, Oliver North, John Poindexter, plus those working with them, and the very large number of people who heatedly defend what they have done, all consider themselves agents of a nobler cause than either the law or the Congress provides. . . . They will believe that breaking or evading the law is for heroes."[37] Observing the almost apocalyptic mood of the cold war that provided the backdrop of such behavior, he pointed to the spiritual and moral price of such "subversion of representative government and of the Constitution." He concludes that such people "are patriots, in their way, but they are zealots; in the end, they are not in democracy's camp but in the other. This is too bad for them; but if they had their way it could also prove too bad for the rest of us."[38]

Benjamin R. Barber infers from the popularity of such figures that "if American democracy falls . . . it will slide into the hands of some reluctant oligarchy or an overzealous domestic party with no foreign connections that will assume power by default because the public has inadvertently abjured its citizenship."[39] Foreign observers who had admired our constitutional democracy were particularly struck by the disparity of the North phenomena. In an interview for the *New York Times*, Mexican novelist Carlos Fuentes said, "What impressed me in Oliver North's testimony was his nostalgia for a United States that had a Soviet coherence. . . . He wished his country could behave like the Soviets, without consultation, without Congressional oversight, without answering the media—beyond the law."[40] Viennese columnist Hilde Saltz observed that:

> an explosive mixture of patriotism and religion . . . has been spreading. The soberly analytical East coast establishment has been replaced by ideologues with an intolerant sense of mission. . . . The Iran-Contra scandal, personified by Oliver North, is symptomatic of this deep crisis in American political culture. Lt. Col. North's view of the world is one of missionary simplicity. For him, saving what he understands to be democracy is a task that justifies trampling on democratic principles.[41]

The serious threat of zealous extremism was driven home by the congressional hearings concerning the Iran-Contra scandal. The message was essentially what Paul was talking about in Romans: that zeal without understanding is dangerous. In the most sustained civics lesson that Americans have had in this generation, the underlying ideals of our democracy were explained and clarified. Here are some of the points that bear on Paul's thesis about "zeal without knowledge":

> That patriotism can be measured by zealous adherence to stereotypical ideals was repudiated by Senator George J. Mitchell, who told North that "it is possible for an American to disagree with you on aid to the contras and still love God and still love this country just as much as you do. In America, disagreement with the policies of the Government is not evidence of lack of patriotism. Although he's regularly asked to do so, God does not take sides in American politics. And in America, disagreement with the policies of the Government is not evidence of lack of patriotism."[42]

> That superwarriors should retain secrecy and deniability so as not to become accountable to the public was dealt with by Senator William S. Cohen. He expressed skepticism that deception should "be practiced upon Congress by deletion, or official documents reduced to confetti, while false statements are given to public officials" in covert operations."[43] Along

with others, Representative Lee H. Hamilton pointed to North's violation of the principle of accountability.[44]

On the issue of telling the truth, which zealots may believe they can abandon for the sake of the higher cause, there were many testimonies to its necessity in a democratic society. Secretary of State George P. Schultz, who strongly agreed with Senator Inouye on the need for truthfulness, was particularly impressive: "Public service is a very rewarding and honorable thing, and nobody has to think they need to lie and cheat in order to be a public servant or to work in foreign policy. Quite to the contrary. If you are really going to be effective . . . you have to be straightforward, and you have to conduct yourself in a basically honest way."[45]

Finally, in relation to our perception that North's behavior resulted in a politics of undemocratic and destructive zealotism, Representative Dante Fascell contended that the National Security Council had "adopted the methods of a totalitarian government in pursuing democratic goals." North sharply disagreed, and Fascell backed off from this penetrating and accurate observation with the admission that he was not talking about a "substitution of values."[46] But the substitution was there for all to see. This theme was reiterated in the dramatic highpoint of the hearings. Senator Daniel K. Inouye was rudely interrupted during his statement at the close of North's testimony while arguing that no military personnel should obey unlawful orders. "This principle was considered so important that we, we the Government of the United States, proposed that it be internationally applied in the Nuremberg trials. And so in the Nuremberg trials we said that the fact that the defendant—" At this point defense attorney Brendan V. Sullivan shouted,

> "I find this offensive. I find you're engaging in a personal attack on Colonel North and you're far removed from the issues of this case. To make reference to the Nuremberg trials I find personally, professionally distasteful and I can no longer sit here and listen to this. . . . Why don't you listen to the American people and what they've said as a result of the last week. There are 20,000 telegrams in our room outside the corridor here that came in this morning. The American people have spoken."[47]

This impassioned exchange revealed the profound disparity between what some of the telegrams favored and the American principle of lawful obedience. The reference to Nuremberg infuriated Sullivan because it indicated the similarity between his client's behavior and Fascist politics. What the public was allowed to glimpse in this exchange was that patriotism of the zealous type cannot be followed without grave threats to a constitutional democracy.

The Global Issues of Zeal and Democracy

When we look beyond our shores to the conflicts in the Persian Gulf, in India, in Northern Ireland, in the areas of the former Yugoslavia, in Georgia, in Armenia and Azerbaijan, and in Israel, the West Bank, and Gaza, it becomes clear that fanatical zeal is a problem of global significance. Its exercise prevents the successful development of democratic societies and political systems. Those of us who are Christian need to acknowledge that our tradition has contributed more than its share to such destructive zeal and that indeed some of our most devoted Christian brothers and sisters are committed to it today. Oliver North and John Poindexter are both devoted Christians, and they are passionately supported by millions of Christian patriots. What is required now in our society is to combine zeal with understanding, and that calls for discussion, argument, debate, and clarification. We have an opportunity now that the cold war is over to come to terms with a dangerous virus in our culture, one that infects religion as well as politics, business as well as education. The best antidote is to practice the democratic arts of equal opportunity, equal participation, responsibility for the welfare of others, of freely speaking and carefully listening, and of public evaluation.

Pauline theology could thus provide a decisive resource to retain what Josiah Royce called "wholesome provincialism" in American culture, which must always be held in tension with the claims of the universal "Beloved Community."[48] He defined provincialism as "first, the tendency of such a province to possess its own customs and ideals; secondly, the totality of these customs and ideals themselves; and thirdly, the love and pride which leads the inhabitants of a province to cherish as their own these traditions, beliefs, and aspirations."[49] Royce argued that while "we must first be loyal to a province, which entails following its interpretive guidelines, we must . . . realize that true loyalty seeks to protect the loyalty of other individuals and provinces."[50] A healthy form of patriotism thus remains tolerant and open not only to contrary voices within our society but also to the larger claims of the world community.

If we wish to preserve and improve this distinctive democratic legacy, we would do well to make the words concerning zeal without understanding, the only citation from the Apostle to America carved into an official government building, into a beacon light probing into the heart of our culture. The cold war may well be over, but the perennial threats of mobocracy and blind zealotism described by Lincoln still have the ability to poison the "land of the free and the home of the brave."

Notes

Introduction

1. For a discussion of the rhetorical structure of this passage, see Johannes Weiss, "Beiträge zur Paulinischen Rhetorik," in *Theologische Studien. Herrn Professor D. Bernhard Weiss zu seinem 70 Geburtstage dargebracht*, ed. C. R. Gregory, et al. (Göttingen: Vandenhoeck & Ruprecht, 1897), 165–247.

2. James D. G. Dunn, *Romans 1—8*, Word Biblical Commentary 38A (Waco, Tex.: Word Books, 1988), 36.

1. Overcoming the Eurocentric View of Paul

1. For a discussion of the translation of regarding and knowing "according to the flesh," see Robert Jewett, *Paul's Anthropological Terms: A Study of Their Use in Conflict Settings* (Leiden: E. J. Brill, 1971), 127–128.

2. See Jewett, *Paul's Anthropological Terms*, 125–127. For a parallel critique of Eurocentric scholarship, see Cain Hope Felder's introduction to *Stony the Road We Trod: African American Biblical Interpretation* (Minneapolis: Fortress Press, 1991), 6–7.

3. Stuart Miller, *Painted in Blood: Understanding Europeans* (New York: Atheneum, 1987).

4. Ibid., 28.

5. See, for example, Ferdinand Christian Baur, *Paul the Apostle of Jesus Christ* (London: Williams and Norgate, 1876); R. A. Lipsius, *Die paulinische Rechtfertigungslehre unter Berücksichtigung einiger verwandten Lehrstücke nach der vier Hauptbriefen des Apostels* (Leipzig: 1853); Hermann Lüdemann, *Die Anthropologie des Apostels Paulus und ihre Stellung innerhalb seiner Heilslehre. Nach den vier Hauptbriefen* (Kiel: Universitäts-Buchhandlung, 1873); Otto Pfleiderer, *Paulinism: A Contribution to the History of Primitive Christian Theology* (London: Williams and Norgate, 1891); C. H. Dodd, *The Meaning of Paul for Today* (New York: Doran, 1920); Herman Ridderbos, *Paul: An Outline of His Theology*, trans. J. R. DeWitt (Grand Rapids: Wm. B. Eerdmans Publishing Co., 1975).

6. See Jewett, *Paul's Anthropological Terms*; Jouette M. Bassler, ed., *Pauline Theology I. Thessalonians, Philippians, Galatians, Philemon* (Minneapolis: Fortress Press, 1991).

7. Calvin Roetzel, *The Letters of Paul: Conversations in Context* (Louisville, Ky.: Westminster/John Knox Press, 1991, 3d ed.).

8. J. Christiaan Beker, *Paul the Apostle: The Triumph of God in Life and Thought* (Philadelphia: Fortress Press, 1984), 39–40.

9. Miller, *Painted in Blood*, 23.

10. Ibid., 25.

11. See Robert Jewett, *Christian Tolerance: Paul's Message to the Modern Church* (Philadelphia: Westminster Press, 1982), for a corrective of this tendency.

12. Auguste Sabatier, *The Apostle Paul: A Sketch of the Development of His Doctrine*, trans. A. M. Hellier (London: Hodder and Stoughton, 1893).

13. Ibid., 124.

14. Ibid., 125.

15. Ibid., 126.

16. Ibid., 136.

17. Ernst Käsemann, *Commentary on Romans*, trans. G. W. Bromiley (Grand Rapids: Wm. B. Eerdmans Publishing Co., 1980), 102.

18. There is a ten-page section of my Romans bibliography devoted to the topic of Paul and the law since the 1950s containing a fraction of these studies. A full-length book by Stephen Westerholm, *Israel's Law and the Church's Faith: Paul and His Recent Interpreters* (Grand Rapids: Wm. B. Eerdmans Publishing Co., 1988), is required to sort out a portion of the recent debate.

19. Miller, *Painted in Blood*, 224.

20. For example, see Günter Klein's theory of apostolic power in "Paul's Purpose in Writing the Epistle to the Romans," in *The Romans Debate: Revised and Expanded Edition*, ed. Karl P. Donfried (Peabody, Mass.: Hendrickson, 1991), 29–43; full-length studies of this issue in English are John Howard Schütz, *Paul and the Anatomy of Apostolic Authority* (Cambridge: Cambridge University Press, 1975); Bengt Holmberg, *Paul and Power: The Structure of Authority in the Primitive Church as Reflected in the Pauline Epistles* (Philadelphia: Fortress Press, 1978); Winsome Munro, *Authority in Paul and Peter: The Identification of a Pastoral Stratum in the Pauline Corpus and 1 Peter* (Cambridge: Cambridge University Press, 1983); G. Shaw, *The Cost of Authority: Manipulation and Freedom in the New Testament* (London: SCM, 1982; Philadelphia: Fortress Press, 1983).

21. See Walter Schmithals, *The Office of the Apostle in the Early Church*, trans. J. E. Steely (Nashville: Abingdon Press, 1969), 32–40.

22. See the extensive survey by Duane F. Watson, "The New Testament and Greco-Roman Rhetoric: A Bibliography," *Journal of the Evangelical Theological Society* 31 (1988): 466–72, and also the collection of essays edited by Duane F. Watson, *Persuasive Artistry: Studies in New Testament Rhetoric in Honor of George A. Kennedy* (Sheffield: JSOT Press, 1991).

23. See Jewett, *Paul's Anthropological Terms*; Abraham J. Malherbe, *Paul and the Thessalonians: The Philosophic Tradition of Pastoral Care* (Philadelphia: Fortress Press, 1987); Paul W. Gooch, *Partial Knowledge: Philosophical Studies in Paul* (Notre Dame, Ind.: University of Notre Dame Press, 1987).

24. Miller, *Painted in Blood*, 155.

25. Ibid., 147.

26. See, for instance, the critique of one of the major alleged divisions within early Christianity in the study by Craig C. Hill, *Hellenists and Hebrews: Reappraising Division within the Earliest Church* (Minneapolis: Augsburg Fortress, 1992). Classic statements of such conflicts are available in the various studies by Walter Schmithals: *Paul and James*, trans. D. M. Barton (London: SCM Press, 1965); *Gnosticism in Corinth: An Investigation of the Letters to the Corinthians*, trans. J. E. Seeley (Nashville: Abingdon Press, 1971).

27. Miller, *Painted in Blood*, 148.

28. A recent effort to counterbalance this tendency is found in Klaus Schäfer, *Gemeinde als "Bruderschaft." Ein Beitrag zum Kirchenverständnis des Paulus* (Frankfurt: Lang, 1989).

29. For instance, the discussion of the nature of the early Christian communities has been dominated by the debate over the leadership roles and offices. See Schmithals, *Office*; Joseph Brosch, *Charismen und Ämter in der Urkirche* (Bonn: Hanstein, 1951); Ulrich Brockhaus, *Charisma und Amt. Die paulinische Charismenlehre auf dem Hintergrund der frühchristlichen Gemeindefunktionen* (Wuppertal: Verlag Rolf Brockhaus, 1972); John N. Collins, *Diakonia: Reinterpreting the Ancient Sources* (New York: Oxford University Press, 1990); Josef Hainz, *Kirche im Werden. Studien zum Thema Amt und Gemeinde im Neuen Testament* (Munich: Schöningh, 1976); Joachim Rohde, *Urchristliche und frühkatholische Ämter. Eine Untersuchung zur frühchristlichen Amtsentwicklung im Neuen Testament und bei den apostolischen Vätern* (Berlin: Evangelische, 1976); Karl Kertelge, *Gemeinde und Amt im Neuen Testament* (Munich: Kösel, 1972); Andrè Lemaire, *Les ministères aux origines de l'Église. Naissance de la triple hiérarchie: évêques, presbytyres, diacres* (Paris: du Cerf, 1971); John Kelman S. Reid, *The Biblical Doctrine of the Ministry* (Edinburgh: Oliver & Boyd, 1955); Alfred F. Zimmermann, *Die urchristlichen Lehrer* (Tübingen: Mohr-Siebeck, 1988); Jürgen Roloff, *Apostolat-Verkündigung—Kirche. Ursprung, Inhalt und Funktion des kirchlichen Apostelamtes nach Paulus, Lukas und den Pastoralbriefen* (Gütersloh: Gerd Mohn, 1965).

30. For example, see Gerd Theissen, *The Social Setting of Pauline Christianity: Essays on Corinth*, trans. J. H. Schütz (Philadelphia: Fortress Press, 1982), 69–101.

31. Miller, *Painted in Blood*, 91.

32. The best introduction to this huge debate in English is I. Howard Marshall, *Last Supper and Lord's Supper* (Exeter: Paternoster, 1980); a comprehensive discussion of the historical-religious background is available in Hans-Josef Klauck, *Herrenmahl und hellenistischer Kult. Eine religionsgeschichtliche Untersuchung zum ersten Korintherbrief* (Münster: Aschendorff, 1982). See also the accounts of the Roman Catholic discussion in J. Delorme, ed., *The Eucharist in the New Testament: A Symposium* (Baltimore: Helicon, 1964), Jerome Kodell, *The Eucharist in the New Testament* (Wilmington: Glazier, 1988), and Xaviar Leon-Dufour, *Sharing in the Eucharistic Bread: The Witness of the New Testament*, trans. M. J. O'Connell (New York: Paulist Press, 1987). Significant Protestant discussions may be found in Markus Barth, *Rediscovering the Lord's Supper: Communion with Israel, with Christ, and among the Guests* (Atlanta: John Knox Press, 1988); and Bernd Kollmann, *Ursprung und Gestalt der frühchristlichen Mahlfeier*

(Göttingen: Vandenhoeck & Ruprecht, 1990). A recent ecumenical discussion is available in Ben F. Meyer, ed., *One Loaf, One Cup: Ecumenical Studies on 1 Cor. 11 and Other Eucharistic Texts* (Macon: Mercer University Press, 1991).

33. Elisabeth Schüssler Fiorenza, *In Memory of Her: A Feminist Theological Reconstruction of Christian Origins* (New York: Crossroad, 1984), 198–99.

34. A study of this was written in 1970 by E. Earle Ellis, "Paul and his Co-Workers," reprinted in Ellis, *Prophecy and Hermeneutic in Early Christianity: New Testament Essays* (Grand Rapids: Wm. B. Eerdmans Publishing Co., 1978), 3–22; the definitive study of Paul's collegial mission is by Wolf-Hennig Ollrog, *Paulus und seine Mitarbeiter. Untersuchungen zu Theorie und Praxis der paulinischen Mission* (Neukirchen-Vluyn: Neukirchener, 1979).

35. Fiorenza, *In Memory of Her,* 169, citing Ellis's article on "Paul and His Co-Workers."

36. Miller, *Painted in Blood,* 81.

37. Jeffrey A. Crafton, *The Agency of the Apostle: A Dramatistic Analysis of Paul's Responses to Conflict in 2 Corinthians,* Journal for the Study of the New Testament Supplement Series 51 (Sheffield: Sheffield Academic Press, 1991), 61.

38. Ibid., 100.

39. See my article, "Paul, Phoebe and the Spanish Mission," in *The Social World of Formative Christianity and Judaism: Essays in Tribute to Howard Clark Kee,* ed. P. Borgen, et al. (Philadelphia: Fortress Press, 1988), 144–64.

40. See Ronald F. Hock, *The Social Context of Paul's Ministry: Tentmaking and Apostleship* (Philadelphia: Fortress Press, 1980).

41. Richard I. Pervo, *Profit With Delight* (Philadelphia: Fortress Press, 1987), 12–85.

42. See F. Stanley Jones, *"Freiheit" in den Briefen des Apostels Paulus. Eine historische, exegetische und religionsgeschichtliche Studie* (Göttingen: Vandenhoeck & Ruprecht, 1987); and Samuel Vollenweider, *Freiheit als neue Schöpfung. Eine Untersuchung zur Eleutheria bei Paulus und in seiner Umwelt* (Göttingen: Vandenhoeck & Ruprecht, 1989).

43. Miller, *Painted in Blood,* 144.

44. Ibid., 152–53.

45. Ibid., 126.

46. Sydney E. Mead, *The Nation with the Soul of a Church* (New York: Harper & Row, 1975).

47. Miller, *Painted in Blood,* 30.

48. Beker, *Paul the Apostle,* 366.

49. Miller, *Painted in Blood,* 33.

50. Ibid., 140.

51. See my studies, *The Captain America Complex: The Dilemma of Zealous Nationalism* (Philadelphia: Westminster Press, 1973; rev. ed., Santa Fe: Bear & Company, 1984); *The American Monomyth,* with John Shelton Lawrence, with a forward by Isaac Asimov (Garden City, N.Y.: Doubleday/Anchor Press, 1977; 2d ed., Lanham, Md.: University Press of America, 1988); *Jesus Against the Rapture: Seven Unexpected Prophecies* (Philadelphia: Westminster Press, 1979); *Letter to Pilgrims: A Commentary on the Epistle to the Hebrews* (Philadelphia: United Church Press, 1981); and *Christian Tolerance.*

2. Interpreting Paul in the American Context

1. See the discussion of the strophic pattern in Gordon D. Fee, *The First Epistle to the Corinthians* (Grand Rapids: Wm. B. Eerdmans Publishing Co., 1987), 423.

2. J. Christiaan Beker, *Heirs of Paul: Paul's Legacy in the New Testament and in the Church Today* (Minneapolis: Fortress Press, 1991), 100–101.

3. Ibid., 101–2.

4. See Robert S. Corrington, *The Community of Interpreters* (Macon: Mercer University Press, 1988), chapters 4–5; also John E. Smith and William Kluback, eds., *Josiah Royce: Selected Writings* (New York: Paulist Press, 1988), 195–218; Frank M. Oppenheim, *Royce's Mature Philosophy of Religion* (Notre Dame, Ind.: University of Notre Dame Press, 1987).

5. Beker, *Heirs of Paul*, 100–101.

6. Ibid., 101.

7. Susanne Heine, *Women and Early Christianity: A Reappraisal*, trans. J. Bowden (Minneapolis: Augsburg Press, 1987), 82.

8. See the extensive bibliography in endnote 1 of chapter 12 in my *Saint Paul at the Movies* (Louisville, Ky.: Westminster/John Knox Press, 1993), dealing with the post-Pauline provenance of the pastoral epistles.

9. Cited by David L. Jeffrey and Camille R. La Bossière, "Paul," in *A Dictionary of Biblical Tradition in English Literature*, ed. David Lyle Jeffrey (Grand Rapids: Wm B. Eerdmans Publishing Co., 1992), 592.

10. Ibid., 592.

11. Ibid.

12. Gooch, *Partial Knowledge*, 46.

13. For example, the premise of Pauline authorship of the pastorals led to Nancy van Vuuren's assessment of Paul's "fear of women and a limited recognition of women as persons," in *The Subversion of Women as Practiced by Churches, Witch-Hunters, and Other Sexists* (Philadelphia: Westminster Press, 1973), 29. Dorothy D. Burlage works from the same premise to conclude that "the Pauline texts of the New Testament not only add dimensions of discrimination against women, but also carry an anti-sex, anti-marriage message," in "Judaeo-Christian Influences on Female Sexuality," in *Sexist Religion and Women in the Church: No More Silence!* ed. Alice L. Hageman (New York: Association Press, 1974), 99.

14. Munro, *Authority in Paul and Peter*, 27–94.

15. This typical assessment is cited by Derrick Sherwin Bailey, while providing a more balanced analysis of the Pauline evidence, in *Sexual Relation in Christian Thought* (New York: Harper & Brothers Publishers, 1959), 11.

16. Cited by Wayne A. Meeks from George Bernard Shaw, "Preface on the Prospects of Christianity" to *Androcles and the Lion*, in *The Writings of St. Paul* (New York: W. W. Norton & Co., 1972), 299.

17. Mary Daly, *Pure Lust: Elemental Feminist Philosophy* (Boston: Beacon Press, 1984), 8.

18. See especially *In Memory of Her*, 160–235.

19. Rosemary Radford Ruether, *Faith and Fratricide: The Theological Roots of Anti-Semitism* (New York: Crossroad, 1979), 95. See chapter 3 below for a detailed evaluation of her approach.

20. Hyam Maccoby, *The Mythmaker: Paul and the Invention of Christianity* (New York: Harper & Row, 1986).

21. See my review of Maccoby, *The Myth-Maker*, in the *Philadelphia Inquirer* (October 26, 1986), S6, and the discussion in chapter 3 below.

22. See Howard Thurman, *Jesus and the Disinherited* (Nashville: Abingdon Press, 1949), 31–35. This episode is described by Amos Jones, Jr., in *Paul's Message of Freedom: What Does It Mean to the Black Church?* (Valley Forge, Pa.: Judson Press, 1984), 5–6.

23. Ibid., 17–18; see also 30–31.

24. Clarice J. Martin, "The *Haustafeln* (Household Codes) in African American Biblical Interpretation: 'Free Slaves' and 'Subordinate Women,'" in *Stony the Road*, ed. Felder, 206.

25. Rollin H. Walker, *Paul's Secret of Power* (New York: Abingdon Press, 1935), 9.

26. Ibid., 7.

27. Ibid., 81.

28. Ibid., 97.

29. Holmes Rolston, *The Social Message of the Apostle* (Richmond: John Knox Press, 1942).

30. See ibid., 230–31.

31. John Knox, *Life in Christ Jesus: Reflections on Romans 5—8* (Greenwich, Conn.: Seabury, 1961), 15–16.

32. Ibid., 43.

33. Kingsley G. Rendell, *Expository Outlines from 1 and 2 Corinthians* (Grand Rapids: Baker Books, 1970).

34. Ibid., 39.

35. See, for example, ibid., 128–29.

36. Lewis B. Smedes, *Love Within Limits: A Realist's View of 1 Corinthians 13* (Grand Rapids: Wm. B. Eerdmans Publishing Co., 1978).

37. William Baird, *Paul's Message and Mission* (Nashville: Abingdon Press, 1960).

38. Ibid., 164–66, 17–32.

39. Ibid., 59.

40. Ibid., 82.

41. Ibid., 161.

42. Ibid., 167: "This is the eternal message from God which is relevant to all the needs of modern men."

43. Roy A. Harrisville, *Romans*, Augsburg Commentary on the New Testament (Minneapolis: Augsburg Press, 1980).

44. Paul J. Achtemeier, *Romans*, Interpretation: A Bible Commentary for Teaching and Preaching (Atlanta: John Knox Press, 1985).

45. Ralph P. Martin, *Colossians and Philemon* (London: Oliphants, 1974).

46. James M. Reese, *1 and 2 Thessalonians* (Wilmington, Del.: Michael Glazier, Inc., 1979).

47. Markus Barth, *Ephesians: Introduction, Translation, and Commentary* (Garden City, N.Y., Doubleday, 1974).

48. Victor P. Furnish, *II Corinthians: Translated with Introduction, Notes, and Commentary* (Garden City, N.Y.: Doubleday, 1984).

49. William F. Orr and James Arthur Walther, *I Corinthians: A New Translation, Introduction, with a Study of the Life of Paul, Notes, and Commentary* (Garden City, N.Y.: Doubleday, 1976).

50. Fee, *1 Corinthians*.

51. James D. G. Dunn, *Romans 1—8; Romans 9—16* (Waco, Tex.: Word Books, 1988).

52. John Paul Heil, *Paul's Letter to the Romans: A Reader-Response Commentary* (New York: Paulist Press, 1987).

53. Graydon F. Snyder, *First Corinthians: A Faith Community Commentary* (Macon, Ga.: Mercer University Press, 1992).

54. Robin Scroggs, *Paul for a New Day* (Philadelphia: Fortress Press, 1977). A more recent effort along these lines, though including only one chapter on an indisputable Pauline letter, is provided by Wilhelm H. Wuellner and Robert C. Leslie, *The Surprising Gospel: Intriguing Psychological Insights from the New Testament* (Nashville: Abingdon Press, 1984).

55. Martin Luther King Jr., *Strength to Love* (New York: Harper & Row, 1963); *Stride Toward Freedom: The Montgomery Story* (New York: Harper & Row, 1958); *Where Do We Go From Here: Chaos or Community?* (New York: Harper & Row, 1967).

56. Joseph A. Grassi, *The Secret of Paul the Apostle* (Maryknoll, N.Y.: Orbis, 1978), 169–70.

57. Ibid., 137–49.

58. Ibid., 93.

59. William G. Thompson, *Paul and His Message for Life's Journey* (New York: Paulist Press, 1986).

60. See ibid., especially 139–44.

61. Ibid., 2.

62. Ibid., 15, 72, 63–68, 85–88.

63. Jones, *Paul's Message*, 25.

64. Ibid., 31.

65. Ibid., 60.

66. Ibid., 64.

67. Ibid., 85.

68. Ibid., 100–110.

69. Ibid., 202.

70. J. Paul Sampley, *Walking Between the Times: Paul's Moral Reasoning* (Minneapolis: Fortress Press, 1991).

71. Ibid., 37–38, 63–69.

72. Ibid., 87–91.

73. Ibid., 117.

74. Ibid., 107.

75. Jewett, *Christian Tolerance*, 10.

76. Ibid., 38.

77. Robert Jewett, *Romans*, Genesis To Revelation Adult Bible Series 20 (Nashville: The Graded Press of the United Methodist Publishing House, 1986); *Romans*, Cokesbury Basic Bible Commentary series (Nashville: United Methodist Publishing House, 1988).

78. Marva J. Dawn, *The Hilarity of Community: Romans 12 and How to Be the Church* (Grand Rapids: Wm. B. Eerdmans Publishing Co., 1992), x.

79. Ibid., xi.

80. Ibid., xiii, 15–17.

81. Ibid., 81.

82. Ibid., 215.

83. E. P. Sanders, *Paul and Palestinian Judaism: A Comparison of Patterns of Religion* (Philadelphia: Fortress Press, 1977); also *Paul, the Law, and the Jewish People* (Philadelphia: Fortress Press, 1983).

84. Sanders, *Paul, the Law,* 209.

85. Beker, *Paul the Apostle,* 331.

86. Ibid., 334.

87. Ibid., 366.

88. J. Christiaan Beker, *Paul's Apocalyptic Gospel: The Coming Triumph of God* (Philadelphia: Fortress Press, 1982), 120.

89. J. Christiaan Beker, *Suffering and Hope: The Biblical Vision and the Human Predicament* (Philadelphia: Fortress Press, 1987), 88.

90. Ibid., 90.

91. See Wayne A. Meeks, *The First Urban Christians: The Social World of the Apostle Paul* (New Haven, Conn: Yale University Press, 1982), ix.

92. Wayne A. Meeks, *The Moral World of the First Christians* (Philadelphia: Westminster Press, 1986), 98–120.

93. Ibid., 162.

94. Wayne A. Meeks, "A Hermeneutics of Social Embodiment," *Harvard Theological Review* 79 (1986): 175–86.

95. John G. Gager, *Kingdom and Community: The Social World of Early Christianity* (Englewood Cliffs, N.J.: Prentice-Hall, 1975).

96. Schütz, *Apostolic Authority.*

97. Norman R. Petersen, *Rediscovering Paul: Philemon and the Sociology of Paul's Narrative World* (Philadelphia: Fortress Press, 1985).

98. Abraham J. Malherbe, *Social Aspects of Early Christianity* (Baton Rouge, La.: Louisiana State University Press, 1977); most of Malherbe's work concentrates on the classical background as the crucial constituent of the social setting, as for example *Paul and the Popular Philosophers* (Minneapolis: Fortress Press, 1989).

99. Dale B. Martin, *Slavery as Salvation: The Metaphor of Slavery in Pauline Christianity* (New Haven, Conn.: Yale University Press, 1990).

100. Bruce J. Malina, *The New Testament World: Insights from Cultural Anthropology* (Atlanta: John Knox Press, 1981); *Christian Origins and Cultural Anthropology: Practical Models for Biblical Interpretation* (Atlanta: John Knox Press, 1986).

101. Jerome H. Neyrey, *Paul, in Other Words: A Cultural Reading of His Letters* (Louisville, Ky.: Westminster/John Knox Press, 1990).

102. Robert A. Atkins, Jr., *Egalitarian Community: Ethnography and Exegesis* (Tuscaloosa, Ala.: The University of Alabama Press, 1991).

103. Robert Jewett, *The Thessalonian Correspondence: Pauline Rhetoric and Millenarian Piety* (Philadelphia: Fortress Press, 1986).

104. Hans Dieter Betz, *Galatians: A Commentary on Paul's Letter to the Churches in Galatia* (Philadelphia: Fortress Press, 1979); *2 Corinthians 8 and 9: A*

Commentary on Two Administrative Letters of the Apostle Paul (Philadelphia: Fortress Press, 1985).

105. Wilhelm Wuellner, "Greek Rhetoric and Pauline Argumentation," in *Early Christian Literature and the Classical Intellectual Tradition: In honorem Robert M. Grant*, ed. W. R. Schoedel and R. L. Wilken, Theologie historique 53 (Paris: Beauchesne, 1979), 177–88; "Paul's Rhetoric of Argumentation in Romans," *Catholic Biblical Quarterly* 38 (1976): 330–51; reprinted in *Romans Debate*, ed. Donfried, 128–46; "Toposforschung und Torahinterpretation bei Paulus und Jesus," *New Testament Studies* 24 (1978): 463–83; "Paul as Pastor: The Function of Rhetorical Questions in First Corinthians," in *L'Apôtre Paul: personalitè, style et concêption du ministère*, ed. A. Vanhoye (Leuven: Leuven University Press, 1986), 49–77; "Where Is Rhetorical Criticism Taking Us?" *Catholic Biblical Quarterly* 49 (1987): 448–63.

106. David E. Aune, ed., *Greco-Roman Literature and the New Testament: Selected Forms and Genres*, Society of Biblical Literature Sources for Biblical Study 21 (Atlanta: Scholars Press, 1988); "Romans as a *Logos Protreptikos*," in *Romans Debate*, ed. Donfried, 278–96.

107. Stanley K. Stowers, *The Diatribe and Paul's Letter to the Romans*, Society of Biblical Literature Dissertation Series 57 (Chico, Calif.: Scholars Press, 1981); *Letter Writing in Greco-Roman Antiquity* (Philadelphia: Westminster Press, 1986).

108. George A. Kennedy, *Classical Rhetoric and Its Christian and Secular Tradition from Ancient to Modern Times* (Chapel Hill, N.C.: University of North Carolina Press, 1980); *New Testament Interpretation through Rhetorical Criticism* (Chapel Hill, N.C.: University of North Carolina Press, 1984).

109. Frank Witt Hughes, *Early Christian Rhetoric and 2 Thessalonians* (Sheffield: JSOT Press, 1988).

110. Crafton, *Agency of the Apostle*.

111. See Jewett, *Thessalonian Correspondence*; "Romans as an Ambassadorial Letter," *Interpretation: A Journal of Bible and Theology* 36 (1982): 5–20; "Following the Argument of Romans," *Word and World: Theology for Christian Ministry* 6 (1986): 382–89. Revised and reprinted in *Romans Debate*, ed. Donfried, 265–77; "Numerical Sequences in Paul's Letter to the Romans," in *Persuasive Artistry*, ed. Watson, 227–45.

112. Hans Dieter Betz's study of Paul's critique of the superapostles in 2 Corinthians remains highly relevant for the critique of similar phenomena in American culture: *Der Apostle Paulus und die sokratische Tradition. Eine exegetische Untersuchung zu seiner "Apologie" 2 Kor 10—13* (Tübingen: J. C. B. Mohr-Paul Siebeck, 1972).

113. Krister Stendahl, *Paul Among Jews and Gentiles and Other Essays* (Philadelphia: Fortress Press, 1976), containing articles that have influenced the scholarly discussion since the early 1960s.

114. Ibid., 1.

115. John Gager, *The Origins of Anti-Semitism: Attitudes Toward Judaism in Pagan and Christian Antiquity* (New York: Oxford University Press, 1983).

116. Lloyd Gaston, *Paul and the Torah* (Vancouver: University of British Columbia Press, 1987).

117. Norman A. Beck, *Mature Christianity: The Recognition and Repudiation of the Anti-Jewish Polemic of the New Testament* (Selinsgrove, Pa.: Susquehanna University Press, 1985).

118. Samuel Sandmel, *The Genius of Paul: A Study in History* (Philadelphia: Fortress Press, 1979).

119. Ibid., 24, 28.

120. Ibid., 34, 114–16.

121. Ibid., 219.

122. Richard L. Rubenstein, *My Brother Paul* (New York: Harper & Row, Publishers, 1972).

123. Ibid., 7.

124. Ibid., 112.

125. Ibid., 172.

126. Ibid., 173.

127. Alan F. Segal, *Paul the Convert: The Apostolate and Apostasy of Saul the Pharisee* (New Haven, Conn.: Yale University Press, 1990), 35, 51.

128. Ibid., 57.

129. Ibid., 60.

130. Ibid., 68.

131. Ibid., 271.

132. Ibid., 182.

133. Daniel Patte, *Preaching Paul* (Philadelphia: Fortress Press, 1984).

134. Daniel Patte, *Paul's Faith and the Power of the Gospel: A Structural Introduction to the Pauline Letters* (Philadelphia: Fortress Press, 1983).

135. Patte, *Preaching Paul*, 64–65.

136. Ibid., 75–76.

137. Ibid., 84.

138. Robert Hamerton-Kelly, *Sacred Violence: Paul's Hermeneutic of the Cross* (Minneapolis: Fortress Press, 1992).

139. Ibid., 63.

140. Ibid., 87.

141. Ibid., 111.

142. Ibid., 12.

143. Walter Wink, *Naming the Powers: The Language of Power in the New Testament* (Philadelphia: Fortress Press, 1984), 107.

144. Walter Wink, *Unmasking the Powers: The Invisible Forces That Determine Human Existence* (Philadelphia: Fortress Press, 1986).

145. Walter Wink, *Engaging the Powers: Discernment and Resistance in a World of Domination* (Minneapolis: Fortress Press, 1992).

146. Ibid., 139–56.

147. Richard B. Hays, *Echoes of Scripture in the Letters of Paul* (New Haven, Conn.: Yale University Press, 1989).

148. Ibid., 16.

149. Ibid., 183–86.

150. Jouette M. Bassler, ed., *Pauline Theology I. Thessalonians, Philippians, Galatians, Philemon* (Minneapolis: Fortress Press, 1991).

151. Robert Jewett, "A Matrix of Grace: The Theology of 2 Thessalonians as a Pauline Letter," in *Pauline Theology*, ed. Bassler, 63–70.

152. Dieter Georgi, *Theocracy in Paul's Praxis and Theology*, trans. by D. E. Green (Minneapolis: Fortress Press, 1991), 92–93.

153. Ibid., 92, n. 24. See also the foreward by Georgi in Oppenheim's study of *Royce's Mature Philosophy of Religion*, ix: "The particular communal experience of Pauline Christianity becomes for Royce a valuable hermeneutical model. . . . In the *Problem*, then, Royce sensed and stressed the corporate and historical dynamisms at work within the interpretation process more concretely and skillfully than Bultmann or Heidegger have done. For these reasons, in his mature work, Royce considerably surpassed Bultmann as an interpreter of the New Testament."

154. Josiah Royce, *The Problem of Christianity. I. The Christian Doctrine of Life* (New York: Macmillan Company, 1913), 156–57.

155. Ibid., 157–58.

156. Ibid., 159.

3. Law and the Coexistence of Jews and Gentiles

1. For a discussion of the rhetorical structure of this passage, see Otto Michel, *Der Brief an die Römer* (Göttingen: Vandenhoeck & Ruprecht, 1955), 291; Weiss, "Beiträge," 238; Johananes P. Louw, *A Semantic Discourse Analysis of Romans* (Pretoria, South Africa: University of Pretoria, 1979), 2:97.

2. Calvin L. Porter, "A New Paradigm for Reading Romans. Dialogue Between Christians and Jews," *Encounter* 39 (1978): 257–72; see also Gager, *Origins*, 198–201.

3. Segal, *Paul the Convert*, ix.

4. Krister Stendhal, "The Apostle Paul and the Introspective Conscience of the West," *Harvard Theological Review* 56 (1963): 199–215; reprinted in *Paul Among Jews and Gentiles and Other Essays* (Philadelphia: Fortress Press, 1976), 78–96.

5. Ibid., 132.

6. Nils Alstrup Dahl, *Studies in Paul: Theology for the Early Christian Mission* (Minneapolis: Augsburg, 1977).

7. Ibid., 190.

8. Ruether, *Faith and Fratricide*, 95–107; a comprehensive response to Ruether's challenge, with extended references to the intervening scholarly debate, is provided by Franz Mussner, *Tractate on the Jews: The Significance of Judaism for Christian Faith*, trans. Leonard Swidler (Philadelphia: Fortress Press, 1984).

9. Ruether, *Faith and Fratricide*, 101.

10. Ibid., 102–3.

11. Ibid., 104.

12. Ibid., 102.

13. Ibid., 107.

14. Gager, *Origins*, 29.

15. Lloyd Gaston, "Abraham and the Righteousness of God," *Horizons in Biblical Theology* 2 (1980): 39–68; "Israel's Enemies in Pauline Theology," *New Testament Studies* 28 (1981–82): 400–423, revised and reprinted in *Torah*.

16. Beker, *Paul the Apostle*, 328–47.

17. Sanders, *Paul, the Law*, 143–210.

18. Cf. Johannes Munck, *Christ and Israel: An Interpretation of Romans 9—11*, trans. I. Nixon from a 1956 German ed. (Philadelphia: Fortress Press, 1967); Peter Richardson, *Israel in the Apostolic Church* (Cambridge: Cambridge University Press, 1969); Christoff Müller, *Gottes Gerechtigkeit und Gottes Volk. Eine Untersuchung zu Röm 9—11* (Göttingen: Vandenhoeck & Ruprecht, 1964).

19. Stendahl, *Paul*, 1; see also Halvor Moxnes, *Theology in Conflict: Studies in Paul's Understanding of God in Romans* (Leiden: E. J. Brill, 1980), 78–107; 216–30.

20. Moxnes, ibid., 28.

21. See Käsemann, *Romans*, 69–104.

22. Ibid., 4.

23. Nils A. Dahl, "The Future of Israel," in *Studies in Paul*, 137–58.

24. Ibid., 141–42.

25. Ibid., 153.

26. Ibid., 157.

27. Ibid., 158.

28. Beker, *Paul the Apostle*, 340.

29. Ibid., 331.

30. Ibid., 332.

31. Ibid., 333.

32. Ibid., 334.

33. Ibid.

34. Ibid., 346.

35. Pinchas Lapide and Peter Stuhlmacher, *Paul: Rabbi and Apostle*, trans. W. W. Denef from the 1981 German ed. (Minneapolis: Augsburg, 1984), 48.

36. Ibid., 51.

37. Ibid., 74.

38. Ibid., 54.

39. Sanders, *Paul and Palestinian Judaism*; *Paul, the Law*.

40. Sanders, *Paul, the Law*, 171–74.

41. Ibid., 196.

42. Ibid., 208.

43. Gager, *Origins*, 262–63.

44. Ibid., 262.

45. Ibid., 251–52.

46. Ibid., 164.

47. Beck, *Mature Christianity*, 40–50.

48. Ibid., 71.

49. Segal, *Paul the Convert*, 279.

50. Ibid., 279–80.

51. Ibid., 281.

52. Ibid., 283.

53. Ibid., 284.

54. Ibid., 280–81.

55. Jewett, *Christian Tolerance*, 121–48.

56. Sanders, *Paul, the Law*; Gerard Sloyan, *Is Christ the End of the Law?* (Philadelphia: Westminster Press, 1978); Heikki Räisänen, *Paul and the Law*

(Tübingen: Mohr-Siebeck, 1983); Hans Hübner, *Law in Paul's Thought*, trans. J.C.G. Grieg (Edinburgh: T. & T. Clark, 1984); Westerholm, *Israel's Law*.

57. Cf. Günther Bornkamm, *Das Ende des Gesetzes. Paulusstudien. Gesammelte Aufsätze I* (Munich: Kaiser Verlag, 1963); Rudolf Bultmann, "Christ and the End of the Law," in *Essays, Philosophical and Theological*, trans. J.C.G. Grieg (London: SCM Press, 1955); Peter Stuhlmacher, "'Das Ende des Gesetzes': Über Ursprung und Ansatz der paulinischen Theologie," *Zeitschrift für Theologie und Kirche* 67 (1970): 14–39. A Roman Catholic title using the same motif is Franz Mussner, "'Christus (ist) des Gesetzes Ende zur Gerechtigkeit für jeden, der glaubt' (Röm 10,4)," in *Paulus—Apostat oder Apostel? Jüdische und christliche Antworten* (Regensburg: Pustet, 1977), 31–44. Other Roman Catholic scholars favoring this translation include, for example, Joseph A. Fitzmyer, "Paul and the Law," in *A Companion to Paul: Readings in Pauline Theology*, ed. M. J. Taylor (New York: Alba, 1975).

58. Käsemann, *Romans*, 282.

59. Ibid., 283; for a similar view, see Stuhlmacher's contention in "Das Ende des Gesetzes," 30, that "the end of the law" is "the quintessence of what God at Damascus had impressed upon the legalistic zealot Paul in the shape of the crucified and resurrected one."

60. Representatives of this view are Andrew John Bandstra, *The Law and the Elements of the World: An Exegetical Study in Aspects of Paul's Teaching* (Kampen: Kok, 1964), 101–6; Ragnar Bring, "Paul and the Old Testament: A Study of the Ideas of Election, Faith and Law in Paul with Special Reference to Romans 9:30–10:30," *Studia Theologica* 25 (1971): 21–60; C.E.B. Cranfield, "St. Paul and the Law," *Scottish Journal of Theology* 17 (1964): 43–68; George E. Howard, "Christ the End of the Law: The Meaning of Romans 10:4ff.," *Journal of Biblical Literature* 88 (1969): 331–37; C. Thomas Rhyne, *Faith Establishes the Law* (Chico, Calif.: Scholars Press, 1981), 95–116.

61. C.E.B. Cranfield, *A Critical and Exegetical Commentary on the Epistle to the Romans* (Edinburgh: T. & T. Clark, 1979), 2:519. For a more nuanced view of the very real discrepancies between Paul's polemic against the law in Galatians and his defense against misunderstandings in Romans, see Hübner, *Law*, 24–86, where a developmental perspective is offered. Räisänen, *Paul and the Law*, 11, perceives internal discrepancies within both Galatians and Romans, rejecting any developmental scheme: "Contradictions and tensions have to be *accepted* as *constant* features of Paul's theology of the law" (italics in original).

62. Cranfield, *Romans*, 853.

63. Ibid., 862, italics in the original.

64. Paul W. Meyer, "Romans 10:4 and the 'End' of the Law," in *The Divine Helmsman: Studies on God's Control of Human Events, Presented to Lou H. Silberman*, ed. J. L. Crenshaw and S. Sandmel (New York: KTAV, 1980), 61.

65. Ibid., 63; Meyer identifies the rock that causes Israel to stumble in its race (Rom. 10:33) as the Torah rather than Christ, which causes an unexplained discrepancy with the latter part of this verse, "and he who believes in him will not be put to shame."

66. Ibid., 68.

67. Ibid., 67.

68. Ibid., 71.

69. Rhyne, *Faith Establishes the Law*, 119–20; italics in the original.

70. C. K. Barrett, *The Epistle to the Romans* (New York: Harper, 1957), 197–98; Otto Kuss, *Der Römerbrief* (Regensburg: Pustet, 1978), 3:752–53; Franz J. Leenhardt, *The Epistle to the Romans*, trans. H. Knight (London: Lutterworth, 1961), 266; F. F. Bruce, *The Epistle of Paul to the Romans: An Introduction and Commentary* (London: Tyndale, 1963), 203.

71. Bruce, *Romans*, 203.

72. John W. Drane, *Paul: Libertine or Legalist?* (London: SPCK, 1975), 133.

73. Robert Badenas, *Christ the End of the Law: Romans 10:4 in Pauline Perspective*, Journal for the Study of the New Testament Supplement 10 (Sheffield: JSOT, 1985).

74. Rhyne, *Faith Establishes the Law*, 104–16; John E. Toews, "The Law and Paul's Letter to the Romans: A Study of Romans 9:30–10:13" (Ph.D. diss., Garrett-Evangelical Theological Seminary—Northwestern University, 1978).

75. See Jewett, *Christian Tolerance*, 43–67.

76. See Jewett, *Captain America Complex*, 1–5, 63–64.

4. The Sexual Liberation of Paul and His Churches

1. For a discussion of the strophic pattern, see Betz, *Galatians*, 181; and Dennis Ronald MacDonald, *There Is No Male and Female: The Fate of a Dominical Saying in Paul and Gnosticism* (Philadelphia: Fortress Press, 1987), 7–9.

2. See, for instance, Heinrich Baltensweiler, *Die Ehe im Neuen Testament: Exegetische Untersuchungen über Ehe, Ehelosigkeit und Ehescheidung* (Zurich: Zwingli Verlag, 1967).

3. Letha Scanzoni and Nancy A. Hardesty, *All We're Meant to Be* (Waco, Tex.: Word Books, 1974; 3d ed., Grand Rapids: Wm. B. Eerdmans Publishing Co., 1992); Richard and Joyce Boldrey, *Chauvinist or Feminist: Paul's View of Women* (Grand Rapids: Baker Book House, 1976); Victor Paul Furnish, *The Moral Teaching of Paul: Selected Issues* (Nashville: Abingdon, 1979); Gilbert Bilezikian, *Beyond Sex Roles: A Guide for the Study of Female Roles in the Bible* (Grand Rapids: Baker Book House, 1985), 126–53; Mary Hayter, *The New Eve in Christ: The Use and Abuse of the Bible in the Debate about Women in the Church* (London: SPCK, 1987), 118–45; Ruth A. Tucker and Walter Liefeld, *Daughters of the Church: Women and Ministry from New Testament Times to the Present* (Grand Rapids: Akademie Books, 1987), 75–83. See also the recent study by C. S. Keener, *Paul, Women and Wives: Marriage and Women's Ministry in the Letters of Paul* (Peabody, Mass.: Hendrickson Publishers, 1992).

4. See for instance John Piper and Wayne Grudem, eds., *Recovering Biblical Manhood and Womanhood: A Response to Evangelical Feminism* (Wheaton, Ill.: Crossway Books, 1991).

5. Michael L. Barré, "To Marry or to Burn: *Purousthai* in I Cor. 7,9," *Catholic Biblical Quarterly* 36 (1975–76): 193–202; Fiorenza, *In Memory of Her*; Wayne A. Meeks, "The Image of the Androgyne: Some Uses of a Symbol in Earliest Christianity," *History of Religions* 13 (1973–74): 165–208; Robin Scroggs, "Paul and

the Eschatological Woman," *Journal of the American Academy of Religion* 40 (1972): 283–303; Scroggs, "Paul and the Eschatological Woman: Revisited," *Journal of the American Academy of Religion* 42 (1974): 532–49; for a critique of Scroggs, see Derwood C. Smith, "Paul and the Non-Eschatological Woman," *Journal of Religious Studies* 4 (1976): 11–19; Graydon F. Snyder, "The *Tobspruch* in the New Testament," *New Testament Studies* 23 (1976–77): 117–20; Mac-Donald, *There Is No Male and Female*; Antionette Clark Wire, *The Corinthian Women Prophets: A Reconstruction through Paul's Rhetoric* (Minneapolis: Fortress Press, 1990).

6. Beginning with Krister Stendahl's pathbreaking study, *The Bible and the Role of Women: A Case Study in Hermeneutics* (Philadelphia: Fortress Press, 1966), a series of hermeneutical options have embraced a wide range of theological orientations. For example, see David Cartlidge, "I Corinthians 7 as a Foundation for a Christian Sex Ethic," *Journal of Religion* 55 (1975): 220–34; W. E. Hull, "Women in Her Place: Biblical Perspectives," *Review and Expositor* 72 (1975): 5–17; George W. Knight III, *The New Testament Teaching on the Role Relationship of Men and Women* (Grand Rapids: Baker Book House, 1977); John P. Meier, "On the Veiling of Hermeneutics (I Cor. 11:2–16)," *Catholic Biblical Quarterly* 40 (1978): 212–26; Grant R. Osborne, "Hermeneutics and Women in the Church," *Journal of the Evangelical Theological Society* 20 (1977): 337–52.

7. Madeleine Boucher, "Some Unexpected Parallels to I Cor. 11:11–12 and Gal. 3:28: The New Testament and the Role of Women," *Catholic Biblical Quarterly* 31 (1969): 56; Elaine H. Pagels, "Paul and Women: A Response to Recent Discussion," *Journal of the American Academy of Religion* 42 (1974): 543–44; William O. Walker, Jr., "1 Corinthians 11:2–16 and Paul's Views Regarding Women," *Journal of Biblical Literature* 94 (1975): 109.

8. Winsome Munro, "Patriarchy and Charismatic Community in Paul," *Women and Religion*, ed. Judith Plaskow, et al. (Missoula, Mont.: Scholars Press, 1974), 189.

9. Pagels, "Paul and Women," 545–46.

10. Rosemary Radford Ruether, "The Subordination and Liberation of Women in Christian Theology: St. Paul and Sarah Grimke," *Soundings* 61 (1978): 173.

11. Fiorenza, *In Memory of Her*, 236.

12. This hypothesis was first developed in my study, "The Sexual Liberation of the Apostle Paul," *Journal of the American Academy of Religion*, Supplement 47 (1979): 55–87.

13. See E. Earle Ellis, *Prophecy and Hermeneutic in Early Christianity: New Testament Essays* (Grand Rapids: Wm. B. Eerdmans Publishing Co., 1978), 6; also Ollrog, *Paulus und seine Mitarbeiter*, 9, 111–50.

14. See Ben Witherington III, *Women and the Genesis of Christianity* (Cambridge: Cambridge University Press, 1990), 185–86.

15. See Jewett, "Paul, Phoebe, and the Spanish Mission," 144–64.

16. Ellis, *Prophecy and Hermeneutic*, 3–22.

17. Constance F. Parvey, "The Theology and Leadership of Women in the New Testament," *Religion and Sexism: Images of Women in the Jewish and Christian Traditions*, ed. Rosemary Radford Ruether (New York: Simon & Schuster, 1973),

142–46; see also the more recent assessment by Fiorenza, *In Memory of Her*, 162–68.

18. Christian Maurer, "*Skeuos*," *Theological Dictionary of the New Testament* (1971), 7:361–67. The NRSV disguises this problem by mistranslating both the verb *ktasthai* ("take, procure") and the noun *skeuos* ("vessel"), producing the unlikely rendering: "that each one of you know how to control your own body."

19. Ernest Best, *A Commentary on the First and Second Epistles to the Thessalonians* (London: Adam & Charles Black, 1972), 165–66. The NRSV disguises the sexist implications of 4:6 by replacing the clear reference to defrauding *ton adelphon autou* ("his brother") with the benign but misleading translation, "that no one wrong or exploit a brother or sister."

20. Snyder, *First Corinthians*, 91; see also his article, "*Tobspruch*," 119.

21. See the commentaries by Heinrich Schlier, *Der Brief an die Galater*, (Göttingen: Vandenhoeck & Ruprecht, 1962; 12th ed.), 174–75; Jürgen Becker, *Der Brief an die Galater* (Göttingen: Vandenhoeck & Ruprecht, 1976), 45–46; Betz, *Galatians*, 195. The most comprehensive recent treatment is by MacDonald who makes a strong case for the pre-Pauline origin of the formula. See *There Is No Male and Female*, 14–16.

22. For an account of the history of exegesis of this passage, see Linda Mercadante, *From Hierarchy to Equality: A Comparison of Past and Present Interpretations of 1 Cor. 11:2–16 in Relation to the Changing Status of Women in Society* (Vancouver: G-M-H Books, 1978).

23. See Robert Jewett, "The Redaction of 1 Corinthians and the Trajectory of the Pauline School," *Journal of the American Academy of Religion* 44.4 (December 1978): Suppl. B, 389–444.

24. Jerome Murphy-O'Connor, "The Non-Pauline Character of I Cor. 11:21–16," *Journal of Biblical Literature* 95 (1976): 621, in response to Walker, "Paul's Views," 94–110. More recent discussions of the authenticity issue may be found in Lamar Cope, "1 Cor. 11:2–16: One Step Further," *Journal of Biblical Literature* 97 (1978): 435–36; and G. W. Trompf, "On Attitudes Toward Women in Paul and Paulinist Literature: 1 Corinthians 11:3–16 and Its Context," *Catholic Biblical Quarterly* 42 (1980): 196–215.

25. The definitive case on this issue was made by Abel Isaksson, *Marriage and Ministry in the New Testament: A Study with Special Reference to Mt. 19:3–12 and 1 Cor. 11:3–16* (Copenhagen/Lund: Gleerup, 1965), 155–77; he has been supported by James B. Hurley, "Did Paul Require Veils or the Silence of Women? A Consideration of I Cor. 11:2–16 and I Cor. 14:33b–36," *Westminster Theological Journal* 35 (1973): 190–220; Alan Padgett, "Paul on Women in the Church: The Contradictions of Coiffure in I Corinthians 11:2–16," *Journal for the Study of the New Testament* 10 (1984): 69–86; Jerome Murphy-O'Connor, "Sex and Logic in 1 Corinthians 11:2–16," *Catholic Biblical Quarterly* 40 (1978): 212–26.

26. See Cynthia L. Thompson, "Hairstyles, Head-coverings, and St. Paul: Portraits from Roman Corinth," *Biblical Archaeologist* 51 (June 1988): 112.

27. See Parvey, "Theology and Leadership of Women," 134–35, and Meeks, "Image," 199–200.

28. Wire, *Corinthian Woman Prophets*, 183, cited approvingly by Ross Shepard Kraemer's survey, *Her Share of the Blessings: Women's Religions Among Pagans*,

Jews, and Christians in the Greco-Roman World (Oxford: Oxford University Press, 1992), 148.

29. Snyder, *First Corinthians*, 151.

30. See Jean Hering, *The Second Epistle of Saint Paul to the Corinthians*, trans. A. W. Heathcote and P. J. Allcock (London: Epworth, 1967), 51; E. B. Allo, *Saint Paul: seconde épître aux Corinthiens* (Paris: Gabalda, 1956; 2d ed.), 187; J. F. Collange, *Enigmes de la deuxième épître de Paul aux Corinthiens. Etude exegetique de 2 Cor. 2:14–7:4* (Cambridge: Cambridge University Press, 1972), 312.

31. See Jewett, *Paul's Anthropological Terms*, 260–63. To follow Robert H. Gundry, *Sôma in Biblical Theology with Emphasis on Pauline Anthropology* (Cambridge: Cambridge University Press, 1976), 77, in defining *sôma* in this passage as nothing more "than the physical body" would miss the force of the argument that "the Lord is for the body," i.e., that God relates to the *sôma* as the whole person.

32. Consistent with this observation, Snyder discusses this section of 1 Corinthians under the heading of "Christian mutuality," *First Corinthians*, 212–17.

33. See ibid., 91–92.

34. See Snyder, *"Tobspruch,"* 117–20; Cartlidge, "Sex Ethic," 233; Wolfgang Schrage, "Zur Frontstellung paulinischer Ehebewertung in 1 K 7, 1–7," *Zeitschrift für die neutestamentliche Wissenschaft* 67 (1976): 215–17.

35. Barré, *"Purousthai,"* 199-201.

36. The clear sense of 1 Cor. 7:7 has been repudiated by ascetically inclined interpreters. Kurt Niederwimmer insists, for example, that "marriage for Paul is not a charisma but a sign of the lack of a charisma, namely: whoever is obliged to marry lacks the charisma of continence"; "Zur Analyse der asketischen Motivation in I Kor 7," *Theologische Literatur Zeitung* 99 (1977): 247. A similar orientation surfaces in Vincent L. Wimbush, *Paul the Worldly Ascetic: Response to the World and Self-Understanding according to 1 Corinthians 7* (Macon: Mercer University Press, 1987), 17, 63.

37. Else Kähler, *Die Frau in den paulinischen Briefen. Unter besonderer Berücksichtigung des Begriffes der Unterordnung* (Frankfurt/Zurich: Gotthelf, 1960), 24.

38. Ibid., 17–21; see also Fee, *1 Corinthians*, 277–86.

39. The contrast with the somewhat unequal definition of conjugal obligations in Jewish Halakhic regulations is undeniable; Paul has moved a long way from the Judaic premises visible in the earlier stages of his development. See Raphael Loewe, *The Position of Women in Judaism* (London: SPCK, 1966), 39–42.

40. Scroggs, "Eschatological Woman," 291.

41. Cartlidge, "Sex Ethic," 222.

42. For a further elaboration of this perspective, see MacDonald, *There Is No Male and Female*, 5–10, 92–98. See also Fiorenza, *In Memory of Her*, 218–20.

43. Meeks, "Image," 165–208.

44. Elaine H. Pagels, *The Gnostic Paul: Gnostic Exegesis of the Pauline Letters* (Philadelphia: Fortress Press, 1975).

45. See Eduard Schweizer, *The Letter to the Colossians*, trans. Andrew Chester (Minneapolis: Augsburg, 1976), 15–24.

46. James E. Crouch, *The Origin and Intention of the Colossian Haustafel* (Göttingen: Vandenhoeck & Ruprecht, 1972), 141–45.

47. See the discussions of this puzzling disparity in J. Paul Sampley, *"And the Two Shall Become One Flesh"*: *A Study of Traditions in Eph. 5:21–33* (Cambridge: Cambridge University Press, 1971); and Andrew T. Lincoln, *Ephesians*, Word Biblical Commentary 42 (Waco, Tex.: Word Books, 1990), 357–67.

48. See Jewett, "The Redaction of 1 Corinthians," 429–32.

49. The definitive case about these verses as an interpolation was made by Gottfried Fitzer, *"Das Weib schweige in der Gemeinde." Ueber den unpaulinischen Charakter der mulier-tacet-Verse in 1. Korinther 14* (Munich: Kaiser, 1963). See also Max Küchler, *Schweigen, Schmuck und Schlier. Drei neutestamentliche Vorschriften zur Verdrängung der Frauen auf dem Hintergrund einer frauenfeindlichen Exegese des Alten Testaments im antiken Judentum* (Freiburg, Switzerland: Universitätsverlag; Göttingen: Vandenhoeck & Ruprecht, 1986), 54–63.

50. Ibid., 63.

51. This text-critical evidence leads Gordon D. Fee to view 1 Cor. 14:34–35 as an interpolation, but he does not include 14:33b, which was not involved in the Western text variations; *1 Corinthians*, 699–705. It is possible that the placement of vv. 34-35 in a position after v. 40 in some Western texts is explainable as a later effort to incorporate the chauvinistic message into a textual tradition that had not yet been altered.

5. Slavery and the Tactful Revolution of the New Age

1. Translation adapted from S. Scott Bartchy, ΜΑΛΛΟΝ ΧΡΗΣΑΙ: *First-Century Slavery and the Interpretation of 1 Corinthians 7:21*, Society of Biblical Literature Dissertation Series 11 (Missoula, Mont.: Society of Biblical Literature, 1973), 183.

2. See particularly Thomas Hoyt, Jr., "Interpreting Biblical Scholarship for the Black Church Tradition," and William H. Myers, "The Hermeneutical Dilemma of the African American Biblical Student," in *Stony the Road*, ed. Felder, 17–39, 40–56.

3. See the contribution of Jones to this reappraisal in *Paul's Message*, 27–112.

4. See Keith R. Bradley, "On the Roman Slave Supply and Slavebreeding," in *Classical Slavery*, ed. M. I. Finley (London: Frank Cass & Company, 1987), 43–46.

5. Ibid., 48–59.

6. Bartchy cites R. H. Barrow, *Slavery in the Roman Empire* (New York: Barnes & Noble, 1968), 12, on this point in *First-Century Slavery*, 46.

7. See William L. Westermann, *The Slave Systems of Greek and Roman Antiquity* (Philadelphia: The American Philosophical Society, 1955), 102–117.

8. Ibid., 14.

9. Ibid., 104.

10. See Bartchy, *First-Century Slavery*, 63–67.

11. See Giuseppe Cambiano, "Aristotle and the Anonymous Opponents of Slavery," in *Classical Slavery*, ed. M. I. Finley, 39.

12. Zvi Yavetz, *Slaves and Slavery in Ancient Rome* (New Brunswick, N.J.: Transaction Books, 1988), 117.

13. See Bartchy, *First-Century Slavery*, 85–91.

14. Keith R. Bradley, *Slaves and Masters in the Roman Empire: A Study in Social Control* (Brussels: Latomus: Revue d'ètudes latines, 1984), 81–112, esp. 96.

15. Martin, *Slavery as Salvation.*

16. Ibid., 7.

17. Ibid., 14–15.

18. Ibid., 22.

19. Ibid., 35–42.

20. Ibid., 48–49.

21. Everett Ferguson, *Backgrounds of Early Christianity* (Grand Rapids: Wm. B. Eerdmans Publishing Co., 1987), 46.

22. Bradley, *Slaves and Masters,* 97–99.

23. Quoted from Seneca *Moral Epistles* 47 by Peter Richardson, *Paul's Ethic of Freedom* (Philadelphia: Westminster Press, 1979), 47.

24. See Fee, *1 Corinthians,* 315.

25. See Bartchy, *First-Century Slavery,* 180: "As in the case of the Christian in slavery, the Christian freeman has been called by God without regard for his social status. 'In the Lord,' his social-legal status was irrelevant."

26. See ibid., 142–55.

27. Fee, *1 Corinthians,* 310.

28. See Martin, *Slavery as Salvation,* 146, epitomizing a discussion from 50–146.

29. Fee, *1 Corinthians,* 316.

30. Hans Conzelmann, *A Commentary on the First Epistle to the Corinthians,* trans. J. W. Leitch, ed. G. W. MacRae (Philadelphia: Fortress Press, 1975), 127.

31. See Bartchy, *First-Century Slavery,* 120; Fee, *1 Corinthians,* 317–18.

32. Fee, *1 Corinthians,* 320; Conzelmann, *1 Corinthians,* 128.

33. Bartchy, *First-Century Slavery,* 181.

34. Bartchy points to the striking parallelism between these two passages in ibid., 181.

35. David L. Barr, *New Testament Story: An Introduction* (Belmont, Calif.: Wadsworth, 1987), 54.

36. Robert Jewett, the fold-out "Graph of Dates and Time-Spans," in *A Chronology of Paul's Life* (Philadelphia: Fortress Press, 1979).

37. Edgar J. Goodspeed, *The Key to Ephesians* (Chicago: University of Chicago Press, 1956).

38. John Knox, *Philemon Among the Letters of Paul* (Nashville: Abingdon Press, 1959; rev. ed.).

39. Petersen, *Philemon,* 68–78.

40. Ibid., 78.

41. Ibid., 292.

42. Peter Lampe, "Keine 'Sklavenfluct' des Onesimus," *Zeitschrift für die neutestamentliche Wissenschaft* 76 (1985): 135–37; and B. M. Rapske, "The Prisoner Paul in the Eyes of Onesimus," *New Testament Studies* 37 (1991): 187–203.

43. F. Forrester Church, "Rhetorical Structure and Design in Paul's Letter to Philemon," *Harvard Theological Review* 71 (1978): 17–33.

44. Lloyd A. Lewis, "An African American Appraisal of the Philemon-Paul-Onesimus Triangle," in *Stony the Road,* ed. Felder, 245.

45. G. B. Caird, *Paul's Letters from Prison: Ephesians, Philippians, Colossians, Philemon* (Oxford: Oxford University Press, 1976), 223.

46. Larry R. Morrison, "The Religious Defense of American Slavery Before 1830," *Journal of Religious Thought* 37.2 (1980–81): 16–29.

47. Ibid., 19.

48. H. Shelton Smith, *In His Image, But . . . : Racism in Southern Religion, 1780–1910* (Durham, N.C.: Duke University Press, 1972), 134.

49. Ibid., 135.

50. Ibid., 136.

51. See David Daube, "Onesimus," in *Christians Among Jews and Gentiles: Essays in Honor of Krister Stendahl on His Sixty-Fifth Birthday*, eds. G. W. E. Nickelsburg and G. W. MacRae (Philadelphia: Fortress Press, 1986), 41.

52. Orlando Patterson, "Our History vs. Clinton's Covenant," *New York Times* (November 13, 1992), A13, based on his book *Freedom* (New York: Basic Books, 1991).

6. Tenement Churches and Pauline Love Feasts

1. See Raymond F. Collins, ed., *The Thessalonian Correspondence* (Leuven: Peeters, 1990); Bassler, *Pauline Theology*; Charles A. Wanamaker, *The Epistles to the Thessalonians: A Commentary on the Greek Text* (Grand Rapids: Wm. B. Eerdmans Publishing Co., 1990).

2. See Wanamaker, *Thessalonians*, 159–64, 279–90; I. Howard Marshall, *1 and 2 Thessalonians* (Grand Rapids: Wm. B. Eerdmans Publishing Co., 1983), 114–17, 218–31; Gerhard Friedrich, *Der erste Brief an die Thessalonicher* (Göttingen: Vandenhoeck & Ruprecht, 1976); Friedrich, *Der zweite Brief an die Thessalonicher* (Göttingen: Vandenhoeck & Ruprecht, 1976); Traugott Holtz, *Die erste Brief an die Thessalonicher* (Zurich/Neukirchen: Neukirchener Verlag, 1986).

3. Reese, *Thessalonians*, 47: "affection for members of the believing community."

4. Wanamaker, *Thessalonians*, 160.

5. Marshall, *Thessalonians*, 117.

6. Wanamaker, *Thessalonians*, 163.

7. See Wanamaker's caption for 2 Thess. 3:7–15 in ibid., 279–90.

8. See ibid., 164; the Bauer-Arndt-Gingrich-Danker, *Greek-English Lexicon*, 885, translates this phrase in terms of having need of something.

9. See Friedrich Hauck, "*Koinos ktl*," *Theological Dictionary of the New Testament* (1965), 3:789–800.

10. See George Panikulam, *Koinônia in the New Testament: A Dynamic Expression of Christian Life*, Analecta Biblica 85 (Rome: Biblical Institute Press, 1979), 5, 29–30. He refers to Paul's approach as "Christocentric and communitarian," 30, but only develops the Christocentric part of the equation.

11. Mark Holloway, *Heavens on Earth: Utopian Communities in America 1680–1880* (New York: Dover, 1966, 2d ed.). For an account of the estimated 140 communal groups founded between 1860 and 1914, see Robert S. Fogerty, *All Things New: American Communes and Utopian Movements 1860–1914* (Chicago: University of Chicago Press, 1990).

12. See John A. Hostetler, *Hutterite Life* (Scottdale, Pa.: Herald Press, 1983).

13. See Johannes Halkenhäuser, *Kirche und Kommunität. Ein Beitrag zur Geschichte und zum Auftrag der kommunitären Bewegung in der Kirchen der Reformation*, Konfessionskundliche und kontroverstheologische Studien 42 (Paderborn: Verlag Bonifacius, 1978), 135–43, referring in n. 96 to the emigration of communal groups in response to such pressures in the nineteenth century.

14. See the survey by Thomas P. Rausch, *Radical Christian Communities* (Collegeville, Minn.: Liturgical Press, 1990).

15. See Andrew Lockley, *Christian Communes* (London: SCM Press, 1976), 4–9.

16. Marguerite Bouvard, *The Intentional Community Movement: Building a New Moral World* (Port Washington, N.Y.: Kennikat Press, 1975), 27.

17. Bernard J. Lee and Michael A. Cowan, *Dangerous Memories: House Churches and Our American Story* (Kansas City, Mo.: Sheed and Ward, 1986), 45–56.

18. Ibid., 1–19.

19. Frances FitzGerald, *Cities on a Hill: A Journey through Contemporary American Cultures* (New York: Simon & Schuster, 1981).

20. Ibid., 23.

21. Ibid.

22. A recent discussion of the appropriateness of the term "cult" for such groups, containing an estimate of 1,500 to 2,500 "religious communities" in the U.S. today, was reported by Ari L. Goldman in "Religion Notes," *New York Times* (April 24, 1993), 8. Whether this estimate includes groups like the Hutterites and monastic communities remains unclear. Bouvard's survey in the 1970s refers to "literally thousands of these small communities," referring to a *New York Times* survey of 100,000 such groups in 1966; *Intentional Community Movement*, 4, 18. Richard Fairfield reported a *New York Times* survey of December 17, 1970 that identified 2,000 communes; see *Communes USA: A Personal Tour* (New York: Penguin Books, 1972), 3.

23. Rom. 16:5; 1 Cor. 16:19; see also 1 Cor. 1:11 and 16:15.

24. Hans-Josef Klauck, *Hausgemeinde und Hauskirche im frühen Christentum* (Stuttgart: Katholisches Bibelwerk, 1981), 15–20. See also Robert Banks, *Paul's Idea of Community: The Early House Churches in Their Historical Setting* (Grand Rapids: Wm. B. Eerdmans Publishing Co., 1980), 37–39, and Vincent Branick, *The House Church in the Writings of Paul* (Wilmington, Del.: Michael Glazier, 1989), 13–28.

25. For example, Floyd V. Filson uses the model of the free-standing house at Dura-Europos as the basis for understanding house churches in "The Significance of Early House Churches," *Journal of Biblical Literature* 58 (1939): 107–09; Willy Rordorf follows this line of thinking in "Was wissen wir über die christlichen Gottesdiensträume der vorkonstantinischen Zeit?" *Zeitschrift für die neutestamentliche Wissenschaft* 55 (1964): 112–18; see also Joan M. Petersen, "House Churches in Rome," *Vigilae Christianae* 23 (1969): 264–72; and Banks, *Paul's Idea of Community*, 14–15.

26. Jerome Murphy-O'Connor, *St. Paul's Corinth: Texts and Archaeology* (Wilmington, Del.: Michael Glazier, 1983), 156.

27. Jerome Murphy-O'Connor, "Prisca and Aquila," *Bible Review* 8 (December 1992): 49–50.

28. See August Strobel, "Der Begriff des 'Hauses' im griechischen und romischen Privatrecht," *Zeitschrift für die neutestamentliche Wissenschaft* 56 (1965): 91–100.

29. Meeks, *First Urban Christians*, 76.

30. See Theissen, *Social Setting*, 11; 107: "This love-patriarchalism takes social differences for granted but ameliorates them through an obligation of respect and love, an obligation imposed upon those who are socially stronger. From the weaker are required subordination, fidelity, and esteem."

31. Peter Lampe, *Die stadtrömischen Christen in den ersten beiden Jahrhunderten: Studien zur Sozialgeschichte* (Tübingen: Mohr-Siebeck, 1987).

32. Ibid., 38.

33. Ibid., 35.

34. Ibid., 43.

35. Ibid., 52.

36. Ibid., 153; see also Peter Lampe, "The Roman Christians of Romans 16," in *Romans Debate*, ed. Karl P. Donfried, 216–30.

37. Cf. Lampe, *Stadtrömischen Christen*, 301.

38. Heikki Solin, *Beiträge zur Kenntnis der griechischen Personennamen in Rom*, Commentationes humanarum litterarum 48 (Helsinki: Societas Scientiarum Fennica, 1971), 1:135–38.

39. See Lampe, *Stadtrömischen Christen*, 40–52; Rodney Stark, "Antioch as the Social Situation for Matthew's Gospel," in *Social History of the Matthean Community: Cross-Disciplinary Approaches*, ed. David L. Balch (Minneapolis: Fortress Press, 1991), 192.

40. Bruce W. Frier, *Landlords and Tenants in Imperial Rome* (Princeton: Princeton University Press, 1980); James E. Packer, "Housing and Population in Imperial Ostia and Rome," *Journal of Roman Studies* 57 (1967): 80–95, and *The Insulae of Imperial Ostia*, Memoirs of the American Academy in Rome 31 (Rome: American Academy in Rome, 1971).

41. Frier, *Landlords*, 15.

42. Ibid., 28.

43. John E. Stambaugh, *The Ancient Roman City* (Baltimore: Johns Hopkins University Press, 1988), 337.

44. See Stark, "Social Situation," 192.

45. See Branick, *House Church*, 71, where he says that meeting in such spaces would be impossible, which reveals the overwhelming weight of the traditional model of a patriarchal house church on the imagination of current scholars.

46. Bo Reicke, *Diakonie, Festfreude und Zelos in Verbindung mit der altchristlichen Agapenfeier*, Uppsala Universitets Arsskrist 1951:5 (Uppsala: A. B. Lundequistska Bokhandeln, 1951).

47. Ibid., 14.

48. Ibid., 244–45.

49. Ibid., 282.

50. For a full development of this hypothesis, see Robert Jewett, "Tenement Churches and Communal Meals in the Early Church: The Implications of a Form-Critical Analysis of 2 Thessalonians 3:10," *Biblical Research* 38 (1993).

51. See Edgar V. McKnight, *What Is Form Criticism?* (Philadelphia: Fortress Press, 1969); Klaus Berger discusses casuistic formulations under the rubric of "Congregational Order" but does not deal with 2 Thess. 3:10 in *Formgeschichte des Neuen Testaments* (Heidelberg: Quelle und Meyer, 1984), 214–16.

52. See James Everett Frame, *A Critical and Exegetical Commentary on the Epistles of St. Paul to the Thessalonians* (New York: Charles Scribner's Sons, 1912), 304–5; Marshall, *Thessalonians*, 223–24; Wanamaker, *Thessalonians*, 285–86; for the typical perspective, see also Christopher Rowland, *Christian Origins: An Account of the Setting and Character of the Most Important Messianic Sect of Judaism* (London: SPCK, 1985), 273.

53. B. W. Winter, "If Any Man Does Not Wish to Work . . ." A Cultural and Historical Setting for 2 Thessalonians 3.6–16," *Tyndale Bulletin* 40 (1989): 309; see also 314: "Christians were not only to command the respect of outsiders by being self-sufficient, but they were to seek the welfare of their city by having the wherewithal to do good to others." For a critique of this interpretation, see John S. Kloppenborg, *"PHILADELPHIA, THEODIDAKTOS* and the Dioscuri: Rhetorical Engagement in 1 Thessalonians 4.9–12," *New Testament Studies* 39 (1993): 276–77.

54. The classification of conditional legal material as "casuistic" by Albrecht Alt has been generally accepted; see Alt, "The Origins of Israelite Law," in *Essays on Old Testament History and Religion*, trans. R. A. Wilson (Oxford: Blackwell, 1966), 88–103.

55. See Bernard S. Jackson, "Law," *Harper's Bible Dictionary* (New York: Harper & Row, 1985), 548–51, esp. 549.

56. See the standard studies by Hans Jochen Boecker, *Law and the Administration of Justice in the Old Testament and Ancient Near East*, trans. J. Moiser (Minneapolis: Augsburg, 1980), 150–55; and B. N. Kaye and C. J. Wenham, eds., *Law, Morality and the Bible* (Leicester: Inter-Varsity Press, 1978).

57. See Berger, *Formgeschichte*, 214–15.

58. See 1QS 6:24–7:24.

59. A helpful listing of editions of some seventeen penal codes from guilds and religious associations is available in Moshe Weinfeld, *The Organizational Pattern and the Penal Code of the Qumran Sect: A Comparison with Guilds and Religious Associations of the Hellenistic-Roman Period*, Novem Testamentum et Orbis Antiquus 2 (Göttingen: Vandenhoeck & Ruprecht, 1986), 9.

60. An example from Lucian *Parasite* 13 is provided by Bauer, et al., *Greek-English Lexicon*, 313.

61. Even the imaginative portrayal of Aristophanes suggesting the reduction of food as a social control was in the context of a utopian vision of a communist society; *Ecclesiazusae* 665f. See the R. G. Ussher edition, *Aristophanes. Ecclesiazusae* (Oxford: Clarendon Press, 1973).

62. See Wanamaker, *Thessalonians*, 285–86.

63. See Gottlob Schrenk, *"Thelō ktl,"* *Theological Dictionary of the New Testament* (1965), 3:44–46; the odd disinterest in 2 Thess. 3:10 among New Testament scholars is indicated by a lack of any reference in this standard dictionary article.

64. See Gene M. Tucker, *Form Criticism of the Old Testament* (Philadelphia: Fortress Press, 1971), 15–17, and McKnight, *Form Criticism*, 20.

65. See Boecker, *Law*, 153.

66. Gerhard Liedke, *Gestalt und Bezeichnung alttestamentlicher Rechtssätze. Eine formgeschichtlich-terminologische Studie*, Wissenschaftliche Monographien zum Alten und Neuen Testament 39 (Neukirchen-Vluyn: Neukirchener, 1971), 56; cited by Boecker, *Law*, 153–54. Liedke shows that even in instances where Israelite law replicates Ancient Near Eastern jurisprudence there is evidence of its reformulation in juridical situations; see the summary in *Rechtssätze*, 59.

67. See Wanamaker, *Thessalonians*, 285.

68. Ibid., 160.

69. See Meeks, *First Urban Christians*, 85–92.

70. Wanamaker, *Thessalonians*, 160; Calvin J. Roetzel, "*Theodidaktoi* and Handwork in Philo and I Thessalonians," in *L'Apôtre Paul. Personnalité, style et conception du ministère*, ed. A. Vanhoye (Leuven: University Press, 1986), 330; Kloppenborg, "*PHILADELPHIA*," 281–82.

71. Malherbe, *Thessalonians*, 102.

72. Roetzel, "*Theodidaktoi*," 330.

73. Kloppenborg, "*PHILADELPHIA*," 283–89.

74. Ibid., 286.

75. Ibid.

76. Ibid., 288: "Paul coins 'god-taught' to convey the idea of divine instruction without thereby confusing God with the *legomenoi theoi* (as he will later call pagan deities in 1 Cor. 8.5)."

77. See Marshall's critique of the "general injunction" construal in *Thessalonians*, 226: "It is probable that the thought of caring for the needy is still in mind here."

78. Wanamaker, *Thessalonians*, 287.

79. John Dominic Crossan, *The Historical Jesus: The Life of a Mediterranean Peasant* (San Francisco: Harper & Row, 1991), 341.

80. Lee and Cowan, *Dangerous Memories*, 82.

81. See Russell E. Richey, "Family Meal, Holy Communion, and Love Feast: Three Ecumenical Metaphors," in *Ecumenical and Interreligious Perspectives: Globalization in Theological Education*, ed. R. E. Richey (Nashville: Quarterly Review Books, 1992), 17–29.

82. See Dawn, *Hilarity of Community*, 76–91; 121–29.

83. Josiah Royce, *The Problem of Christianity. II. The Real World and the Christian Ideas* (New York: Macmillan, 1913), 90.

84. Ibid., 94.

7. Discharged from the Law of Consumerism

1. The rhetorical structure is adapted from Weiss, "Beiträge," 230–31, and Stowers, *Diatribe*, 148–49.

2. Lisa Birnbach, ed., *The Official Preppie Handbook* (New York: Workman, 1980).

3. Marissa Piesman and Marilee Hartley, *The Yuppie Handbook: The State-of-the-Art Manual for Young Urban Professionals* (New York: Long Shadow Books, 1984).

4. For instance, William Sanday and Arthur C. Headlam, *A Critical and Exegetical Commentary on Paul's Epistle to the Romans* (Edinburgh: T. & T. Clark, 1895), 170, paraphrased the thought of Rom. 7:1–8 as "you are free from the law of Moses." Similarly, Heinrich August Wilhelm Meyer, *Critical and Exegetical Handbook to the Epistle to the Romans*, trans. J. C. Moore (Edinburgh: T. & T. Clark, 1876), 314; and James M. Stifler, *The Epistle to the Romans: A Commentary, Logical and Historical* (New York: Fleming H. Revell, 1897), 122.

5. For a classic statement, see Fréderic Godet, *Commentaire sur l'Epître auz Romains* (Genève: Labor et Fides, 1968), 267–68. See also the typical chapter entitled "Paul's Conversion.—The Triumph of the Christian over the Jewish Principle," by Sabatier, *The Apostle Paul*, esp. 55–69. A British statement of the same viewpoint is available in H.A.A. Kennedy, *The Theology of the Epistles* (London: Duckworth, 1919), 31–33. Dieter Lührmann tones down the classic position while suggesting that Paul's Pharisaic background is similar to the *Psalm of Solomon* in "Paul and the Pharisaic Tradition," *Journal for the Study of the New Testament* 36 (1989): 75–94.

6. Sabatier, *The Apostle Paul*, 55.

7. For example, Kennedy writes that Paul came "to estimate the Law no more as an end in itself, but as a preparatory discipline for the individual, making him fully aware of his own helplessness in the presence of sin, and compelling him to look for aid to One who is the medium of the very might of God"; *Theology of the Epistles*, 43–44.

8. Stendahl, *Paul*, 78–96.

9. Sanders, *Paul, the Law*, 93–136; Dahl, *Studies*, 4–5.

10. See Beverly Roberts Gaventa, *From Darkness to Light: Aspects of Conversion in the New Testament* (Philadelphia: Fortress Press, 1986), 28, 32.

11. Birnbach, *Official Preppie Handbook*, 59.

12. Ibid., 122.

13. Piesman and Hartley, *Yuppie Handbook*, 71.

14. *The Enterprise* (August 17, 1983).

15. Cranfield comments that Paul's citation of the command on coveting "directs attention to the inward root of man's outward wrong-doing"; *Romans*, 349. Bruce contends that "Coveteousness . . . is indeed a basic element in most forms of sin"; *Romans*, 148. For a detailed analysis of this verse, see S. Lyonnet, "'Tu ne convoiteras pas' (Rom. 7.7)," *Neotestamentica et Patristica: Eine Freundesgabe, Herrn Prof. Dr. Oscar Cullmann zu seinem 60. Geburtstag überreicht*, ed. W. C. van Unnik (Leiden: Brill, 1962), 157–65. For a review of the Jewish discussion of the tenth commandment and an argument that coveting is a concept that Paul uses to encompass all inappropriate desires, see Dieter Zeller, *Der Brief an die Römer. Übersetzt und erklart*, Regensburger Neues Testament (Regensburg: F. Pustet, 1985), 139.

16. Barrett, *Romans*, 141.

17. Piesman and Hartley, *Yuppie Handbook*, 12.

18. Walter Grundmann describes Paul's peculiar emphasis on sin as coming from "the tendency of man to assert himself against God and to try to will in independence of Him. This desire of man to dispose concerning himself is opposition to the will of God. Once this became clear, he [Paul] was insistent that sin

is . . . active hostility to God and resistance to His will on the part of the man who wills to be independent and to rule his own life. This thought of hostility is the constitutive element in Paul's doctrine of sin"; "*hamartanô*," *Theological Dictionary of the New Testament* (1964), 1:309.

19. Saul Bellow, *Henderson The Rain King* (Greenwich, Conn.: Fawcett, 1959), 24–25.

20. Michael Kinsley, "Dressing Down: Why My Friends Don't Wear Alligators on Their Shirts," *Harper's Magazine* 276 (February, 1983), 10.

21. Ibid., 10.

22. Ibid., 11.

23. Ibid.

24. *Connoisseur*, May 1984.

25. Scroggs, *Paul for a New Day*, 12–13.

26. See Jewett, *Captain America Complex*, 68–69; Martin Hengel, *The Zealots: Investigations into the Jewish Freedom Movement in the Period from Herod I until 70 A.D.*, trans. D. Smith (Edinburgh: T. & T. Clark, 1989), 156–82. For a balancing view, see David Rhoads, *Israel in Revolution: 6–74 C.E.: A Political History Based on the Writings of Josephus* (Philadelphia: Fortress Press, 1976).

27. Gaventa, *Darkness to Light*, 26.

28. Klaus Haacker, "Die Berufung des Vervolgers," *Theologische Beiträge* 6 (1975): 1–19, develops the theme of violent religious intolerance revealed in Phil. 3:5–6. See also Seyoon Kim, *The Origin of Paul's Gospel* (Tübingen: Mohr-Siebeck, 1981), 44–50.

29. Gaventa, *Darkness to Light*, 40.

30. See Kim, *Origin*, 73–74.

31. Karl Barth, *The Epistle to the Romans* (London: Oxford University Press), 248.

32. See Grundmann, "*hamartanô*," 309–11.

33. Bellow, *Henderson the Rain King*, 7.

34. Ibid., 284.

35. Stendahl, *Paul*, 9, has stressed that Paul refers to a "call" rather than to a "conversion": "his call brings him to a new understanding of his mission, a new understanding of the law which is otherwise an obstacle to the Gentiles."

36. Ibid., 15; see also Dahl, *Studies*, 178–91.

37. See Ernst Käsemann, *An die Römer* (Tübingen: Mohr-Siebeck, 1974), 170: "Paul is concerned to eliminate the possibility of neutrality" (my translation).

38. Cranfield, *Romans*, 339–40, draws the contrast between the "newness" of the Spirit and the "oldness" of the letter that "the legalist is left with as a result of his misunderstanding and misuse of the law. It is the letter of the law in separation from the Spirit."

39. See the section entitled "Spirit as Openness for God and One's Neighbor," by Eduard Schweizer, "*pneuma, pneumatikos*," *Theological Dictionary of the New Testament* (1968), 6:430–32.

40. Piesman and Hartley, *Yuppie Handbook*, 89.

41. Ibid., 88.

8. Truth and Dark Mirrors: The Opening of the American Mind

1. The rhetorical structure of this passage is adapted from Weiss, "Beiträge," 198.

2. Allan Bloom, *The Closing of the American Mind: How Higher Education Has Failed Democracy and Impoverished the Souls of Today's Students* (New York: Simon & Schuster, 1987).

3. Wilhelm Bousset, *Der erste Brief an die Korinther, Die Schriften des Neuen Testaments neu übersetzt und für die Gegenwart erklärt* (Göttingen: Vandenhoeck & Ruprecht, 1917), 2:142.

4. Archibald Robertson and Alfred Plummer, *A Critical and Exegetical Commentary on the First Epistle of St. Paul to the Corinthians* (Edinburgh: T. & T. Clark, 1914; 2d ed.), 298.

5. Seneca *Quaest. nat.* 1.15.7.

6. Norbert Hugedé, *La metaphore du miroir dans les Épîtres de Saint Paul aux Corinthiens* (Neuchâtel and Paris: Delachaux et Niestle, 1957).

7. Frederick W. Danker, "The Mirror Metaphor in 1 Cor. 13:12 and 2 Cor. 3:18," *Concordia Theological Monthly* 3 (1960): 428–29.

8. Ibid., 428.

9. For a more balanced view, see Gooch, *Partial Knowledge*, 142–61.

10. Ibid., 153.

11. *Odes of Solomon* 13:1f., cited by Conzelmann, *1 Corinthians*, 227.

12. Cf. John Wesley, *Explanatory Notes upon the New Testament* (London: Epworth, 1966 reprint ed.), 627: "The wisest of men have here but short, narrow, imperfect conceptions, even of the things round about them, and much more of the deep things of God." He goes on to suggest that "at death and in the last day" both the "imperfect" knowledge and the "slow and unsatisfactory methods of attaining" knowledge will be brought to an end.

13. Gooch, *Partial Knowledge*, 187.

14. Ibid., 187.

15. See for instance John Wesley's sermon, "The Case of Reason Impartially Considered," *The Works of John Wesley* (1872; reprint, Grand Rapids: Zondervan, 1958), 6:350–60 (page citations are to the reprint edition).

16. Jacob Bronowski, "The Principle of Tolerance," *Atlantic* 266 (December, 1973), 65; cited in Jewett, *Christian Tolerance*, 90.

17. After an initial presentation of this chapter in a college convocation, Professor David H. Mickey of Nebraska Wesleyan University pointed to the parallel insight of the Grimm fairy tale that depicts the wicked queen gazing at the mirror with the admiring words, "Mirror, mirror on the wall, who is fairest of them all?"

18. See the fuller development of these ideas in the chapter entitled "Faith Without Tolerance and Tolerance Without Faith" in Jewett, *Christian Tolerance*, 68–91.

19. Bronowski, "The Principle of Tolerance," 59.

20. Dan O. Via, Jr., *Self-Deception and Wholeness in Paul and Matthew* (Minneapolis: Fortress Press, 1990).

21. Ibid., 16.

22. Ibid., 27.

23. Ibid., 22.

24. Ibid., 28–29.

25. Ibid., 30.

26. Ibid., 43.

27. Daniel Goleman, "Insights into Self-Deception," *New York Times Magazine* (May 12, 1985), 36–43. The article is adapted from his book *Vital Lies, Simple Truths: the Psychology of Self-Deception* (New York: Simon & Schuster, 1985).

28. Goleman, "Insights," 38.

29. Ibid., 41–43.

30. Ibid., 43, 36.

31. See the discussion of this connection by Gooch, *Partial Knowledge*, 154–61.

32. See Robert Jewett, "*Star Wars* and the Force of Paul's Gospel," chap. 1 in *Saint Paul at the Movies* (Louisville, Ky.: Westminster/John Knox Press, 1993).

33. Royce, *Problem of Christianity II*, 148.

34. Gooch, *Partial Knowledge*, 98.

35. Bloom, *Closing*, 34.

36. Ibid., 41.

37. Ibid., 141.

38. Ibid., 147.

39. Ibid., 381.

40. Karl R. Popper, *The Open Society and Its Enemies. Volume I. The Spell of Plato* (Princeton: Princeton University Press, 1971, paperback ed. based on the 5th ed. 1966), 120–37.

41. Ibid., 132; the quoted line is from Plato's *Republic* 540c.

42. Ibid., 90; the Plato quotes are from the *Republic* 433–41.

43. See Bloom, *Closing*, 39.

44. See ibid., 95–96.

45. Ibid., 97–108.

46. Popper, *Open Society and Its Enemies*, 139–41.

47. Ibid., 43–47.

48. Ibid., 256–57, quoting Plato *Politics* III, 9, 1, 1280a, 1282b–1284b, and 1301b.

49. Plato *Laws* 942a, f, quoted by Popper, *Open Society and Its Enemies*, 103.

50. Ibid., 19.

51. Ibid., 20–21.

52. Ibid., 137.

53. Plato *Republic* 415c, discussed by Popper, *Open Society and Its Enemies*, 140.

54. Plato *Republic* 389b.

55. Popper, *Open Society and Its Enemies*, 144.

56. Ibid., 68–81.

57. Robert L. Gale, "Scanning the Future of Higher Education," *AGB Reports* 34 (November/December, 1992): 6.

58. Ibid.

59. Edward Farley, *The Fragility of Knowledge: Theological Education in the Church and the University* (Philadelphia: Fortress Press, 1988), 17.

60. Ibid., 18.

61. Henry James Young, *Hope in Process: A Theology of Social Pluralism* (Minneapolis: Fortress Press, 1990), 47–74.

62. See Corrington's discussion of Josiah Royce's concept of "wholesome provincialism" that needs to be held in tension with loyalty to the universal community of love, which can only be fully embodied at the end of history with the full coming of the kingdom of God; *Community of Interpreters*, 74–75. Royce develops his concept of loyalty on the basis of Pauline categories in *Problem of Christianity I*, 100–106.

63. See, for instance, Bruce Buursma's article, "Education Secretary's Call for Religion . . . ," *Chicago Tribune* (September 21, 1986), 5.4, referring to William J. Bennett's "aggressive call to restore Judeo-Christian values to American public life and classrooms . . . . Bennett's forceful plea for the teaching of moral and ethical values grounded in the nation's general religious tradition has been joined by New York Gov. Mario Cuomo, who recently proposed that public schools in his state inculcate students with such values as 'love thy neighbor,' a Biblical injunction."

64. Norman Lamm, "A Moral Mission for Colleges," *New York Times* (October 14, 1986), A35.

65. See Henry A. Giroux and Peter L. McLaren, *Critical Pedagogy, the State, and Cultural Struggle* (Albany, N.Y.: State University of New York Press, 1989), xi–xxvi.

66. See the classic summary by G. Max Wingo, *Philosophies of Education: An Introduction* (Lexington, Mass.: D. C. Heath and Co., 1974), 49–136.

67. Ibid., 137–194.

68. Royce, *Problem of Christianity* 2:362.

69. See Oppenheim, *Royce's Mature Philosophy of Religion*, 286–91.

9. Paul and the Democratic Prospect

1. James Hastings Nichols, *Democracy and the Churches* (New York: Greenwood Press, 1969; reprint of 1951 ed.), 17–18.

2. "The Testimony," *New York Times*, July 25, 1987, Section 1.6.

3. Alfred Lief, ed., *The Brandeis Guide to the Modern World* (Boston: Little, Brown, 1941), 50.

4. David Rhoads, "Zealots," *Anchor Bible Dictionary* (Garden City, N.Y.: Doubleday, 1992), 6:1044.

5. See Martin Hengel, *The Zealots: Investigations into the Jewish Freedom Movement in the Period from Herod I until 70 A.D.*, trans. D. Smith (Edinburgh: T. & T. Clark, 1989), xv, 146–212. For a balanced appraisal of the complex evidence concerning the impact of zealous ideology on the war, see Rhoads, "Zealots," 1045–52.

6. Ibid., 183.

7. Ibid., 224–28.

8. Rhoads, *Israel in Revolution*, 170.

9. In contrast to S.G.F. Brandon, *Jesus and the Zealots: A Study of the Political Factor in Primitive Christianity* (Manchester: Manchester University Press, 1967),

my research in *Captain America Complex* and *Jesus Against the Rapture* follows the mainstream of scholarship on this point, represented in recent studies by Richard Horsley, *Jesus and the Spiral of Violence: Popular Jewish Resistance in Roman Palestine* (San Francisco: Harper & Row, 1987), E. P. Sanders, *Jesus and Judaism* (Philadelphia: Fortress Press, 1985), and Marcus Borg, *Jesus, A New Vision: Spirit, Culture and the Life of Discipleship* (San Francisco: Harper & Row, 1987).

10. Snyder, *First Corinthians*, 171.

11. See Otto Michel, *"oikodomeô," Theological Dictionary of the New Testament*, (1967), 5:140–42.

12. David E. Aune, *Prophecy in Early Christianity and the Ancient Mediterranean World* (Grand Rapids: Wm. B. Eerdmans Publishing Co., 1983), 47.

13. Robertson and Plummer, *First Epistle . . . to the Corinthians*, 323.

14. See Aune, *Prophecy*, 219.

15. Ibid., 51–52.

16. Christopher Hill, *Intellectual Origins of the English Revolution* (Oxford: Clarendon Press, 1965), 2.

17. Ralph Barton Perry, *Puritanism and Democracy* (New York: Vanguard Press, 1944), 195.

18. Nichols, *Democracy and the Churches*, 31.

19. Perry, *Puritanism and Democracy*, 32.

20. Ibid., 32.

21. Ibid., 34.

22. Jewett, *Captain America Complex*, 33–35.

23. Cited by Harry V. Jaffa, *Crisis of the House Divided: An Interpretation of the Issues in the Lincoln-Douglas Debates* (Garden City, N.Y.: Doubleday & Company, Inc., 1959), 196.

24. Cited in ibid., 210.

25. Ibid., 215.

26. John Dean, "John Dean on Ollie: The Ugly Road Ahead," *Newsweek*, July 20, 1987, 29.

27. Jonathan Alter, "Ollie Enters Folklore," *Newsweek*, July 20, 1987, 19.

28. Cf. also Tom Brokaw, "If Only He'd Known What He Knows Now When He Met North in 1985," *Des Moines Register*, July 7, 1987, 6a: on the basis of an interview in 1985, Brokaw reported that Oliver North said, "Not so long ago, I fought in a far-off war we were not allowed to win. I vowed it would never happen again."

29. Cheryl Lavin, "Ollie's War Captivates a Nation," *Chicago Tribune*, July 12, 1987, Section 5.1.

30. R. W. Apple, Jr., "Fighting the Good Fight," *New York Times*, July 9, 1987, Section 1.8.

31. Fox Butterfield, "A Correction: *Times* Was in Error on North's Secret Fund Testimony," *New York Times*, July 13, 1987, Section 1.1.

32. Alter, "Folklore," 19.

33. Lavin, "Ollie's War," Section 5.1.

34. David Broder, "King in This Land of the Blind," *Chicago Tribune*, July 15, 1987, Section 1.15.

35. Wayne King, "Cards and Calls (and Cash) Pour In for North, a Hero to Many Americans," *New York Times* , July 11, 1987, Section 1.5.

36. Wade Huntley, "The United States Was the Loser in the Cold War," *The Chronicle of Higher Education*, March 31, 1993, A40.

37. William Pfaff, "Casey and Zealots Who Are Not in Democracy's Camp," *Chicago Tribune*, October 2, 1987, Section 1.21.

38. Ibid.

39. Benjamin R. Barber, "The Real Lesson of 'Amerika,'" *New York Times*, March 1, 1987, Section E.25.

40. Barbara Gamarekian, "Fuentes a World Citizen at Home in Washington," *New York Times*, May 30, 1988, Section 1.10.

41. Hilde Saltz, "The Value System Has Come Apart," reprinted from *Die Presse* of Vienna by *World Press Review*, September, 1987, 14.

42. "The Committee's Turn," *New York Times*, July 14, 1987, Section 1.8.

43. "Legislators Seize Spotlight from North," *New York Times*, July 14, 1987, Section 1.8.

44. R. W. Apple, Jr., "North is Dismissed," *New York Times*, July 15, 1987, Section 1.1.

45. "Testimony Continues," *New York Times*, July 24, 1987, Section 1.8.

46. Testimony taken from the televised hearings on July 9, 1987.

47. "Panel's Case: Bullets and the Rule of Law," *New York Times*, July 15, 1987, Section 1.5; punctuation corrected.

48. See Corrington, *Community of Interpreters*, 74–78.

49. Quoted in ibid., 74, from Royce's 1908 article titled "Provincialism," in Josiah Royce, *Basic Writings*, ed. John J. McDermott (Chicago: University of Chicago Press, 1969), 2: 1069.

50. Corrington, *Community of Interpreters*, 75.

Index of Passages

Index of Authors Cited

Index of Subjects

171

Jewett, Robert
Paul: The apostle to America

227.
060
973
JEW

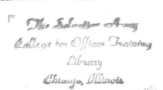